Police in Contradiction

Recent Titles in
Contributions in Criminology and Penology

Waging the Battle Against Drunk Driving: Issues, Countermeasures, and Effectiveness
Gerald D. Robin

Policing Western Europe: Politics, Professionalism, and Public Order, 1850–1940
Clive Emsley and Barbara Weinberger, editors

Policing a Socialist Society: The German Democratic Republic
Nancy Travis Wolfe

Domestic Marijuana: A Neglected Industry
Ralph A. Weisheit

Personality and Peer Influence in Juvenile Corrections
Martin Gold and D. Wayne Osgood

Bad Guys and Good Guys: Moral Polarization and Crime
Daniel S. Claster

Innovative Approaches in the Treatment of Drug Abuse: Program Models and Strategies
James A. Inciardi, Frank M. Tims, and Bennett W. Fletcher, editors

Coca and Cocaine: An Andean Perspective
Felipe E. Mac Gregor, editor

Police Under Pressure: Resolving Disputes
Robert Coulson

Punishing Criminals: Developing Community-Based Intermediate Sanctions
Malcolm Davies

Crack and the Evolution of Anti-Drug Policy
Steven R. Belenko

In Defense of Prisons
Richard A. Wright

POLICE IN CONTRADICTION

The Evolution of the Police Function in Society

CYRIL D. ROBINSON,
RICHARD SCAGLION,
with J. MICHAEL OLIVERO

Contributions in Criminology and Penology, Number 44

GREENWOOD PRESS
Westport, Connecticut • London

Library of Congress Cataloging-in-Publication Data

Robinson, Cyril D.
    Police in contradiction : the evolution of the police function in
society / Cyril D. Robinson, Richard Scaglion, with J. Michael
Olivero.
        p.   cm.—(Contributions in criminology and penology, ISSN
0732–4464 ; no. 44)
    Includes bibliographical references and index.
    ISBN 0–313–28891–7 (alk. paper)
    1. Police—History. I. Scaglion, Richard. II. Olivero, J.
Michael. III. Title. IV. Series.
HV7903.R63   1994
363.2′09—dc20   93–25071

British Library Cataloguing in Publication Data is available.

Library of Congress Catalog Card Number: 93–25071
ISBN: 0–313–28891–7
ISSN: 0732–4464

First published in 1994

Greenwood Press, 88 Post Road West, Westport, CT 06881
An imprint of Greenwood Publishing Group, Inc.

Printed in the United States of America

The paper used in this book complies with the
Permanent Paper Standard issued by the National
Information Standards Organization (Z39.48–1984).

10 9 8 7 6 5 4 3 2 1

CONTENTS

PREFACE

This book takes preliminary steps toward formulating a theory of the origin and evolution of the police function. Our theory suggests that the police function, in its modern form, is linked to economic specialization and differential access to resources which characterize class-dominated rather than kinship-based societies. The special contribution of our theory is to explicate the incremental changes in the police function associated with the transition from kinship-based to class-dominated societies, both historically and cross-culturally, and to examine the implications of these changes for modern police-community relations.

The theory proposed in this book is constructed from both anthropological and historical materials. It consists of four interdependent propositions: (1) specialized police agencies are generally characteristic only of societies politically organized as states; (2) the origin of the specialized police function is associated with the division of society into dominant and subordinate classes, that is, classes with antagonistic interests; (3) in a period of transition, the crucial factor in delineating the modern specialized police function is an ongoing attempt at conversion of the social control (policing) mechanism from an integral part of the community structure to an agent of an emerging dominant class; and (4) the police is created by the emerging dominant class as an instrument for the preservation of its control over restricted access to basic resources, over the political apparatus governing this access, and over the labor force necessary to provide the surplus upon which the dominant class lives.

Thus, our theory suggests that developmentally, the police institution has a double and contradictory origin and function. At the same time, and in the same society, it may be the agent of both the people it polices and the dominant class controlling these same people. An analysis linking the origin of the modern police function to social change in stateless societies has important implications for an understanding of contemporary problems in police-community relations. It allows the dynamics of the social control function of police in small homogeneous social units to be integrated with a consideration of its role in a complex society. In addition, it illuminates how an understanding of this specialized role may be obscured by the more general social control function of police displayed in simple social units, resulting in differential and conflicting expectations about the role and functions of police in the modern world.

The original idea for this book originated with Robinson, who as a lawyer had had considerable experience with cases involving the police; had been interested in and had written articles on police history, and had become frustrated with the sources of police history that normally stopped at the organization of the English police in 1829. One of his law school professors had counseled that legal analysis consisted in always taking one step backwards. In this instance, that meant looking at police institutions in pre-state societies. Robinson developed the basic theory of transition of the police institution from pre-state to state societies, and then sought the help of an anthropologist, Richard Scaglion, with whom he collaborated to complete the manuscript. Scaglion, a legal anthropologist, has published on police-community relations in Pittsburgh, Pennsylvania; but specializes in the study of "pre-state" societies, which he prefers to call non-state, tribal, or kinship-based societies.

We were fortunate in obtaining a faculty development loan from Southern Illinois University and support from the Crime Study Center at the University for a then graduate assistant, Michael Olivero, who under the direction of Scaglion, did most of the cross-cultural tabulation and data collection. A preliminary summary of our work was initially published by Robinson and Scaglion as "The Origin and Evolution of the Police Function in Society: Notes Toward a Theory" (*Law and Society Review,* 1987, vol. 21:109–152). Olivero discussed our research method in "Research Notes—A New Look at the Evolution of Police Structure" (*Journal of Criminal Justice,* 1990, vol. 18: 171–176).

Along the way we have had critical help from a number of people whose useful comments improved this work, including Jane Adams, Michael Banton, Paul Chevigny, Charles Cobb, and David Greenberg. We also wish to thank the staff at Southern Illinois University's Morris Library staff, especially James Fox and Walter Stubbs; and for the innumerable drafts ably executed by Kieshia Cobb, Jennifer Gist, Margaret Highland,

Thara Plumb, Sarah Schrader, and Melinda Tripp under the always tolerant and good-humored direction of Linda Patrick, head of the College of Education's Operations Support Center.

Police in
Contradiction

1

INTRODUCTION

The whole enormous apparatus of "law and order" associated with modern life is absent among village and band-level cultures. Yet there is no "war of all against all." The Eskimo, the Bushmen of the Kalahari, the Australian aborigines, and many other cultures enjoy a high degree of personal security without having any "sovereign" in Hobbes's sense. They have no kings, queens, dictators, presidents, governors, or mayors; police officers, National Guard soldiers, sailors, or marines; CIA, FBI, Treasury agents, or federal marshalls. They have no written law codes and no formal law court, no lawyers, and no patrol cars, paddy wagons, jails or penitentiaries. People managed to get along without these means of law enforcement for tens of thousands of years. Why are contemporary state-level societies so dependent upon them?
—Marvin Harris, *Culture, People, Nature: An Introduction to General Anthropology,* 1975, pp. 355–356

The heathen clan or tribe may be relatively egalitarian, and poverty may be more or less equally distributed among its members, but it can never move forward in mass order towards higher civilization and the freedom of the individual. When men collectively are very poor some few must be made rich if there is to be any accumulation of wealth for civilized purposes. When men collectively are very ignorant, progress is only possible through the endowment of an educated few. In such a world, organization can only begin through personal ascendancy and can only be rendered permanent through privilege. . . . In our own democratic and partially scientific age these conditions of progress in the past may seem strange to some, but they are a large part of the secret of early English history. . . .

So the ploughman ceased more and more to be a warrior, and the warrior ceased to be a ploughman. Differentiation of function led away from equality—away from liberty even. But it led to settled order, to civilization, to wealth, and finally in the course of centuries to a much fuller liberty for the individual than the freeman of a savage tribe can possibly enjoy.
　　—G. M. Trevelyan, *History of England*, vol. 1, 1953, pp. 73, 125

Conventional evolutionary anthropologists . . . tend to enumerate progressive trends such as productivity of human labor power, variety and quantity of goods available, and proliferation of occupational and life-style choices. But instead of being counted as social gains, these criteria should be looked at as gains for ruling classes and a small proportion of unruling but affluent people. Such criteria, or analytic centers, obscure evolutionary losses for the majority of humanity. Workers, for example, do not own the results of their productivity, and most of the world's population is denied even an adequate diet and has little meaningful choice of occupation or life style. In nonclass societies, necessities were generally available and fairly equally distributed. Although occupational or life-style choices were indeed limited, the lack of specialization forced adults to command a wide range of mental and manual occupations. From this perspective, then, the rise of the ruling classes and state formations initiated a long and uneven process of destroying kin corporations.
　　—Karen Sacks, *Sisters and Wives: The Past and Future of Sexual Equality*, 1979, pp. 194–195

As the three preceding quotes amply demonstrate, there is no clear consensus concerning the benefits of civilization. In the first extract, simple and complex societies are seen merely as alternatives, whereas in the second and third extracts, complex society is seen as a "positive" and as a "negative" development, respectively. For better or worse, however, complex, that is, civilized societies, are almost universally characterized by the police function, which supports "the whole enormous apparatus of 'law and order' " present in such societies. Why should this be so? What aspects of complex society necessitate the modern police function? What implications have these associations for the relationships between police and people in the modern world?

This book attempts to formulate a theory of the origin and evolution of the police function. We believe that a society dominated by a ruling class needs a coercive instrument to maintain its control over basic resources and over a labor force necessary to produce the surplus product to support and sustain that ruling class (Haas 1982:173–174). Our theory contrasts the police function in kinship-based, stateless societies with the police function in state societies (Claessen and Skalník:1978b), arguing that the development of the police function parallels and is dependent upon the development of the state. By a series of almost imperceptible changes, the police function existing within a kinship society, as a product of and serving the whole society, is transformed into a police function that predominantly represents the interests of the dominant class in a class-dominated society, while at the same time purporting to and appearing to represent the entire society. We attempt to reconstruct the means by which this transformation may have occurred. Because we consider the kinds of changes in community organization that make a police "necessary," such an analysis has important implications for an understanding of contemporary problems in police-community relations. The very fact that one important arm of police reform is composed of the "community police" movement (considered in chapter 6) gives credence to the crucial significance of the concept of community.

From the very beginning, a disclaimer is in order. By use of the word "evolution," we do not wish to associate ourselves with any particular school of anthropological or social theory. By "evolution," we mean merely social change in the most general sense. Nor do we believe that there are rigid, preordained or inevitable stages of social development. Obviously, social development proceeds in many different ways in many different places. Although we find them useful, we do not strictly subscribe to the neoevolutionary schemes arising from Service (1962) and Fried (1967), among others, popular in the 1960s and 1970s, schemes that promoted a rather simplistic "stagal" approach to social change and development.

Despite innumerable local and regional variations in the social process, we believe that there are certain trends and relationships discernible in the development of state society that are worth investigating. We should not necessarily abandon the search merely because general evolutionary trends are difficult to discern and not without exceptions.

We have drawn heavily on a few theoretical schools of discourse because, despite its obvious importance, the nature and development of the police function in modern society has generated surprisingly little literature. Modern writers on social control, both in criminal justice and in anthropology, have been especially deficient in developing a conceptual and theoretical approach to the police function.[1] Although almost every introductory text in anthropology discusses the nature of social control in tribal societies, fundamental questions about the development of the police function remain unanswered. In fact, these sorts of questions are infrequently posed: To what kind(s) of social and political organizations is the specialized police function linked? From what sort of conflict management institutions did the police function develop into a specialized institution? Out of what need did such a specialized form of social control evolve? What is the relation of the incipient police to the community? What are the modifications in the political, economic, and social relations within a community that may encourage the development of the police function?

Despite the enormous amount of writing on various aspects of police behavior, function, and history, no one has attempted to directly answer such questions or to construct a cross-cultural, evolutionary theory of the police function. This lapse is perhaps explainable from the point of view of the two disciplines most likely to be concerned with construction of such theory: history and anthropology. Historians normally specialize in a limited time period or in some limited area of police history itself. For English and American historians, the accepted focal beginning of police history has been the formation of the English organized police in 1829.[2]

Although the pre-1829 period seems to have been adequately documented by competent authors, especially Reith (1952), dealing with the years 600 to 1950; Critchley (1967), studying the period 900 to 1966; and Radzinowicz (1956), examining the years 1750 to 1850, their purpose has been restricted to recounting the events leading up to the formation of the organized police (Robinson 1979). No historian has been interested in the prestate police institution for its own sake, perhaps because materials were relatively unavailable for these earlier periods or perhaps because the documents that were available were understandable only by experts in ancient history, who were themselves uninterested in the police function. In addition, the method used by most historians has not been designed to concentrate on questions involving the transition from one form of society to another (Terray 1972:32; Lewis 1968:x). In this work we draw upon both pre- and post-1829 police historical literature in examining and integrating a theory of the development of the policy function.

In anthropology, contemporary analysis of state formation[3] and the related development of police function seem to have been hampered by a widening gap between ethnology and archeology and a concomitant tendency on the part of anthropologists to specialize in one or the other subdiscipline.[4] As Flannery (1972:404) points out,

Most recent evolutionary studies by ethnologists are *synchronic*; they take a series of unrelated, contemporary societies on different levels of development and by comparing them, try to imagine which institutional changes could have turned the simpler into the more complex. Most archeological studies on the other hand, have been diachronic, tracing the development of society through time in a single region.

The problem for ethnologists has been that, while they have rich data for contemporary societies, there are few societies for which the time depth for a diachronic study is possible.[5] As a result, most ethnologists seem to have lost interest in investigating specific aspects of social evolution, such as the development of the police function, as a step in theory building. Archeologists, on the other hand, can provide considerable continuity in a single region, but lack the richness of behavioral data found in ethnological studies. Wright (1986:359), in arguing for an approach combining ethnology and archeology, pointed out that "the fine details of sociopolitical process . . . are difficult to evaluate unambiguously for the earlier civilizations known solely from archeological research." Archeologists have tended to concentrate more on variables such as production of surplus or systems of distribution that are more observable "on the ground" than on the police function.

This book combines the diachronic approach favored by archeologists with the synchronic approach more characteristic of ethnologists. In chapter 4, we examine in detail several ethnographic examples for which extensive diachronic data exist. In chapter 5 we test our theory on a large sample of societies, using synchronic data. While each approach is not without its problems, we believe that a combined synthetic methodology provides the best test of our theories.

One might also expect to find a comparative analysis of the police function among the writings of Marxist sociologists, because the class-based theories of Marx and Engels seem to accept as their analytic focus the workings of the entire social system and employ what appears to be an evolutionary perspective as an integral part of that analysis. Marx and Engels, however, had shown only limited interest in precapitalist modes of production, concentrating principally on capitalist class relations (Hindess and Hirst 1975:33). On the police, they wrote little (Pearce 1976:61–66). It is understandable, therefore, that even Marxist scholars concerned with police history have largely ignored early police forms, preferring to center attention on the function of the police during the more recent industrial era. Despite a lack of specific focus on the police function, however, all of the literature reviewed above together provides a framework and analytic vocabulary for such an analysis. Anthropologists, who have written extensively on differences between state and stateless societies, have provided a starting point.

The state is generally defined as the societal institution having a monopoly of legitimate force over a specified territory.[6] In contrast, stateless societies are commonly agreed to have social control mechanisms characterized by kinship-based, communal security arrangements. Resources are often collectively owned within significant social units, and there is evidence that the police function, to the extent that such specialized functions exist in the absence of state structure, remains part of and serves the entire social unit or community. Even in those few egalitarian societies that have a formalized police function, the police themselves are not specialists, but serve only temporarily. In societies organized as states, however, the community social control mechanism is replaced by a permanent bureaucratic apparatus which appears to serve the dominant class. Haas (1982:15), for example, sees states as possessing "a ruling body controlling production or procurement of basic resources and exercising economic power over its population."

In developing our theory, we make use of the framework and analytic vocabulary just presented, and in so doing, draw from all of the disciplines reviewed above. We see no meaningful analytical difference between "general evolution" (constructing theories of evolutionary change based on the studies of many societies) and "specific evolution" (the study of the social systems of one society). We believe that a general theory of cultural evolution involves principles that subsume specific cases, and that specific cases can inform the development of more general principles. The application of the principles varies due to historical-particularist situations. Thus, social evolution cannot be predicted, but post facto it can be understood. We seek to derive general principles concerning the evolution of the police function from both diachronic case studies and synchronic cross-cultural research. Our basic principles involve four interdependent propositions:

1. Specialized police agencies are generally characteristic only of societies politically organized as states.
2. The origin of the specialized police function is associated with the division of communal (kinship) society into dominant and subordinate classes, that is, classes with antagonistic interests.

3. In a period of transition, the crucial factor in delineating the modern specialized police function is an ongoing attempt at conversion of the social control (policing) mechanism from an integral part of the community structure to an agent of an emerging dominant class.

4. The police institution is created by the emerging dominant class as an instrument for the preservation of its control over restricted access to basic resources, over the political apparatus governing this access, and over the labor force necessary to provide the surplus upon which the dominant class lives.

Thus, our theory suggests that developmentally the police have a double, contradictory, and dynamic origin and function leading to their contemporary schizophrenic image: as the agent of the people they police and, at the same time, as an agent of the dominant class controlling these people in the interest of that class (Reiner 1978:183–184; Robinson 1978; Monkkonen 1981; Kent 1986:15–23). Such a concept of the police, not surprisingly, is a reflection of the same contradiction in the structure of the state itself. As one commentator stated: "The state *tends* to be an expression of facts of domination, to act coherently as a corporate unit, to become an area of social conflict, and to present itself as a guardian of universal interests. Clearly, these tendencies stand in contradiction to each other" (Rueschemeyer and Evans 1985:48; emphasis in original). Later chapters develop our theory by the diachronic examination of societies known to have developed state organizations. Sacks (1979:106–107) states the rationale for such an approach:

Looking backward, comparative analysis allows us to make nonteleological guesses at the possible developments of contradictory forces that may have precipitated change. It will not tell us what really happened, but as historical material is sought, comparative analysis may generate hunches for its analysis.

To test the cross-cultural validity of our theory, we examine the relationship between developmental typologies in our model and the police function in various types of societies. We do not here seek to provide a complete cross-cultural theory of the police function. Rather, with particular emphasis on state development, and with supporting cross-cultural evidence, we test the validity of our belief that, at some point in the developmental sequence, there exists a perceived need on the part of a dominant group to protect restricted access to basic resources. For such a group, the police provide one means by which to protect this privileged position. This task, both of formulating hypotheses that specify the connections between these variables and a methodology capable of testing the empirical validity of the hypotheses, is a rare anthropological event (Newman 1983:4), full of conceptual and methodological pitfalls (Olivero 1990).

Of the four propositions of our theory set forth above, it is the third that is both the structural and ideological support for the other three. Social control by police agencies is itself dependent on an ideological structure that legitimizes the stratification benefiting a ruling elite. One important task of such ideology is to fit the police into the general ideological framework of that society. This task involves two interlocking requirements: to convince the populace that they need a police agency for their own control, and to convince the police of their own legitimate right to control their fellows in the name of the state. For the purpose of understanding the development of the police function, the essential step is the transfer of allegiance and loyalty of the police to the state from the community of which they were historically a part (Robinson 1978).

The idea that the police really issue from the community and are a part of that community has been a pervasive and essential prop to concepts of modern policing (Robinson 1979). It supplies the continuity between the ancient structural change from "police" in and of the community to police as an agent of the state. Therefore, before proceeding to develop our theory, it is essential to examine the assumptions that give ideological sustenance to the modern police function.[7]

Traditional writing regarding the police function does not view the police as an instrument of the state conceived to protect the interests of the few at the expense of the many.[8] On the contrary, police, both in England and the United States, are most often generally seen as protectors of the law and order that allow democratic institutions to operate. Early police history, from an American perspective, is English history, and most writers who have written on this period are English (Robinson 1979). To them, England is a democracy and the police, like other English institutions, is either identical with or is representative of her people. American writers have generally accepted these propositions without question. What follows is a discussion of the logic behind these assumptions.

Crucial to the notion of the police as a democratic institution are the ideas that (1) the police institution in England has deep historical roots and is said to have experienced a slow but consistent growth (many writers call it "progress") from ancient to modern times; (2) the police institution is unique to the English people, originates from the people, and is dependent upon them for its support in the sense that without it, its effectiveness, even its existence, would be in doubt (in effect, the people are the police and police are the people);[9] (3) the community is divided into a majority of good, law-abiding people and a minority of lawbreakers, and therefore, one police function is to protect this virtuous majority from the criminal minority (Robinson 1979).

A well-known English police historian (Lee 1971:xxvii) expresses the first two themes as follows:

Our English police system . . . rests on foundations designed with the full approval of the people, we know not how many hundreds of years before the Norman conquest, and has been slowly molded by the careful hand of experience, developing as a rule along the line of least resistance, now in advance of the general intelligence of the country, now lagging far behind but always in the long run adjusting itself to the popular temper, always consistent with local self-government and even at its worst, always English.

This past is said to continue into the present. No structural or ideological breach between the police and the community is recognized. On the contrary, the unity of the two is affirmed. "The police . . . represent the collective interests of the community. . . . The device which is most characteristically English has been to arm the police with prestige rather than power, thus obliging them to rely on popular support" (Critchley 1967:xiii–xiv).

One of the most important assertions is that far from being policed from above, the English people police themselves. That the police and the people are one is embodied in the Seventh Principle adopted at the time of the formation of the English police:

The police at all times should maintain a relationship with the public that gives reality to the historic tradition that the police are the public and that the public are the police; the police are the only members of the public who are paid to give full-time attention to duties which are incumbent on every citizen in the interest of the community welfare. (Radelet 1986:4)

This same idea continues today to influence American literature on police-community relations (Trojanowicz and Bucqueroux 1990:ix–x, 45; Holden 1986:242–243; Radelet 1986:30; Skolnick and Bayley 1986:9–11; Greene 1981:234). Charles Reith (1975:14–15) makes the same point, suggesting an evolutionary perspective for the police function, but with a heavy ideological overlay.

Firstly, there is a coming together of individuals or small-group community units in search of collective security. . . . *Secondly*, there is discovery or recognition of the need of rules or laws for smooth and cooperative action and living, and the making of these makes necessary, also, the setting-up of authority of one kind or another. . . . *Thirdly*, there comes, always and inevitably, discovery or recognition of the facts that some members of the community will not keep some or all of the rules; that by their behavior in this respect they weaken and endanger the welfare and lives of other members and the existence of the community as a whole; and that to ensure its continuing welfare and survival, means must be found for compelling observances of rules. *Fourthly*, in one form or another, these means are found and established. Their effectiveness is the key-stone of community existence. (Emphasis in original)

This stress on rules or norms of behavior is at variance with what anthropologists know about dispute management in stateless societies. In kinship-oriented societies, norms or rules are subordinated to a desire for peace and mutual cooperation. Disputes are generally handled on a case-by-case basis without regard to formal rules. Only in hierarchically organized societies is substantive law predominant. As we shall demonstrate, the substantive model of conflict management, accompanied by rules of behavior for finding those who break them and making such persons deviant and subject to punishment, is in itself supportive of a ruling elite. Certainly Reith's (1975:19) assertion that centralized authority is necessary for collective security is better ideology than history:

Somewhere in history, a ruler . . . found . . . a solution which in the course of its evolution through the ages has become the basis on which, at the present day, true democracy depends for its existence. This is the system by which a chief or any other form of ruling authority in a community . . . confers, on the members of the community as a whole, responsibility for securing and maintaining observance of laws. . . . From Saxon England we can trace its further evolution in detail and its survival . . . in the English parish-constable police system and the present-day police forces of Britain, the British Commonwealth and Empire, and the United States.

Reith (1975:20) then concludes that the world knows two police systems:

The kin police or Anglo-Saxon police system, and the ruler-appointed, *gendarmerie*, or despotic totalitarian police system. The first represents, basically, force exercised indirectly, by the people, from below, upwards. The other represents force exercised, by authority, from above, downwards. (Emphasis in original)

This history is haunted by a search for a once-idyllic community of people and police. What is the significance of this search? Is there really continuity between the Anglo-Saxon community described by Reith and the community of today? The now-defunct Law Enforcement Assistance

Administration (LEAA 1978:3–4), reviewing police-community relations efforts, combined these ideas into a modern police-community relations philosophy:

Sir Robert Peel, in the early 1800's set forth law enforcement principles which are particularly interesting today because of a notable prevailing emphasis on the important role to be played by the ordinary citizen in police service. . . . Within the context of the Peel philosophy and its assimilation into our society, at least three strongly prevailing themes have managed to stand the test of time. These points are:

1. The police are the public and the public are the police, the police accurately mirror the general culture of the society they represent;
2. The police function depends on a considerable amount of self-policing by every citizen. The system is rooted in personal responsibility—police officers, even under conditions of intensive specialization and extensive training, cannot possibly perform their duties effectively without abundant self-policing by the citizen. This custom is not merely a matter of cooperation or good relations between police and community. Ideally, it is a matter of organic union, with police as part of, and not apart from the community they serve; and
3. The police are a living expression, and embodiment, an implementing arm of democratic law.[10]

These assumptions, which traditional police historians have denoted as conclusions from observed historical facts, could not help but hinder analysis of the police function, for they serve an ideological rather than an analytic end (Robinson 1979) and obscure class formation and domination (Corrigan and Sayer 1985). In particular, they obscure both the structural changes resulting from state formation—the switch in "police" loyalty from the community to the state—and the consequent conflicts between police and community groups.

Continuing clashes between the police and the unempowered or underempowered repeatedly suggest the questions: Who do the police really represent? Who *does* and who *should* control the police? If control is to be exercised by the community, how is such control possible with a structure in which the police are the legal agents of a state dominated by a class with its own interests, perhaps antagonistic to those of the community? These and other issues are explored in the chapters to follow.

NOTES

1. See, for instance, Galliher (1971:308) and Center for Research on Criminal Justice (1977:5). Manning (1979:42) notes that "there is no comprehensive analysis of the rise of the police." Newman (1983:2) finds that

we still know very little about why particular kinds of societies exhibit the structures of conflict resolution they do. There has been a dearth of modern *comparative* work attempting to formulate typologies of legal institutions and determine what, if any, systematic causal links may be found between these institutions and the *types* of societies in which they occur. (Emphasis in original)

One response to this asserted lack of theory is that because of its diversity and the different perspectives of different groups with an interest in the police function, "it is doubtful that a single comprehensive definition of the police function is possible or desirable" (Perry 1975:xiii).

    2. Richardson (1979) concludes that

academic or professional historians largely ignored the police until the 1960s when Roger Lane (1967) and James Richardson (1970) produced their accounts of the formative years of the Boston and New York departments respectively. Lane and Richardson concentrate on the political and administrative side of the story. . . . Both employ . . . an organization–social control explanation of the development of salaried, bureaucratic police agencies in a society with a tradition of opposition to anything resembling a standing army and a long-standing fear of the coercive power of government.

In recent years, the literature on the police has grown enormously. Police history has shared this trend. A summary of much of this literature is found in Walker 1977 and Robinson 1983. A critical view is found in Center for Research on Criminal Justice 1977. A few exceptions to the lack of attention to preindustrial police are collected in Greenberg (1976:9 n. 1). Monkkonen (1981:24) takes a stab at the problem in stating that "any historical analysis" must "question the necessity of the police." But in looking into the origins of the English police, he disposes of the matter in a page and a half, beginning with the Statute of Winchester (1285), when, he is able to conclude, there is already a "compulsory social control system" (ibid.: 32–33). Duffee (1990:13) notes the "integral connection of 'police power' with the concept of the state."

    3. For example, Fried (1967); Krader (1968, 1976); Carneiro (1970); Leacock (1972); Service (1975); Saxe (1977); Wright (1977); Sacks (1979); Haas (1982); and Newman (1983). Haas (1982: 1, 132) notes that "there have been few research projects aimed at systematically collecting data directly relevant to questions of state evolution. . . . Only within the past decade has archaeology turned its attention to such problems."

    4. Most ethnologists investigate non-Western societies. But even in these societies police have received surprisingly little academic attention. A bibliographic search using Hewitt 1965, Becker and Felkenes 1968, McGehee 1970, International Police Association 1968, and *Dissertation Abstracts* revealed a dearth of substantial work specifically related to the police function in non-Western cultures. The few studies that exist are primarily organizational in nature (e.g., Ashburn 1967; Coats 1969; Chen 1963; Foran 1962; Hagan 1980; Petty 1961; Romay 1963–1966; Vanderwood 1970). As a result, little theory has been developed concerning the nature of the police function in non-Western societies. Some discussion of police in non-Western, principally American

Indian, societies, can be found in Lowie (1927); MacLeod (1924, 1937); and Llewellyn and Hoebel (1941). These latter readings will be discussed below.

5. One exception is Moore (1987:1), discussed later, who studies the Cheyenne nation from the sixteenth through the nineteenth centuries, criticizing anthropologists who "have seen variability and reported normality, have seen open conflict and reported only resolution, have witnessed vast complexity and reported a single and fantastic crystallography of social structure."

6. A critical review of attempts to define the state from a Marxist perspective will be found in Balandier (1970:123–157) and Newman (1983). See also Krader (1968:9, 21) and Vinogradoff (1920:Vol. 1,93). For more traditional definitions, see Sahlins (1972:140, 179); Service (1962:171, 175:10, 1975:2); Adams (1966:14); Cohen (1978a:52); Wright (1977:52); Weber (1976:10); Harris (1975:370); and Wright and Fox (1978:73). Haas (1982:2–3, 20) suggests that theories of states can be divided into those characterized by integration ("governing institutions of the state first developed as integrative mechanisms to coordinate and regulate the different parts of complex societies") and those characterized by conflict ("governing institutions of the state initially developed as coercive mechanisms to resolve intra-societal conflict arising out of economic stratification"). "Most researchers have concluded that the achievements of civilizations could have been accomplished only through the coordinating and/or coercive efforts of a formal institution of government" (Haas 1982:131–132). For an attempt to apply the conflict theory, see Moore (1987).

7. These assumptions are more explicitly set forth by English than by American police historians, although these themes become more evident in American writing on police-community relations (Robinson 1979). See chapter 6.

8. We summarize only some of the major writers on early police history, that is, those writing about the period before the organized London police of 1829. Much relevant writing about law courts, prisons, local government, and the church is therefore not included. Our purpose here is not to set forth all information available on English prestate police, but rather to expose the analytic framework used by police historians.

9. Apparently this idea derives from the larger eighteenth-century notion of the role of private persons in government. "Most officeholding was still regarded . . . as a public obligation that private persons 'serving gratis or generously' " owed to the community. Indeed, all government was regarded essentially as the enlisting of "the power of private persons to carry out public ends" (Wood 1992: 82,85).

10. In Marxist theory, such ideas are denoted legal fetishism. According to Collins (1982:11), "There is the thesis that a legal order is necessary for social order: unless there is a system of laws designed to ensure compliance with a set of rules which define rights and entitlements then no civilization is possible; if laws and legal institutions were abolished anarchy would immediately break out." It follows "that laws enacted according to the dictates of a dominant ideology will appear to the members of that society as rules designed to preserve

the natural social and economic order" (ibid., p. 43). The same reasoning would apply to the creation of and the ideology supporting the police institution. See Trojanowicz and Bucqueroux (1990:ix–x; 45).

2

THE POLICE FUNCTION IN KINSHIP-BASED SOCIETIES

Anthropologists have been divided as to the merits of approaching the development of complex society from an evolutionary perspective. Early social evolutionists advocated some kind of "stage" theory in which it seemed to be argued that all civilizations passed through or were destined to pass through specified stages, for example, savage, barbaric, and civilized or hunting-gathering, herding, pastoral, agricultural, and industrial, that were based on economic and social characteristics. Other evolutionists rejected the idea that there is any necessary passage through specified stages and argued that the evolutionary pattern may vary, may progress or regress depending on ecological and cultural conditions to which any particular civilization is subject (Claessen and Skalník 1978b; Sacks 1979:194). Recently, neoevolutionists have focused upon energy capture and utilization as a diagnostic variable indicating social evolution. As to the police function, most anthropologists have been satisfied with concluding that at a certain stage one group in society has acquired a monopoly of force.

There have been few systematic attempts to theoretically reconstitute the development of the police function. Wright and Fox (1978) seek to present the development of criminal justice control mechanisms using anthropological studies (cf. Diamond 1971). The authors analyze a number of civilizations of mounting complexity in order to show the increasing incidence of criminal justice "specialists." Moving through the band, the tribe, the confederation to the primitive state, these authors find increasing political centralization and specialization: big-man, chief, paramount chief, and finally king. Social control mechanisms found in simple societies include private revenge, ridicule, and gossip and insult and scorn; more complex societies may be characterized by use of the mediator and the development in the chief of the implicit threat of force, backed by public opinion. Using the Bantu as an example of the primitive state, there, the king employs quasi-military-age regiments to arrest and to execute criminals and full-time employees to collect fines or to summon or arrest people to bring them to meetings or to court. Wright and Fox, however, express no clear idea of causative factors in passage from a policeless to a political civilization, although by implication they see this transition as one of a series of cumulative changes.

Much of the contemporary writing on the anthropology of law supports such a perspective, although it is rarely phrased in an evolutionary manner. Relationships between societal complexity on the one hand, and such factors as bargaining or authority modes of resolution on the other, are recognized. Kinship-based societies usually settle disputes through negotiation and mediation in loosely structured moot courts characterized by lack of formal proceedings, lack of authority, stress on peacekeeping rather than assessing blame, and an attempt at decision making through consensus. Complex state societies are characterized by dispute management based on adjudication in formal courts having authoritative decisions backed by legitimized coercion (Hoebel 1983). Stress is on unilateral decisions based on rules or norms and fact situations related to the violation of these rules (Nader and Todd 1978). However, these approaches beg the question of causative factors.

Simplistic notions of social development often focus on factors thought to impede social progress. There seems to be an assumption that there is a natural human tendency towards complexity; that humans *want* to develop. Yet, in fact, the members of egalitarian societies are often quite satisfied with their social institutions. To us, Fried (1967:182) has asked the pertinent question: "Why have people permitted themselves to be seduced, bilked, murphied or otherwise conned into relinquishing a condition of egalitarianism for one of inequality?" This is no easy question to answer. Clearly, the benefits of civilization are not obvious, particularly for members of an egalitarian society, who must give up certain advantages for these benefits. It is the social evolutionists who have dealt most directly with problems of causal transitions, and we proceed to a review of their positions.

There have been a number of attempts to express complete theories of social evolution, the most well known of which is that of Morgan (1964), which inspired those of Engels (1972) and Fried (1967). For all three, the crucial point in societal development is the transition from stateless to state society, although for Engels, class division precedes state formation. The latter represents a qualitative change from a noncoercive to a coercive, class-dominated society. Each explains the appearance of the police function by the inability of the kinship means of social control to support or maintain a system of inequality and class domination, because, in the process of formation, these class divisions decimated the kinship organization of society.

According to Engels, a state apparatus evolved as one of the conditions of the continued existence of a class-divided society and as a replacement for the kinship organization. The former "self-acting armed organization" was no longer possible in a society consisting of antagonistic classes—impossible because society was no longer a "self-acting" organism. It was now directed from above. And from above emerged an agent of this state power, the police, "which, apparently standing above the warring classes, suppressed their open conflict and allowed the class struggle to be fought out at most in the economic field, in so-called legal form" (Engels 1972:228). Engels's thesis is useful as a starting point for comparative analysis, but it does not "develop a very adequate theory about the causal mechanisms involved" (Pryor 1977:223; Balandier 1970:157). As Sacks (1979:102–103) points out, "his work is really not a history at all. It is evolution, a logical arrangement of static descriptions of a variety of social systems (or modes of production) frozen in time and truncated in space."

A somewhat different theory has been elaborated by political anthropologist Morton H. Fried (1967), who suggests that three stages of social organization precede the state: egalitarian, ranking, and stratification. In the first two stages, individuals have equal access to basic resources—that which is necessary to maintain human life. In the third stage, stratification, it is the control of these basic resources by some persons that makes possible and necessary means of coercive social control by which such limited access is maintained. Social control mechanisms to preserve such inequality are found within a state organization.

Thus, the police incidentally arise out of the transition from a stateless to a state society in that a society based on state organization, it is argued, is sustainable only through force. Despite general agreement about the association between the two, there is some disagreement among writers about whether a state bureaucracy produces a class structure or whether a class structure produces a state. It will be useful to briefly review some of these efforts before elaborating our theory.

Pryor (1977) attempted to generalize the concept of slavery as a precipitating factor in the development of the police function. Comparing sixty stateless societies at different levels of economic and political development, Pryor (p. 246) related slavery to various other variables, finding that once there is a "family-social structure in which wives do considerably more economic work than their husbands . . . the social structure permits a relatively easy introduction of slavery into the work situation." Such introduction is most likely to take place where farming is the mode of food production (p. 242). A slave-based mode of production posed certain problems of control for the dominant class.

> In societies with slavery as economic capital, serious problems of ruling slaves exist because the slaves can see quite plainly their relatively low living standards vis-à-vis their masters. . . . In order to prevent large-scale political disruptions by slaves or in order to quell slave revolts if they occur, a certain amount of political centralization is necessary. That is, political power must be sufficiently concentrated that decisive repressive actions can be taken whenever trouble might arise; indeed, the very existence of such political concentration is an important assurance that trouble will not arise. Therefore we would hypothesize that the occurrence of political concentration is a necessary condition for the maintenance of slavery as economic capital, an hypothesis receiving empirical confirmation. (Pryor 1977:235)

Many state societies have developed what we have called the "modern" police function without the institution of slavery. But slavery provides the most clear-cut example of what Engels (1972:223) called "a new cleavage of society into classes." In such a system, the need for the ruling class to protect itself is evident. In a less obviously polarized class system, however, *must* a police function arise to control class conflict and/or maintain class division in favor of the dominant class? If so, how would such a function develop?

Barry Hindess and Paul Q. Hirst (1975, 1977) have substantially advanced this analysis. It is our position, which the Hindess and Hirst analysis supports, that the essence of the transition to a coercive societal organization will be found in a series of incremental changes in which "early states developed gradually from earlier-existing organizational forms" (Claessen and Skalník 1978c:619) and in which kinship itself can represent a coercive protostate structure (Claessen and Skalník 1978b:21). Karen Sacks (1979:7) has put it well: "The rise of states was not an event but a process, and an uneven one in time and space at that. It is still a process. The other side of that process is that kin corporations were not totally destroyed overnight. Rather they have been and continue to be slowly subverted, transformed and overcome."

KINSHIP-BASED SOCIETIES

Our purpose here is to explore the development of coercive characteristics of kinship structure. Thereafter, we will show how these characteristics may have evolved into a permanent coercive apparatus. This section is informed by the work of Hindess and Hirst, and again draws upon the work of scholars in theoretical traditions who deal directly with the question of causal relationships. We begin with an examination of the attributes of kinship-based society that are most relevant for our work.

One of the major characteristics of such societies is that the people produce most of what they consume and consume most of what they produce (Fallers 1964:117). However, pictures of such egalitarian, idyllic societies, in which (it is sometimes said) there are no divisions of producers and nonproducers and therefore there is no basis for a class structure, do not, of course, take into consideration sex or age divisions, nor such natural nonproducers as the too young, the too old, and the disabled, for whom some provision must be made. They do not consider intertribal trade and exchange. They do not consider differential access to diverse ecological zones by different kinship groups. Nor do they consider overproducers, or persons of exceptional ability, courage, ambition, energy, acquisitiveness, or inventiveness who may thereby create deviations in the customary straight line.

Stateless societies cannot be distinguished from complex societies merely by determining the stage at which they are capable of producing a surplus of food products that will enable the society to support a class of nonproducers. Such a simplistic analysis leads to an explanation of change based on technological forces rather than on modification in social organization. Another difficulty with such an analysis is that many simple societies are quite capable of producing a surplus. Richard B. Lee's data (1968, 1979) on the Kung bushmen, for example, show that a surplus of mongongo nuts, their staple food, lies rotting on the ground for the lack of someone with a reason to gather them.

Nevertheless, surplus seems to be a necessary if not sufficient condition for the development of social stratification, and a variable worth focusing upon. The question is not whether any particular society has a surplus, but how the labor capable of producing a surplus is *appropriated* and how the surplus products of that labor are distributed.[1] In egalitarian societies, there is no meaningful social distinction between a class of laborers, or direct producers, and a class of nonlaborers, and therefore there are no antagonistic relations of production.[2] There is no overarching political level, and therefore no state. Such a society is organized and governed by and through its ideological formation, that is, by customs, traditional norms of behavior, and rituals organized and enunciated through a kinship system. Such a system includes within it means for directing the labor process so that surplus is appropriated and distributed in accordance with the rules of kinship and reciprocity.

Arrangements that allow for collective and cooperative appropriation are not excluded by such an economic base. Neither does it preclude coercion. But the organization of a kinship-based society does preclude a state apparatus to maintain such coercion (Hindess and Hirst 1975:77). In most cases, production of a large surplus is of little benefit to individuals in kinship-based societies.

At this point, it seems important to make distinctions between types of redistribution systems. *Simple redistribution* consists of the appropriation of natural products ready for use (nuts, roots, animals) and their redistribution by means of a network of relations established on a temporary or semipermanent basis, as illustrated by a hunting-gathering society living in small bands. This type of distribution network may be determined by the fragility and temporary nature of the social organization. Bands are small in size, often variable in composition, and may not endure as units for long periods of time. There is therefore no basis for social relations permanent enough to sustain the cooperation necessary to complete more complex labor tasks. The dominant social division of labor is by age and sex.

Complex redistribution, on the other hand, allows distribution of the product throughout a permanent network of relationships established in advance of any particular labor process. There is the likelihood then of cooperation among work teams. Such redistribution makes possible (1) increased productivity of labor and (2) a greater number of laborers and thus an increase in the amount of surplus labor appropriated for redistribution within the community. Such a community can support specialists who do not engage in food production but can receive their share of food just as if they had produced it themselves. A larger nonproductive population such as children and older persons can be sustained. The presence of these nonproducers has several results: (1) a continued high level of production depends on a continuing division of labor and complex cooperation over long periods of time that in turn encourage mechanisms to supervise and coordinate the labor process, and their appreciation as a necessary part of production of this surplus (an addition to the ideological component); (2) it permits the support of a higher density of population, that is, more producers; (3) it allows the development of persons who can devote time to ceremonial activities (appeasing or opportuning the gods to increase or maintain production); and (4) it encourages the development of relationships with other tribes that tend to promote exchanges of items produced. In societies with such a system of distribution, normally it would be the elders or other leaders who would receive the surplus and direct its redistribution. Distribution would be based not on the relative amount of work done by the team or on temporary relationships that might have been established between individuals, but on the position each person occupied in the kinship network (as determined by age, status, or sex).

Thus, the emergence of particular kinds of complex kinship relations is a necessary condition for the transition from simple to complex redistribution as the dominant form of distribution. Kinship relations, and often very complex ones, exist in societies where there is simple redistribution, but their existence is not critical for the reproduction of the economy. The kinship relations that seem necessary for complex redistribution are those featuring hierarchical relations within the household or lineage, between elders and juniors and between lineages and villages within a tribe (Lowie 1927:82). Although elders and adults of various statuses may supervise and coordinate the labor process, it is the kinship network of relationships that allows the direction, coor-dination, and supervision of labor by elders and other adults so as to extract surplus labor from those lower in the hierarchy. Division of labor, however, is limited by the social organization of kinship that predetermines that the surplus will be redistributed to the community itself according to customary relations.

To illustrate the position outlined above, Hindess and Hirst (1975:46) have used Claude Meillassoux's work with the Gouro of the Ivory Coast, a tribe where both simple and complex distribution are present but where complex distribution is dominant. "The elder (*doyen*) of the community is the pole of the system of circulation. The production of the group makes movement towards him, then returns for the greater part, if not, in its totality, towards the members of the community" (ibid.: 49).

Underlying this means of distribution is the agricultural mode of production.

As soon as agriculture becomes important, the "reproduction" (continuation) of the production community has to be a dominant preoccupation; it becomes of paramount importance to gain (and retain) control over enough women in order to ensure the generation of new members of the group; only then is there the guarantee that the agricultural cycles can be renewed uninterruptedly in the future. It is only under such circumstances—as expression of specific production and reproduction problems—that kinship becomes the dominant organizational principle. (Geschiere 1982:56–57)

Although most tools necessary to set the means of production in motion (wooden tools, mortars, pestles, and canoes) are collectively available, iron tools (machetes) remain in the exclusive possession of the elders (ibid.: 50). The hierarchical relationship between elders and juniors allows elders and other adults to assign land or work and to regulate marriage exchanges; and thus "the primary basis of the elders' authority would lie in [their control over] reproduction" (Geschiere 1982:93). Hindess and Hirst suggest that both the coordination of labor and the regulation of marriages involve some forms of coercion such as deprivation of food or slavery (forced labor). Such a social formation is what Sacks (1979:73) calls corporate kin groups wherein

every individual has access to at least some productive property by virtue of being born into one of these kin-based corporations. Here power exists to the extent that these corporations have unequal amounts of productive property and members within them have unequal access to their corporation's property.

Moreover, there is a different distribution for prestige goods (iron and salt) and subsistence products. The elders are in charge of the former and the women of the latter (Geschiere 1982:98). But neither coercion nor such division of labor signifies that the elders are an exploiting class or that a state exists (Sahlins 1972:93–94, 138; Terray 1974:331). On the contrary, power resides in the customary order carried on by the elders as a group and not in any one person, for there is no institutional base to perpetuate individual power (Copet-Rougier 1986:68). Of course, elders who are "representatives of the gentile community" are well advanced over elders in a simpler society in which elders can command "respect" but where that respect is dependent on their ability to constantly demonstrate their sagacity (Geschiere 1982). Nevertheless,

as far as the position of the leaders is concerned the crucial question is not whether they are elected but whether their position is maintained by means of a state apparatus. The intermittent exercise of coercion in lineage societies does not necessarily imply the presence of a *state* coercive apparatus which enables the elders as a class (or class-like category) to exploit their cadets. The coercion exercised by the elder is strictly limited in scope . . . it is exercised by the individual elders as representatives of the gentile community. (Hindess and Hirst 1975:77–78; see also Geschiere 1982:91. Emphasis supplied.)

The coercive force is thus embodied in the capacity of elders to withhold essential goods and services or to employ supernatural sanctions relating to illness and ill fortune until their demands are complied with (Copet-Rougier 1986:57; Haas 1982:82). By punishing their juniors for violating the rules of hierarchy, elders reproduce the societal hierarchy (Copet-Rougier 1986:64). Similar situations, studied by Malinowski (1921), may be seen in the redistribution of surplus by the Kula chiefs in the Trobriand Islands, and in the mobilization of labor for their seagoing voyages.

We see, therefore, that a kinship-based society with a complex distribution system has, in addition to the usual accoutrements of such a society (reciprocal relations, relatively equal access to basic resources, authority based on kinship rather than on political structure), a hierarchical order of kinship relations that permits coercive use of traditions, rituals, and customs by the elders or others for and on behalf of the tribal unit. We thus have a theoretical umbrella under cover of which a police function can act through the leaders on behalf of the community. At the same time, the structure contains the essential building blocks for a different police function once a class-dominated system forms.

In addition to a hierarchical, coercive organization based on age, there may also be divisions based on other characteristics, including sex. Godelier (1982a) studied the Baruya people, a simple society living in seventeen villages and hamlets in a mountainous region of New Guinea, who until 1951 had not known of the presence of whites (ibid.: 9, 19). The society exhibits two kinds of domination of one group over another: all males over all females, and some males over other males and all females. Sacks (1979) also examines coercive kinship organizations based on sex. We explore both of these studies in greater detail in the next chapter. In fact, in apparently egalitarian societies where status differences seem to be based more on achievement than on ascription, there are nevertheless a variety of differences that can form the basis for coercive kinship differences (see, e.g., Strathern 1982).

Having argued that various social divisions may be the base of a coercive system without the existence of either exploitation or a police mechanism, our next task will be to examine police mechanisms in societies that have a central redistributive authority but where the central authority and the police, acting for that authority, act on behalf of the whole community. Thereafter, we will suggest the transactional steps whereby a coercive, stateless society can be converted to a society with a police institution acting on behalf of a dominant class.

SOCIETIES WITH CENTRAL AUTHORITIES
SERVING THE ENTIRE COMMUNITY

In some societies that have a central authority, that central authority is judged (by the members of that community) as successful,[3] and is perpetuated because it serves the community better than the community can serve itself without the central authority. Among such societies, some have social control mechanisms that are clearly identifiable as a police, but a police that has a function of serving the whole community rather than some part of it.

Service (1975) ties his theory of the rise of the state to the gradual growth of a central authority or bureaucracy out of an egalitarian society. At a point at which this bureaucracy acts for itself rather than for the community, the state is born. While such a summary of Service's theory is a gross oversimplification, it highlights the aspects of Service's account that have particular application to our theory. Service (1975) relates the way a "big-man" and his followers "may resemble an embryonic *chiefdom* . . . : Leadership is centralized, statuses are arranged hierarchically, and there is to some degree a hereditary aristocratic ethos." Such a big-man has "no formal means to enforce his authority and his command elicits only a voluntary response from his followers" (ibid.: 74, emphasis in original).

Redistribution, according to Service, may be closely "allied to the rise of and perpetuation of leadership . . . as [the big-man's] position as redistributor becomes more useful or necessary" (ibid.: 75). Service expands this point, making clear the usefulness of this position of redistributor to the community as a whole:

The most significant group activity in chieftains is redistribution, which not only enables a leader to become a permanent fixture but also requires that he do his job well. This means that he must be able to command labor in agricultural and craft production, and then he must equitably and wisely decide how the goods are to be allocated. Among the important uses of the goods is to store certain of them, not only to later subsidize public labor and craftsmen, but as capital for uses in contingencies like war or a great feast for important visitors.

Such powers are economically and socially useful, having, as mentioned, a politically integrative effect. (Ibid.: 94, 292–293; see also Godelier 1972:113; Malinowski as quoted in Sahlins 1972:189, app. B; White 1959:254; Lenski 1966:165)

By the very nature of an egalitarian, segmentary society, "to be successful, the chief must have the active and willing support of his subjects" (Wright and Fox 1978:73). Thus, far from having the disruptive effect that the "redistribution" function has in a state society in which distribution is by definition unequal, in a stateless society, redistribution and the centralized bureaucracy accompanying it represent an equalizing factor and a benefit to the community (Sahlins 1972:132–133). As Service (1975:95) concludes, "It is evident that a well-managed redistributional system by its very nature, contributes to solidarity. Most obvious, and most often remarked upon, is its organismic quality."

Such a description and interpretation of redistribution need not be an exercise in romanticism or teleology. Social relations of reciprocity within a kinship structure in which there is a central authority converts the apparent generosity of the chief into a "manifest imposition of debt" by placing the "recipient in a circumspect and responsive relation to the donor during all that period the gift is unrequited. The economic relation of giver-receiver is the political relations of leader-follower" (Sahlins 1972:133). "[R]edistribution is conceived and sanctioned as a reciprocal relation, and is in form but a centralization of reciprocities" (ibid., 134 n. 16; see also ibid., 249; Ruyle 1973:615).

Nevertheless, if a chiefdom begins to expand its bureaucracy in the direction of self-aggrandizement without at the same time acquiring a forceful means of maintaining itself, the result may very well be dissolution[4] (Godelier 1977:111; MacLeod 1931:114–116). Thus, Service (1975), quoting Sahlins's study of a Polynesian society, states:

The expansion of a chiefdom seems to have entailed a more-than-proportionate expansion of the administrative apparatus and its conspicuous consumption. The ensuing drain on the people's wealth and expectations was eventually expressed in an unrest that destroyed both chief and chiefdom. (1975:96; see also Sahlins 1972:146)

These instances accord with the well-accepted idea that in stateless societies social control mechanisms act to attempt a reconciliation of differences among individual members of the community in order to restore unity and well-being to the community as a community (Service 1975:126). In a state society, split as it is into classes with a structure to maintain that division, the concept of reconciliation is subordinated to that of coercion (Chambliss 1975:2), a factor that increases community divisions.

What is the nature of the police function in such societies? In many non-Western cultures, sodalities or associations "cutting across kindreds and bands" (Hoebel 1978:40), occupy a transitional position between the absence of formal police functions and the formal police structure of state organization. Since sodalities are "mainly centered on the common experience of the members as warriors, with rituals glorifying and enhancing that experience, and with duties and services performed on behalf of the community at large" (ibid.), sodalities combine both individual and community advancement. From the point of view of social organization, the Plains societies of the American West were perhaps the simplest societies to have such sodalities. Plains military societies policed tribal ceremonies and hunts and aided the tribal council in enforcing customary law such as a sentence of exile (ibid.:42, 55).

Lowie (1927) describes how exigencies of the hunt precipitated the development of the police function in an essentially egalitarian society in which the thought of a chief having absolute, unchecked power over life and property was foreign. In order to prevent a premature attack on the buffalo herd, particular men's societies were empowered to protect communal access to resources through the use of legitimized coercion, including the confiscation of property and corporal or capital punishment. In the words of Lowie (1927:103–104):

The personnel of the constabulary varies with the tribe; the duties may be linked with a particular society (Mandan, Hidatsa), or be assumed by various military societies in turn (Crow), or fall to the lot of distinguished men without reference to associational affiliations (Kansas). But everywhere the basic idea is that during the hunt a group is vested with the power forcibly to prevent premature attacks on the herd and to punish offenders by corporal punishment, by confiscation of the game illegally secured, by destruction of their property generally, and in extreme cases by killing them. . . . If, for example, a man had been murdered by another, the official peacemakers of the tribe—often identical with the buffalo police—were primarily concerned with pacifying the victim's kin rather than with meting out just punishment. There was thus a groping sentiment on behalf of territorial cohesion and against internecine strife. But there was no feeling that any impartial authority seated above the parties to the feud had been outraged and demanded penance or penalty. In juridical terminology, even homicide was a tort, not a crime. But with transgressions of the hunting regulations it was otherwise; they were treated as an attempt against the public, in short, as a criminal act, and they were punished with all the vigor appropriate to political offenses (Lowie 1935:5; see also Hoebel 1978:58).

John H. Provinse saw the functions of these Plains Indian police as extending beyond their function in the hunt. Based on a number of references found in the reports, Provinse (1937:348) concludes that "police duties in connection with settling disputes, punishing offenders, and maintaining order in the camp generally would seem to surpass in importance the police duties at the communal hunt." Plains Indians also used police while engaged in public works such as burial mounds (Black 1976:89).

Black (1976:46, 90) cites a number of other such examples from the literature. There are the Yahgan nomadic bands, where appointed "policemen" police the initiation ceremonies: "They forcibly drag refractory tyros to the initiation lodge, overpower a troublemaker, bind him, and let him lie for half a day without food or drink." The Apinaye Indians of northern Brazil utilized policemen during the growing season. Anyone who harvested before that time was subject to punishment. Likewise, another tribe "punished anyone who prematurely harvested wild rice" and "the early Ontong Javanese had officials . . . who guarded against theft of coconuts and other foodstuffs from the common lands."

Clearly such "police" have coercive temporary powers. What distinguishes them from modern police, however, is first, that they were in some sense ordinary tribal members who held their police powers on a temporary basis, and second, that they served the collective interests.

TRANSITIONAL MECHANISMS

As we have argued, in attempting to construct an evolutionary approach to the police function, it does not seem profitable to try to provide a series of stages through which the police function necessarily progressed to its modern guise; neither does it seem fruitful to search for the point at which the police function suddenly appears (Godelier 1972:124; Price 1978:168; Claessen and Skalník 1978b:15). Rather, we should be searching for key areas of change likely to be related to the police function. We believe that the most pertinent developmental changes are modifications in productive and distributional relations; political and community structure, social relations, and ideology.

Moore (1987:338) describes the historical process as a constantly shifting "natural and political environment." Resources are lost, technology is invented, population characteristics change, and tribal nations immigrate—a whole host of problems are created that are unsolvable within the existing structure, and so the whole process is repeated. That is, the tribe does not evolve slowly through time but bounces through history in a series of national identities, periodically forming and reforming (ibid.).

Sacks suggests the problems in answering transformational questions:

An evolutionary discussion cannot speak to questions of change—the processes by which communal modes were transformed into kin corporations. These questions can be answered only by comparative historical inquiries into particular transformations. . . . The information on such transformations, particularly for the preclass world, is sparse. (1979:193)

Our purpose, then, will be to suggest in each of these areas the transitional mechanisms likely to move a society from a coercive but classless to a class-dominated organization maintained, at least in part, by a coercive state apparatus, of which the police institution is one component. We will describe what we believe to be the sufficient conditions for the development of the police function without at the same time asserting that these are necessary conditions from which the police specialized function must follow.

We agree with the way Fried (1967:182–183) posed and answered the pertinent question mentioned previously:

Why have people permitted themselves to be seduced, bilked, murphied, or otherwise conned into relinquishing a condition of egalitarianism for one of inequality? . . . I believe that stratified society and the state emerged in the same quiet way and were institutionally fully present before anyone fumbled for a word by which to designate them.

Fried's point is important—that the development of stratified society can be a lengthy, subtle, and barely perceptible process. It has already been suggested that the so-called egalitarian society was anything but structureless. Nor was it a society without coercion. Given, then, a kinship-structured, hierarchical society with a complex redistribution system and a coercive order, how did "an institution which began primarily as a functional necessity of group life [become] . . . an instrument employed primarily for self-aggrandizement and exploitation?" (Lenski 1966:168). How was the earlier system converted to one in which a particular group (class) maintains itself in power by means of a permanent, specialized coercive (state) apparatus?[5]

One key would seem to be the ability *and desire* to accumulate a surplus. "In the formation of the early state, the production of a surplus constitutes the pre-eminent factor enabling the development of a governmental apparatus as well as the institutionalization of inequality: a dialectical process" (Claessen and Skalník 1978c:628).

Once one is chief within a complex redistribution system, he has captive the kinds of virtues and material possessions that can attract to him the means to substantially increase his ability to appropriate and thus systematically accumulate surplus. This accumulation of wealth, in turn, increases his capability to add to his work force, and so on (Sahlins 1972: app. B). He remains as chief because he appears to embody the community-approved virtues of liberality, reciprocity, and mutual aid so important to tribal survival, and thus it is upon him that tribal survival seems to depend (Saxe 1977:122). Redistribution of foodstuffs appears to be the material realization of tribal custom and virtues. In fact as well as in appearance, redistribution tends to enhance reciprocity, allowing more cooperative enterprise (Polanyi 1968:225; White 1959:234).

Chiefs may obtain additional workers in numerous ways. Many men need work only part-time in order to obtain enough food for their families, or in some agricultural societies need to do no work at all. Their wives work in the fields while they work for the chief (Fallers 1964:144). A chief may also acquire several wives and thereby acquire sons to work in his fields (Boserup 1970:37–38). Likewise, his marriageable daughters may attract young men as "adopted sons," also increasing his influence by establishing contacts with other lineages (Geschiere 1982:47). Low producers who accept gifts of food from the chief may be in his debt and so will feel obligated to work it off (Sahlins 1972:252; Adams 1966:54); retainers or clients often attach themselves to a chief who is in a position to be generous to them (Mair 1964:chap. 7; Sacks 1979:177). Continuation of this dynamic results in an institutionalization of power:

They are still primitive. The political armature is provided by kinship groups. But these groups make positions of official authority a condition of their organization. Now men do not personally construct their power over others; they come *to* power. Power resides in the office, in an organized acquiescence to chiefly privileges and organized means of upholding them. Included is a specific control over the goods and the services of the underlying population. The people owe in advance their labor and their products. And with these funds of power, the chief indulges in grandiose gestures of generosity ranging from personal aid to massive support of collective ceremonial or economic enterprise. The flow of goods between chiefs and people then becomes cyclical and continual. (Sahlins 1972:139, emphasis in original; see also Mandel 1968:40)

The redistribution system organized around and by the chief means that each family is obligated to the chief and to the community to make a regular contribution. The permanent surplus produced allows the community to support craftsmen, many of whom attach themselves to the chief. Such people are dependent on the chief because they are not producers themselves (Mandel 1968:20). Larger projects requiring cooperative labor, such as irrigation systems and other public works, are now possible. In such a system, mass cooperative labor need not be forced.[6]

Sahlins (1972:130) expresses the contradiction within the stateless system produced by the kinds of systems we have described:

In the course of primitive social evolution, main control over the domestic economy seems to pass from the formal solidarity of the kinship structure to its political aspect. As the structure is politicized, especially as it is centralized in ruling chiefs, the household economy is mobilized in a larger social cause. This impulse transmitted by policy to production is often attested ethnographically. For although the primitive headman or chief may be himself driven by personal ambition, he incarnates the collective finalities; he personifies a public economic principle in opposition to the private ends and petty self-concerns of the household economy. Tribal powers that be and would-be powers encroach upon the domestic system to undermine its autonomy, curb its anarchy, and unleash its productivity.[7]

The essence of the kinship-based society is that it represents a *unity* of economic, social, political, and ideological life (Godelier 1977:67). The transition to a civil society occurs when that unity is ruptured "so that kinship relations *cease to play* the dominant role unifying all the functions of social life" (Godelier 1977:123, emphasis in original). This rupture can best be understood by considering in more detail the ideological evolution suggested earlier by Sahlins—that the chief "personifies a public economic principle in opposition to the private ends . . . of the household economy." Such a change represents a reconstitution of the material foundation of and reconception of community,[8] and as such forms a crucial hinge in our theory of transition from stateless to state society.

As neatly expressed by Sahlins (1972:140), "What begins with the would-be head-man putting his production to others' benefit, ends, to some degree, with others putting their production to the chief's benefit." This transformation in the material social relationship between the chief and his kinsmen is "compensated" for by increased production and the evolution of an ideology unnecessary in earlier stages of development (Service 1962:290–294).

On [the basis of a mode of production founded on cooperative labor] arises the ideology characteristic of all peoples at [the simple] stage: sharing, generosity, hospitality, brotherhood, empathy, humaneness . . . , and equality. This perspective . . . has a material basis. At this stage, however, the idea and reality still coincide. Equalizing the basis and chances of survival and well-being for all individuals is a prerequisite to the survival of the group. A person who suddenly acquires wealth is considered a danger to the community. (Vilakazi, commenting on Ruyle 1973:624)

These individuals are seen by many commentators as the primary driving force in manipulating economic resources, expressing individual private interests clothed in public custom and virtue (Sahlins 1972:130; Krader 1976:35; Lowie 1927:62; Ruyle 1973:627; Rounds 1979; Claessen and Skalník 1978c:621). "An overt display of individual ambition and superiority" produces a "tension between levelling tendencies" of an egalitarian society and "personal ambition" (Geschiere 1982:54). Such men need not be motivated by economic gain, a dynamic more appropriate to a more complex societal organization (White 1959:233–234). Through virtues loudly applauded in tribal society, military leaders may conquer lands and obtain spoils. With liberality and generosity, they may distribute their plunder to the most courageous among them. By attacking an outside enemy, they protect their own kinsmen; the warfare may tend both to unify the tribe and to consolidate their individual power as the ones who lead their kinsmen in a common enterprise (Geschiere 1982:47). Though war may increase stratification, it does not cause it. It does, however, lead to loyalty on the part of the participants; and it encourages the growth of secret military societies, an alternative to kinship ties (Lowie 1927:13; Fried 1967: 214–216; Adams 1966:151–153; Ruyle 1973:614; Hoebel 1978:40); or such men may accumulate (concentrate) powers of visible and invisible (magic) violence to attain, maintain, and even pass on their position (Copet-Rougier 1986:67–68). While as a result of these individual assertions the mass of the people have not basically changed their material being, these "few . . . are torn loose from the community" to form a nucleus of an incipient class structure (Krader 1976:35; Harris 1975:380–382).

Once the socially produced product is directed to the redistributor, it is then the redistributor who appears, after a time, to be the *source* of these goods, and therefore the condition upon which "the *unity* and *survival* of the community as a whole" is assured (Godelier 1977:8, emphasis in original; See also Ruyle 1973:616; Cohen 1978a:67).

Once the *common interests* of all members of a community are incarnated in the person of one of its members (or a section, the family, the clan), this person will represent on a *higher* level the community of which he is a member. He is therefore both in the *centre* of it and *above* it. Responsible for the common interests, he controls the surplus labour destined to satisfy those interests; having more responsibilities than other members in the community, he has more rights and this inequality of status forms a *hierarchy* in the ensemble of community membership. (Godelier 1977:174, emphasis in original; see also Krader 1976:35)

Thus, the redistributive function may lead to hereditary office in which lineage rather than the individual ability of the kinsman is determinate[9] (White 1959:234; Lenski 1966:109; Ruyle 1973). Core or privileged lineages may arise, around which the lesser clans group (Sanders and Price 1968:131–132); slaves may be taken, again distributed unevenly, thereby differentially increasing productive capacity (Terray 1974:328–329); ownership of or symbolic representation of the common lands justifies the chief in levying taxes and rents (Ruyle 1973:614); conquered or community land may become "state" land and thereby be converted into private property of the sovereign (Skalník 1978:604); or the sovereign, in acting as "the ultimate source of order and justice," determines that offenses against his dignity are in contravention of the common good (Mair 1964:204; Lenski 1966:181). Dominant-subordinate relations become the focus of political-social relations, and finally to "*emergent* social classes" (Claessen and Skalník 1978a:642, emphasis in original). Deference, loyalty, and obedience to hierarchical superiors replaces individual striving as a means of achievement (Cohen 1978a:67–69). The former kinsman becomes thereby the ruler-father and the people his subject-children (Rounds 1979:78; Ruyle 1973:616).

While we have discussed such changes in terms of initiatives by chiefs in redistribution patterns, change may also occur as a result of one group's taking power over another group: by capturing slaves in warfare, or through denying to another group access to basic resources. Eventually, what began as a restriction of one group by another becomes by one extension of this same principle of dominance a restriction of most of the dominant group by its own elite, which now demands tribute for access by other tribal members to its own basic resources.

To this point we have relied primarily on the literature and language of social evolution in developing our arguments in this chapter. We recognize that there are many variations on the basic theme of how complex redistribution can act in a particular social milieu to precipitate widespread changes. Since such changes feed back on one another, and take a considerable time to unfold, it is difficult if not impossible to demonstrate an ultimate causal mechanism or mechanisms even for a single society.

One of the most anthropologically interesting cases of the rise of social stratification is that of the Polynesian societies. Kirch (1989) provides a comprehensive summary of literature concerning this case, or rather, these cases. Over a period of approximately a millennium, a relatively homogeneous ancestral society, which Kirch (1989:5) calls APS or Ancestral Polynesian Society, colonized a variety of previously uninhabited island ecosystems. "Over time, the differentiation of Ancestral Polynesian society results from colonization of a range of new and environmentally contrastive islands, and from subsequent internal change, generally in isolation" (ibid.). At the time of European contact, the various Polynesian societies showed great similarities in language and culture, but relatively great differences in social stratification. On smaller, ecologically homogeneous islands, the ramage, or basic kinship unit, of social organization, an internally stratified unit based on primogeniture, was also the basic political unit. There existed relatively few distinctions between ramages. However, on ecologically complex islands, such as Tonga and Hawaii, certain ramages were able to control choice ecological areas, and complex patterns of stratification arose. Complex redistribution patterns appear to have played a central role in this developmental sequence.

The development of late prehistoric Hawaiian society illustrates exactly the sorts of transformations we have been analyzing in this chapter. As Kirch (1989:257–258) puts it,

By the time of European contact, Hawaiian society had undergone two fundamental departures from Ancestral Polynesian Society, which highlight the degree of structural transformation. Both of these changes can be couched in negative terms from the viewpoint of the common people: they lost their genealogies, and they lost direct control of their land. . . . The term for commoners, *maka' ainana*, is of particular interest, since it is the Hawaiian reflex of Proto-Polynesian *kainanga*, a corporate descent group together with its territorial segment. As the "people of the land," the term *maka' ainana* retained one aspect of its ancient semantic value, but the implication of corporate descent had disappeared, as had the implication of ownership. Instead, the term had come to represent the *class* of people who worked the land, and who stood in opposition to the class of landowners (*haku' aiba*)—the chiefs—to whom the *maka' ainana* owed tribute and labour.

Retainers and religious props helped the chiefs maintain dominance:

The Hawaiian polity can be analyzed not only in terms of class stratification and land control, but in terms of its hierarchical, decision-making structure. Aside from the *ahupua's* chiefs and their *konohiki*, there existed a considerable body of councilors, priests, executants, and other retainers who formed a "court" of the paramount chief. Most important of these officials were the *kalaimoku* and the *kahuna nui*. The *kalaimoku* essentially acted on behalf of the paramount in most secular matters, and his position was in many ways analogous to the Tongan *hau*. Though the position was not hereditary it was, significantly, often accorded to affinal relatives of the paramount. Sahlins . . . through an analysis of the Kamehameha polity, makes the reason for this clear: by handing the secular affairs over to the *kalaimoku* the paramount not only preserved his tabu status, but he kept the power out of the hands of close consanguineal relatives, who were always to be suspected as potential usurpers. Also vital to the operation of government, the *kahuna nui*, or high priest of the order of Ku, god of war, assisted the paramount in vital rituals, especially those pertaining to war and conquest. (Kirsch, 1989:258–259)

Clearly, however, complex redistribution was instrumental in maintaining this system:

The system of tribute *(ho'okupu)* upon which the polity depended for its economic support was bound up with another great cult, that of Lono, god of fertility and agriculture. Collection of tribute (in the form of barkcloth, cordage, feathers, dogs, and so on) took place in conjunction with the *makahiki*, an annual four-month-long season devoted to the god Lono, and during which the temples of Ku were dismantled and warfare forbidden. As Handy and Handy (1972:351) pointed out, the *makahiki* had its origins in the first-fruits rites that were certainly a part of Ancestral Polynesian ritual; its evolution as a ritualized form of taxation arose later in conjunction with "the sociopolitical institutions of the late Hawaiian feudal system." In light of the emphasis that has frequently been placed on the concept of redistribution in chiefdom societies . . . , it is important to point out that in Hawai'i redistribution of the *ho'okupu* was essentially limited to the chiefly class. Malo makes this perfectly clear when he states that "the king distributed it among the chiefs and the companies of soldiery throughout the land. . . . No share of this property, however, was given to the people." Thus the *makahiki* served as a political vehicle for the paramount to reward his supporters within the chiefly class. (Kirsch 1989:260)

Why did the common people tolerate this situation?

We should not be misled, however, to believe that the bonds of reciprocity between chief and people were totally severed, that the Hawaiian chiefs had relinquished all obligations to support their followers. Chiefs were, indeed, expected to take care of the people, not only through their ritual mediation with the gods, but more tangibly in providing the means of subsistence when shortage occurred. David Malo, famous custodian of Hawaiian tradition, put it metaphorically: "As the rat will not desert the pantry where he thinks food is, so the people will not desert the king while they think there is food in his storehouse." (Kirsch 1989: 260–261)

In short, while Hawaiian society strained the limits of kinship-based social organization, they never transcended it.

As Sahlins so elegantly demonstrated, the Hawaiian political cycle, and its economic base, reveal an essential truth concerning the most highly developed of the Polynesian chiefdoms. Though the ruling elite had managed to greatly distance themselves from the commoner populace, and though they exercised a majority (but *not* a monopoly) of force, they never managed to completely sever the *kinship* bond between chiefs and people that Hawaiian society inherited from Ancestral Polynesian Society. "They had not broken structurally with the people at large, so they might dishonor the kinship morality only on pain of a mass disaffection" (Sahlins 1972:148). Thus, Hawaiian society pushed the evolution of the chiefdom polity to its structural limits, a threshold which was the "boundary of primitive society itself." (Ibid.: 261–262)

We have already described how the complex redistribution model combined significant political and ideological changes. We now suggest further changes instrumental in the development of state organization. It is at this point that the police institution in our modern sense comes into being.

We have argued that a police in the modern sense can exist only within the context of a class-dominated society. In such a society, the police represent the *force* by which the interests of the dominant class are maintained. Such a police, by definition, cannot be present in an egalitarian society, that is, in a classless society in which social relations are based on kinship. Put another way, how can we explain the means by which an egalitarian society (that is, a society without the sort of inner conflicts inherent in a class-dominated society) experiences a structural change radically modifying its class base? Harris, for example, describes the egalitarian society as one that has the capacity to be fulfilling for all—the strong as well as the weak (1975:308, 366; Leacock 1972:25).

For an egalitarian society to begin exploiting one part of its population for the benefit of another part requires a concept and practice so utterly foreign to egalitarian ethics as to demand an enormous ideological leap. Such a transformation implies a series of evolutionary changes, each of which, at the time, must appear to the individuals in that society to be reasonably consistent with its traditional ways. Thus, where a conquering group treats a defeated enemy as having an "inferior social status," such treatment "must be preceded by an evolution within the conquering group of the ideology, the social differentiations, and the administrative mechanisms" that would allow the conquering group to accept such "treatment of the defeated" (MacLeod 1924:51, quoted portions italicized in original).

In seeking to explain the source of structural change in such an outwardly stable society, we have examined some points of disequilibrium within that society that carry the seeds of change. In proceeding toward a society consisting of dominant and subordinate classes, the dominant class, in becoming dominant, must institutionalize a means of exploiting the subordinate class. Exploitation of one class by another implies that the dominant class determines and dominates the societal mode of production, whose products are produced by the larger subordinate class for the benefit of the smaller dominant class. The position of the dominant class is sustained by a political (a part of which may be a police) and an ideological structure appropriate to the nature of that society (Ruyle 1973:607).

The continuation of communal relations in dimmer form has the important ideological effect of hiding the exploitive character "because the old ideological forms, which now serve different ends, correspond to former, more egalitarian relations of production" (Godelier 1977:69). "In so far as subjects and oppressors shared the same ideology (politico-economic reciprocity and religious displays), real oppression was concealed from both groups; it was therefore fully justified in the eyes of the latter and passively borne, if not accepted, by the former" (Godelier 1977:69).

Thus, a state or protostate may exist with such a strong ideological base that it is able to maintain an essentially class-based system without "any institutionalized coercive force (police, militia) to maintain internal security" (Schaedel 1978:313). At the same time it has been noted that this disassociation from kin relations is class specific, being "of smallest extent in the lower strata (peasantry, urban lower classes); limited in the upper hereditary classes (especially the landed aristocracy); and greatest in the urban and rural middle classes, and in religious elites and organizations"(Eisenstadt 1963:80). One writer has summed up this change from an egalitarian to an early state organization that occurs without seeming to rupture traditional ways:

The early state retained a more or less reciprocal character throughout the period of its existence. This was based mainly on specific ideological convictions, as well as the extension of certain political and/or military services by the governmental apparatus to the common people, for which the populace paid with different kinds of tribute, levies, labor, etc. In part, these contributions were used "for the common good," such as major public works, the administration of state affairs, etc. The members of the ruling hierarchy, for the greater part, supplemented the surplus from their own lands. The mechanism of exploitation represented, in fact, an *unbalanced* reciprocal system. It was a fairly smooth running machine as a result of extra-economic, politicoideological coercion. This mode of exploitation did not yield much income for the ruling stratum, which implies that the standard of living of the latter did not differ too greatly from that of the common people. It did not provoke much protest on the part of the exploited majority, either. That is why it is impossible to speak of any sort of class struggle in the early state. Mutually we can only speak of "emergent" social classes. Exploitation was covert, and was compensated for by a common ideology of reciprocity and mutual aid. Nevertheless, the society of the early state was already divided into the group of those who produced tribute, and those who received it. The dynamics of social inequality were fully operative, though it could, and usually did, take centuries before the class character of the fully developed state was finally established. (Skalník 1978:614, emphasis in original)

We have just shown the insidious means by which the state organization may develop. Before proceeding with evidence of the development of the police mechanism within the bosom of that state evolution, a few comments are appropriate to show how the largest portion of the population is controlled by means other than the police. Police control of large populations over long periods of time is abnormal. In fact, states that endeavor to control their populations by such methods are called "police" states. A much more effective social control mechanism than the police is the economic system itself, especially the market exchange system.

Of supreme importance as a control of peasant populations is the self-regulating market, that is, an economic system regulated and directed by market forces—in which order in the production and distribution of goods is assured by price alone (Polanyi 1957:68). Although true free market systems do not develop before early forms of capitalism, variants of such a system are present in any state society (Smith 1976). The reorganization of the production and distribution process we have described has transformed the egalitarian economic system of occasional (natural) scarcity to one of organized scarcity, that is, productive capacity is organized to serve one part of the population, occasionally or often at the expense of the other. This is the meaning of appropriation of the surplus by an elite (Smith 1976:310 n. 2; see also ibid., 314). One of the precursors of the development of stratified society is the conversion of communal land to private property accompanied by the exclusion of nonowners from access to scarce basic resources (Fried 1967). Where land is such a critical resource, exchange principles and private property form an ideological basis for the elite to

use the legal fiction of land ownership to control exchange with peasants. . . . [T]he classic exploitive production relationship can also be seen as a case of imbalanced exchange: The surplus value created by the producers as "exchange for" their right to have access to the means of production. Stable stratified societies must always have regular exchanges between producers and nonproducers, if for no other reason than that the nonproducing elite must eat and the producing peasantry must be guaranteed a survival amount of the scarce resources that empowers the elite. (Smith 1976:311)

As a free market develops, the function of a police is not to force peasants to work but to preserve order so that the market can work, for it is the market that is the chief means of social control:

Peasants will compete among themselves to produce more goods, thereby driving down the costs of production and increasing the surplus. Moreover, the peasants require little policing and no one need administer production. . . . The administrators do not relinquish economic control. The marketing system is an organ of the state when markets and the bureaucracy are concentrated in a few administrative centers and the much smaller class than the peasantry, merchant artisans, is policed. (Smith 1976:334–335; see also Harris 1975:287)

At least in some societies, courts were actually convened in the marketplace.

Communication was an important function of markets in Aztec society, for only in markets could so many people be contacted at any one time. Announcements and edicts by the state were presented to the polity in marketplaces. Local courts convened there, and criminals were tried publicly. Punishments were also public and most frequently administered in marketplaces. (Kurtz 1978:182)

Together with religion, this same market mechanism supplies an important ideological support to the state organization. "Markets exist in virtually all large hierarchical social systems because, after a certain size is reached, the elite and their retainers (themselves hierarchically organized) must be fed by a system more *efficient* than direct exchange or tribute collection" (Smith 1976:334, emphasis added; cf. Sahlins 1972:187, 215; Kurtz 1978:179).

Attribution of change to more efficient incoming systems is common; thus it is important to elaborate on the point made by Smith earlier.[10] At a certain juncture in the evolution of the state apparatus the concept of efficiency becomes associated with organization, technology, social relations, whatever is advantageous to the appropriation of surplus by or for the elite (Sanders and Price 1968:234). Of all ideological notions, this is perhaps the one that is most pervasive.[11] We now pass on to other ideological supports to state society.

In simple or weak states, religious institutions supply significant overt ideological support. Nevertheless, the main ideological cover continues to come from the apparent fact that nothing seems to have changed in the customary way of doing things (White 1959:218–220; see also Ruyle 1973; Ruyle 1976:24; Cohen 1978b:63–65; Skalník 1978:606).

Adams (1966), for example, suggests that the movement of Aztec society from a stateless to a state organization was accompanied by the transformation of humanlike gods representing growth and fertility to gods "more remote and awesome in their powers . . . , the emergence of representational art [and] an elite . . . that promoted those aspects of individuality for which portraiture became necessary as an enduring symbol and movement" (ibid.: 124; see also Kurtz 1978:178–179).

Like the chief, the temple represented a redistributional center to which offerings could be made, where craftsmen could gather, and where writing could develop and records could be kept. Thus, the temple functioned as an economic as well as a religious institution (Sedov 1978:122). It came to have a life separated from the community, with a monopoly of knowledge, encouraging "a sense of detachment from and superiority to the day-to-day concerns of secular life" (Adams 1966:126; see also Saxe 1977:133; Lenski 1966:208–210).

"Only religion fulfilled the role of disseminating state propaganda and inculcating in the common people a sense of loyalty toward the state and its sovereign" (Skalník 1978:607). Conversely, it was religion that maintained the myth of a continuous, harmonious, integrated, nonexploitative, and ideal community. In emphasizing moral and individual concerns and responsibilities, it replaced kin and territorial loyalties with a universalistic perspective (Skalník 1978:607; Eisenstadt 1963:63–65). The king became the center of a priest-created universe with the priest as the interpreter of the laws of a divine order in which each individual had his preordained place (Campbell 1959:146–149).

Sovereign ideology became a kind of egalitarianism stood on its head (Cohen 1978b:67). Like the egalitarian big man, the chieftain or kingship came to be thought of as an office held by virtue of the peculiar personal qualities of its occupant. But unlike egalitarian society, these qualities could be possessed only by the chief, king, or his lineage. His magnificence derived not from the fact that his chieftainship or kingship had been gained in open competition with his equals in a display of accepted customary values (Fried 1967), but, on the contrary, from the fact that he who occupied the post was guaranteed by divine intervention to possess personal qualities accruing only to him and to which none other could aspire (Balandier 1970:150; Skalník 1978:606–607).

Likewise, manual labor, which had been egalitarian, reciprocal, and communal, had become associated in a stratified society with the status of the worker, lower-class groups, frequently slaves, doing tribal drudgery (Latham 1958:188–189; Ash 1964:73, 14 n. 17). This view was concretized by requiring nobles and commoners to do different types of work

(Weber 1976:60; Ruyle 1973:611), and even to eat different foods. That
of the commoners was designated as "unclean flesh" (Latham 1958:186).
In Natchez society, for example, commoners were called "stinkards"
(Swanton 1911). Coercive force, instead of being seen as occasionally
necessary to return an errant tribesman to customary ways, soon came to
be promoted, by the elite at least, as the sustainer of neighborliness and
egalitarian virtues (Lowie 1927:116–117). Violence, in initiation ceremonies of the Mkako, a West African acephalous society, teaches the young
"controlled violence within the community" by emphasizing "warlike
qualities" (Copet-Rougier 1986:58–59).

War leaders (*bende*) could emerge. When war was threatening, people (mainly
the elders) chose a man to organize war expeditions. If he was prestigious, strong,
had charisma and retained the elders' support, he could try, after a successful war,
to transform his military leadership into political capacities by becoming the chief
of the community. War made chiefship more or less permanent, providing, in this
acephalous society, a measure of centralized authority for external affairs. (Ibid.:
59)

Legitimacy, the recognition by the commoners that they are commoners, and that the sovereign (and the noble class) are sovereign, and
therefore, the fount of authority, is a crucial piece in the formation of the
state. Legitimacy is a process, a matter of inquiry, never a given. The
process involves a shift of allegiance from the local center to the sovereign
(who eventually becomes the state or its representative). This transformation is accomplished through usurping local functions such as child
education, tax collection, power to designate and punish criminals, regulation of marriage and divorce, and raising a military force. At the same
time, the state weakens and replaces "lineages, clans, age sets, secret
societies and the like" (Kurtz 1978:170). This legitimization process has
the effect of linking together an "entire network of rights, duties, obligations, and loyalties" to form "the social structure of the early state, since
all these rights and duties derived from this one relationship, namely that
between the ruler(s) and the ruled" (Claessen 1978:555).

This process of state legitimation has three phases: (1) survival tactics
involving the continual acquisition of more power; (2) validating state
authority "by developing a legal basis for its actions," usually by imbuing
"its political-legal structure with divine sanctity derived from its religious
institutions"; and (3) "political socialization, which involves benevolence,
control of information, and terror" (ibid.).

Legitimation and political socialization by the developing state must be "acquired":

Legitimation of authority in incorporative [inchoate] states is in large measure a legal process. Codification of laws provides a critical mechanism by which incorporative states acquire the right to apply force in order to gain conformity with state goals and values. It also establishes a new set of social norms with reference not only to what most people will do, but what people think ought to be done. In incorporative states especially severe punishments are meted out for offenses which would seem trivial in contemporary Western states.

In Aztec society the death sentence was commonly invoked. However, punishment was not equal for the classes. Although Aztec law presumably was designed to apply to noble and commoner equally, penalties for the nobility for the same infraction committed by a commoner presumably were often more severe. The official state dogma regarding this matter held that greater responsibility went with greater privilege, and the nobility was expected to set an example for the commoners. . . . [T]he relationship between the emergence of an autonomous state and the development of a legal code and formal legal institutions, such as courts, police, and jails, suggest that they are indispensable to the legitimation of state authority. . . .

The legal system was also a mechanism of socialization. It provided a vehicle by which the state could intrude into the daily affairs of the citizenry and could convey its expectations regarding proper social behavior (Kurtz 1978:179–180).

A legal basis of sovereign action is given by restricting the aristocracy and the occupation of high office (the lawgivers) to the sovereign's kin. The priesthood both belongs to this aristocratic clan and proclaims its divine derivation. At the same time, it preaches that commoners are obliged to pay tribute, obey levies, and accept military service. Commoners thus have many obligations and few rights. The earliest "general principle" upon which this disparity is based is the "distance from the sovereign's lineage" (Claessen 1978:568–569, 574). This social distancing translates into social inequality, which in the material world reflects unbalanced reciprocity. Goods and labor are "reciprocated mostly on the ideological level"; actually "a form of redistributive exploitation prevails" (Claessen and Skalník 1978a:638–639).

Ideology may take the form of ceremonially induced myths that justify and reinforce domination of one group over another or a particular world order with the sovereign at its center and elevated above his people (Claessen 1978:555). Likewise, in southern Mesopotamian towns, around 3500–2500 B.C., the "professional, full-time, initiated, strictly regimented temple priest" linked meticulously observed laws of movement of the heavenly bodies to "those governing life and thought on earth" (Campbell 1959:146–147):

The whole city, not simply the temple area, was now conceived as an imitation on earth of the cosmic order, a sociological "middle cosmos," or mesocosm, established by priestcraft between the macrocosm or the universe and the microcosm of the individual, making visible the one essential form of all. The king was the center, as a human representative of the power made celestially manifest either in the sun or in the moon, according to the focus of the local cult. . . . This celestial order then became the model for mankind in the building of an earthly order of coordinated wills—a model for kings and philosophers, inasmuch as it seemed to show forth the supporting law not only of the universe but of every particle within it. (Ibid.: 146–147, 149)

Perhaps the function of the sovereign as the people's protector is closest to the police function. Part of this protective function is illustrated by the ruler's acquisition of the role of benevolent lord in monopolizing the redistributive function (Eisenstadt 1963:128). That function, in its revised form, has three characteristics: food is no longer redistributed on the basis of equality, the redistributed food now belongs to the ruler and is therefore a gift from him to his commoners, and food returned is only a fraction of that contributed by commoners (Claessen 1978:563, 564–565). Moreover, such redistribution may be used to reward those segments of the population that support the rulers (Skalník 1978:609–610). One observer at the court of a Buganda ruler noted that "all acts of the king are counted benefits, for which he must be thanked; and so every deed done to his subjects is a gift received by them, though it should assume the shape of flogging or fine" (cited in Claessen 1978:563).

Together with the sovereign's jobs as supreme lawgiver, judge, and commander of the military forces, he may also be the high priest in touch with supernatural forces (ibid.: 557–559).

The essential aim of all these characteristics is *protection*—against supernatural forces, secular powers, poverty and anarchy. It is believed that wherever the sovereign is, there is safety, order and well-being. The relations between the sovereign and his people can therefore in principle be seen as a *reciprocal* one: the people supply food, goods and services, and the ruler provides protection. (Ibid.: 567; emphasis in original)

Cumulatively, therefore, commoners increasingly supply material goods to the nobility, while the reciprocal return of the nobility is made in symbolic terms, and has symbolic rather than material value. The impact on the relative material prosperity of the two groups is obvious. But there is the ever-present threat that commoners will see through this symbolic veil with the resultant loss of legitimacy, and therefore the necessity for the nobles to have available the naked fist within the velvet glove.

NOTES

1. *Necessary labor* is "that labour time necessary to secure the conditions of reproduction of the labourer." *Surplus labor* is that "labour over and above necessary labour [that] exists in all modes of production because the conditions of reproduction of the labourer are not equivalent to the conditions of reproduction of the economy" (Hindess and Hirst 1975:26). See also Mandel 1968:29. The following analysis substantially relies on Hindess and Hirst (1975, 1977).

2. Hindess and Hirst (1975:27–28) point out that the mechanism of appropriation in all other modes of production involves a class of nonlaborers. They argue that the form of economy and method of appropriation must then involve a political level and determinate form of state in the society since the reproduction of the labor process depends on the mechanisms of extraction and distribution of surplus labor. In such cases, the ruling class and its functionaries control the conditions of production.

3. There is no Berlin Wall in stateless societies to keep people, unhappy with a particular headman or chief, from leaving in order to find a better arrangement (Mair 1964:chap. 7). Judged thus, such terms as "success" and "it serves the community better" are not teleological in the sense discussed in n. 10.

4. Sanders and Price (1968:130–131) suggest that reduction in population (by emigration) would simplify distribution problems among the remaining population and lead to the disappearance of the chiefdom social structure.

5. Balandier, following Engels, posed the problem as follows: "The urgent task now is the search for different processes by which inequality is established and by which contradictions appear in society and necessitate the formation of a differentiated organism whose function is to contain them" (1970:157).

For Godelier (1972:289–290), "The theoretical problem is to know how (in egalitarian societies) inequality becomes more serious and firmly established, how it actually ceases to be challenged (except ritually symbolically when the ruler dies), how a social minority is able to benefit *permanently* by an *exceptional* situation, even if it continues to redistribute part of its possessions" (emphasis in original).

Harris (1975:308) suggests that in a stateless society "people do not voluntarily suffer poverty in order that others stay rich." For the late eighteenth century, E. P. Thompson (1966:375) poses a similar question: "The utility of Methodism as a work-discipline is evident. What is less easy to understand is why so many working people were willing to submit to this form of psychic exploitation. How was it that Methodism could perform with such success this dual role as the religion of both the exploiters and the exploited?" In the modern context,

Gramsci argued that "the most effective form of domination in a capitalist society is achieved not via coercion but via 'the manufacture of consent' " (quoted in Taylor 1987:202).

6. Gabel (1967:49–50), in reviewing various archeological studies of massive projects, concludes that the work could be accomplished by a "voluntary labor force," thereby suggesting that "we may sometimes underrate the extent of cooperative labor organization among prehistoric peoples" and "that at least some ancient public works were cooperative ventures of the community or district and not the result of enforced labor recruitment." But see Haas (1982:127), who questions the likelihood of such projects on a voluntary basis.

7. Cohen (1978a:70), in a review of the literature on state formation, concludes:

Once a society starts to change its authority structure towards greater permanency and stable supra-local hierarchy, then the political realm itself becomes an ever-increasingly powerful determinant of change in the economy, society, and culture of the system. The entire process is a large-scale feedback system in which multiple possible sets of causes in the ecology, economy, society and intersocietal environment singly or in combination produce more permanent centralized hierarchies of political control. After this initial impetus, the hierarchical structure itself feeds back on all societal factors to make them more closely into an overall system that supports the authority structure.

8. The word *community* originally meant "the totality of those who own something in common" (Konig 1968:15). For a modern view of the same kind of reconstitution of the community, see Robinson 1985.

9. There may be an intermediary period prior to full recognition of hereditary chieftainship in which the office passes to the son from the father provided the eldest son "is a good hunter, is mature, and possesses the qualities of leadership" (Holmberg 1969:150). Such a requirement, originally a restriction on selection, over time likely will become assumed to be inherited from the father until the right of inheritance itself obliterates the characteristics that provided the bases for the leader's selection.

10. There is a strong teleological component to many theories of the state, usually based on their superior efficiency over simpler societies (Hindess and Hirst 1975:203–204; Sacks 1979:104). Cohen (1978a:141) describes how state formation theory may be stated in teleological terms: "Service is clearly most impressed by the benefits of statehood, while the materialists stress its cost and inequities. For them the fundamental point is clear: early states are tyrannical and exploitive, and it is to further the class interests of those in power that states come into being."

For Sanders and Price (1968:176–177; see also 206, 209), the state is related to "effective" organization; "the organization of the state gives it competitive advantages" over stateless societies.

Boulding (1981:18) observes that concepts of "efficiency" are similar to the principle of "survival of the fittest," a term borrowed by Darwin from Herbert Spencer [which] was easily interpreted to mean survival of an aggressive, macho-type mentality at the expense of the more cooperative and accommodating patterns of behavior. As even Thomas Huxley showed, "the survival of the fittest" is a quite empty principle, simply because if we ask "Fit for what?" the answer is "To survive," so that all we have is a survival of the surviving, which we knew anyway, and unless fitness—that is, survival value—can be specified in some way, the principle is quite empty.

11. See also Lewis (1983:102), who argues "that the fittest to survive are, in fact, the forms that manage to cooperate the best in symbiosis with their environment, to enhance rather than to overwhelm the environment's ability to sustain them." Sacks (1979:139–140) has given an excellent example of the Lovedu tribe of the northwest Transvaal whose mode of production, agriculture, was decimated by the introduction of the plow. She observed that "conventional evolutionary anthropologists" often misunderstand increased "productivity of human labor power, variety and quantity of goods available and proliferation of occupational and life style choices" as "societal gains" whereas in fact they may represent "gains for ruling classes and a small proportion of nonruling but affluent people" (ibid.: 194). It is just such change that is often seen as more efficient. The fashionable idea that technology is the cause of change has been criticized by E. P. Thompson (1966).

3

THE POLICE IN STATE SOCIETIES

Anthropologists find it profitable to view conflicts in stateless societies as resulting from the mutually incompatible desires of normal individuals. The complex of laws or rules found in state societies is absent, so too is the perception that persons breaking such laws are deviants against whom society at large must be protected. Yet such laws, and the apparatus to enforce them, form an essential prop to state societies. How does such a complex system develop?

From the standpoint of the Fried thesis, the police function emerges when there is the perceived need by the chief or some bureaucratic clique to protect for themselves limited access to basic resources. Engels would place this development at a time when there is a class division of society into rich (those controlling the mode of production) and poor (those working for the rich). To maintain that division, a third power is necessary. It is this third power, the state, that regulates class conflict by acting as a neutral power, ostensibly representing all classes but actually representing the class structure. The state maintains that structure by confining struggle to the legal and economic spheres, thus at the same time maintaining the relative positions of the dominant and subordinate classes.

It follows from this analysis that once there is such a class division, a police agency becomes necessary as one institution to aid in maintaining this equilibrium of inequality. What such a society designates as crime (to be banished or controlled by a police) flows from attempts on the part of the subordinate class to re-equalize distribution of assets either on a collective basis (riot, rebellion, revolution) or on an individual basis (theft, robbery, burglary, fraud). The police represent an active threat of violence to repress or punish any of these acts (Collins 1982:28). "Both the exercise of military force and the criminal justice system are directed towards a common goal with the former acting as a fail-safe mechanism for the latter" (ibid.: 29).

At this juncture, it will be helpful to summarize the progressive transformations we have set forth, including references to changes in policing mechanisms.

1. *Reciprocity and basic redistribution*, collective tribal security as part of a total, reciprocal, mutual-aid system in which economic, social, and ideological functions compose a unitary social formation, containing no specialized police function. Social control is accomplished through ritual, tradition, and custom; disputes within the group are normally resolved through mediation and arbitration.

2. *Redistribution* in which tribal elders or other leaders appropriate a surplus on behalf of the community for almost total redistribution to tribal members. Elders exercise coercive authority based on ritual, tradition, and custom. No class division or state apparatus is available to maintain coercion; usually no specialized police agency is in evidence, but if present, it serves the entire community. Collective tribal security is still employed.

3. *Complex redistribution* in which the chief retains enough of the surplus to attract retainers; the chief manipulates surplus so as to increase his wives, clients, and those personally loyal to him. Tribal loyalty becomes subordinated to personal loyalty. Retainers may act to enforce some orders of the chief, but no class or state apparatus is present to maintain the chief in power.

4. *Complex chiefdom* with complex redistribution and communal appropriation (kinship-based economic system) at the community local level, with the redistributing chief, after a time, appearing to be the source of goods coming to him from the people, and thus the source and symbol of unity and survival of the community as a whole. He controls the surplus labor needed to satisfy his interests; as the ultimate source of order and justice he determines offenses that contravene the common good; the office becomes hereditary; the bureaucratic structure around the chief increases in order to implement his growing centralizing function to carry out the community good.

In the following chapter we describe two additional types of societies in which the police function in its modern form emerges:

5. *Simple state.* A state organization forms, with the incipient class structure gradually seizing and turning to its own purposes the local kinship mode of production while maintaining it on a kinship basis. The local elite is coopted and becomes an important "hinge" in this operation. Collective security, like the local political structure, slowly becomes integrated into the state. The

original clients and retainers of the chief-kin become the nucleus of the police organization to enforce orders of the central bureaucracy.

6. *State*. Gradual absorption by the state organization of the local community structure while the community is engaged in continual struggle with the dominant class and state organization; a high degree of ideological penetration and reduction of participation of the local community in decisions concerning its own affairs. With the subordination and the progressive disintegration of the local community, collective security loses all community cohesion and retains only ideological identity. Organization and centralization of police follow that of a central state structure.

Having shown the means by which a classless, stateless society may become, in incremental steps, a class-dominated, state-organized society, it is now possible to show how the police mechanism fits within such an organization of society.

One of the earliest scholars to deal with this problem was Jean-Jacques Rousseau, in his *Discourse on the Origin of Inequality*, in which he speculated on the origin of government. He hypothesized that as wealth increased, society was divided into those who possessed land and those who did not. This condition led to a "state of war," placing the possession of property in jeopardy. For the rich, this posed the problem of a means of social control that would protect their property. According to Rousseau:

The rich in particular must have soon perceived how much they suffered by a perpetual war, of which they alone supported the expense, and in which, though all risked life, they alone risked any property. . . . [T]he rich man, thus pressed by necessity, at last conceived the deepest project that ever entered the human mind: This was to employ in his favor the very forces that attacked him, to make them adopt other institutions as favorable to his pretensions, as the law of nature was unfavorable to them. (as cited in Haas 1982:29–30)

The theoretical framework provided by Engels suggests that the function of the state in a class-structured society is determined by that class structure:

Such a society could only exist either in the continuous, open fight of these classes against one another or else under the rule of a third power, which, apparently standing above the warring classes, suppressed their open conflict and allowed the class struggle to be fought out at most in the economic field, in so-called legal form. The gentile constitution was finished. It had been shattered by the division of labor and its result, the cleavage of society into classes. It was replaced by the *state*. (1972:278, emphasis in original)

Engels's analysis is consistent with our own. We have shown the development of a class structure out of kin society; in chapter 4, citation will be made to societies—the Gyaman, Aztec, and the Incan—engaged in class struggle. Such struggle need not imply armed combat but rather involves resistance by the subordinate class to control by the dominant class of the appropriation of a disproportionate quantity of scarce economic resources (Haas 1982:107–115). Given this division of economic resources, open conflict may result, either between the classes or among the elite over the spoils (Fried 1967:229–230; Lenski 1966:53; Harris 1975:357–358). To be effective in resolving these basic antagonisms, the evolving political structure must "cut across the divisions" in order to "represent and regulate the divisions that arise from the existence of classes" (Hindess and Hirst 1975:198; see also Sanders and Price 1968:234).

The presence of a state and a political level are, then, conditions of existence for any mechanisms of appropriation of surplus-labour by a class. . . . Raw materials, the means and conditions of production must always be distributed among the agents of production so as to enable existing forms of real appropriation to continue. It follows that in all class societies the state is a condition of existence of the process of real appropriation itself. In that respect the state does indeed perform functions that are absolutely necessary to the existence of society as a whole. . . . the state represents class society *as such*—it is a means of preservation of class domination in so far as it maintains the conditions of existence of class society. (Hindess and Hirst 1975:32,198, emphasis in original; see also Sanders and Price 1968:232–233)

In the very special sense suggested above, the state acts as the *representative* of both classes in regulating the class struggle so as to keep it within legal limits, that is, requiring that the struggle be engaged on economic rather than on physical grounds. Hence, the state's need for a monopoly of force. By standing above the classes, the state appears to act as a neutral arbiter between contending classes, thus ostensibly rendering equal justice under law. One consequence of such a stance is the maintenance of the stratification of society by providing a rationalization for the creation of a specialized organ both to prevent and put down conflict and to provide a neutral forum where such conflict may be resolved (White 1959:232; Hindess and Hirst 1975:198).

Concepts of the state as standing above conflict and restoring order in conflicts between rich and poor (Tigar and Levy 1977:135–136), as being "an essential instrument by which the weak were protected against the strong" (Seneviratne 1978:385; Robinson 1979), or as appealing to rules for justice (Finley 1973:38–39; Mair 1964) are oft-made observations in anthropological literature (MacLeod 1937:181; Adams 1966:151; Lowie 1927). From the standpoint of the ruler, it may frequently be the nobles that create the problem (Rounds 1979:81–82; Thurnwald 1969:11), and the ruler may even be seen by commoners as their protector against overexploitation by nobles (Lloyd 1968:51–52; Diakonoff 1969:192–193).

Fitting within this concept of the state is the police institution and other specialized agencies of social control (White 1959:32–32). According to Engels (1972:230), the state first divides its subjects

on a territorial basis. . . . The second distinguishing characteristic is the institution of a public *force* which is no longer immediately identical with the people's own organization of themselves as an armed power. This special public force [the police] is needed because a self-acting armed organization of the people has become impossible since their cleavage into classes. . . . The public force exists in every state; it consists not merely of armed men but also of material appendages, prisons and coercive institutions of all kinds, of which gentile society knew nothing. (Emphasis in original)

Engels suggests that the division of classes requires the creation of a *public* power, that is, a public power that is private in the sense that it represents not an undivided totality but a class-divided public. This public power replaces the "self-acting armed organization" of kindred society, consisting of the entire population, with a specialized part, a police (White 1959:232). This police can represent *both* contending classes only to the extent and to the degree that these contending classes are themselves represented in the distribution of economic, social, and political state power (Lenski 1966). Appearance and reality of the representation of the state by the gendarmerie can be understood only in terms of its divisive and contradictory position in relation to the state and to the people.

Krader (1978:94) states it well:

The archaic collective institutions had formerly resolved conflicts or maintained the peace internally in the interest of the social whole, in this case the whole community, clan or tribe. The agencies of the state now defended, warred, both in the interest of the state and that of the social whole. It is a double interest, conflicting internally within itself; on the one side, it is the interest of the state as the representative of the social class in whose interest it is organized, on the other, the interest of the social whole.

Earlier we demonstrated how a police could exist in a stateless society and could act on behalf of the whole community. Our present task is to show how a police function fits within a class-dominated society. We have argued that such a society results from a series of incremental steps. A major thesis of this book is that the modern (specialized) police institution is a product of the class organization of the state. We would expect the evolution of the police function to follow and parallel the evolution of class society.

Thus, the appearance of a *specialized police institution* is related to the appropriation of surplus labor. Like other specialists, such as craftsmen, police are nonproducers. Persons substantially engaged in police activity, therefore, must be maintained from the surplus labor appropriated by some central authority (Harris 1975:374). A society that cannot support other specialists because it has no apparatus to appropriate a surplus for an elite class of nonproducers is unlikely to have a police (Lenski 1966:62). In addition, of course, as Engels and Fried have pointed out, a society based on kinship relations has adequate means of mutual aid mechanisms to resolve internal divisions without resort to law-and-order specialists (White 1959:85; Harris 1975:357).

In an egalitarian society, there is a natural order based on horizontal relationships. Self-regulation and social control are parts of this order, consisting of reciprocity in face-to-face relationships (Malinowski 1922, 1926) and customary norms of behavior. Gossip, ridicule, and peer pressure act in concert to help maintain this order. People know one another, and can put pressure on one another to act in a culturally normative manner. In a state- and class-based society, this natural order-keeping function dissipates. Order (the correct way to do things) is determined from above (Corrigan and Sayer 1985:31). There is no longer any "natural" mechanism for maintaining order on a horizontal level. A police, employed from above, becomes "necessary" to enforce a set of "rules."

Anthropologists studying tribal societies often note the absence of abstract "rules of order," and prefer to analyze dispute settlement as a process of mediation and arbitration of individual cases (e.g., Malinowski 1926; Colson 1953; Turner 1957; Gulliver 1971; Koch 1974; Nader and Todd 1978). On the other hand, anthropologists working in more hierarchically organized societies have often found it more convenient to use a rule-oriented analysis (e.g., Rattray 1929; Schapera 1938; Gluckman 1955; Fallers 1969). This choice of paradigm is not accidental. According to Hoebel (1983:26), "The really fundamental *sine qua non* of law . . . is the legitimate use of physical coercion by a socially authorized agent." Egalitarian societies, with small populations and face-to-face contact, generally lack such an agent.

In the case of the simple states we have discussed, the kinship mode of production is maintained for the greatest part of the population. Such a society may well be in transition to an intensive agriculture-based economy in which extra people, instead of being a burden, become a source of prestige and power to the chief through his use of the additional labor to increase his surplus. Thus, "person acquisition" through "increased birth rates . . . adoption, polygyny, bridewealth, clientage, fostering, and even . . . forcible capture and enslavement of strangers" becomes advantageous (Claessen and Skalník 1978b:43). These more densely populated societies carry within them the seeds of a stratified society, often encouraging mechanisms that eventually develop into a police function.

Haas (1982:chap. 4) attempts to determine whether, among theories of state evolution, the integrative or conflict position is supported by the greater weight of empirical evidence. In concluding that the balance is on the side of the conflict position, he cites a number of examples from the literature showing that both force and nonforceful means have been used to maintain unequal access to scarce basic resources. In Hawaii, paramount chiefs used a mix of redistribution and force to maintain their power, exercising

their control over land and water to dispossess from the means of subsistence those persons who failed to produce sufficient resources, or who secretly accumulated resources. More direct physically coercive sanctions were applied against commoners who committed criminal acts or misdeeds. Particularly severe sanctions were applied when the misdeeds affected the paramount chiefs. (Ibid.: 116, original citations omitted)

Haas also cites the Zulu rulers' use of violence against their subordinate chiefs as a "critical component of the governing process" to keep the people in a position of subordination: "the threat of violence, accompanied by limited application, is an effective element in long term stable government" (ibid.: 118). He cites numerous cases of archeological research on stratified societies, concluding that although more evidence supports the conflict theory that force was used to sustain stratification, "it may be further argued that the material benefits gained through centralization would have been used by the rulers of [early stratified societies] as positive mechanisms to govern their respective populations" (ibid.: 128–129).

One such mechanism, clientage, represents a combination of forceful and nonforceful relations, of personal dependence of a subordinate on a superior. It is suggested that the birth of the police institution is to be found in the building up of a system outside of kinship and the gradual replacement of kinship with a system of personal dependency (Skalník 1978:599–600). Although there is no direct description of such evolution of a police institution, there are many references to various types of clientage relationships in which police duties form one part of overall duties owed by the client to his patron.

One of the clearest descriptions of such a relationship is that provided by Mair of several East African societies. Mair herself gives considerable attention to clientage, believing the "relationship to be the germ from which state power springs" (1964:166). "For a Hutu in Ruanda the value of clientship was that it got him the use of cattle even if he did not actually own them, and protection against marauders who might seize them" (ibid.: 172).

Clientage is a reciprocal relationship and is therefore a fictive reproduction of the kinship relationship on a vertical (superior-inferior) rather than on a horizontal (equal) basis. Mair describes the case of the Getutu, a Kenya people who took in refugees from other related tribes that had been driven from their homelands. In exchange for various services such as serving as soldiers or working land or tending cattle, the clients were given cattle, land, and protection. It becomes evident how these clients began to be used for police duties in ways that contributed to the deterioration of kinship ties.

If a man wished to demand payment of a debt from someone at a distance, he would first persuade the elder in his part of the country that he had a good claim. Then the elder would send one of his sons, carrying his staff, to the debtor's home to order him to pay. . . . But if the elder was afraid that the debtor would defy the order, he would send a number of his "bought persons'" to enforce it. If they had to seize a cow from the debtor, and this led to fighting and perhaps killing, it would not be a fight between real "sons of Nyakundi," who ought to remain at peace. (Ibid.: 112)

Like "bought persons," the "broken men" theme is recurrent throughout the literature, referring to people who have lost the protection of their lineage and therefore have to attach themselves to some powerful man for their own protection and advancement. Fox (1971: 146, 148–149), citing Maine, describes the case of the Irish tribes. There, broken men were those "who through some misdeed had been outcast from their original tribal group and were forced to fend for themselves." Alternatively, they may be a conquered people under the chief's protection (Schaedel 1978:310). The acquisition of these men gave a chief a following independent of his kinsmen.

Characteristically, the growth of the state administration and the subsequent bureaucratization were dependent on the sovereign's military following and on military power in general. Bodyguards, and so forth, appeared at first as individuals who had been alienated from their own native communities. They were personally dependent on the sovereign, and thus fully devoted to his service (Skalník 1978:602).

Loyal clients, especially in Africa, were of importance to give a chief power and prestige because the attraction of men to cultivate his fields was "the most problematic factor" in the chief's accumulating a surplus to distribute which in turn would increase the number of his loyal supporters (Fallers 1964:126). Generosity, particularly in the distribution of foodstuffs, was also a source of followers, in that food could be given selectively to those who protect the chief (Pospisil 1971:68–69; Ruyle 1973:610). Fox (1976:111) describes early Scottish society, in which large groups of "broken men," unattached to any kin group, "driven from their natal clan region or having voluntarily foresworn their brethren . . . were a large mobile population allied with any dominant clan or chief who would guarantee them safety and land." In India, "the elite commonly settle foreign families, kin groups and Brahmins on their kin lands in order to establish a loyal class of retainers apart from the kin order" (ibid.: 101). Other sources of retainers were poorer relations and people in debt who placed themselves in pawn (Ruyle 1973:620; Terray 1974:335; Winks 1972:53).

A related institution, slavery, contributes to the possible origin of the police function. Slavery must be considered one aspect of a particular social formation (Hindess and Hirst 1975:116). We discuss it as a component of Gyaman society in chapter 4. Slavery is important because chiefs may use slaves to enforce obedience to orders; slaves are normally outsiders cut off from their lineage group; but ironically, like close relatives, they are the only ones on whom the chief can most surely rely for loyalty—for which reason slaves are said to have been better treated in times of unrest (Ruyle 1973:616; MacLeod 1924:85; Finley 1973:70; Pospisil 1971:123; Skalník 1978:602). "A slave, being cut off from any prospect of escape and completely dependent on his master for his welfare and his life, would find it to his advantage to support his master loyally in warfare and in disputes with commoners" (Ruyle 1973:613).

The fact that slaves are "socially rootless" tends to make them "a formidable weapon of autocratic policy" (Wittfogel 1957:360–363). For this reason they are often used as administrators (Lowie 1927:56). For the slave to rise in the service of the oriental despot, the most important qualification is "total and ingenious servility" (Wittfogel 1957:364). This trait, when translated into the modern version of loyalty, is a continuing demand made by rulers on the police (Miller 1977:214–215; Robinson 1978). The slave, the broken man, and the foreigner all have one thing in common in that their loyalty is based on some tie other than kinship. Thus, at one and the same time, this phenomenon tends to weaken the importance of kinship ties and strengthen the importance of personal loyalty to a sovereign.

Mair (1964), with Engels (1972), develops the specific idea that we believe is crucial to the development of a police as part of a state structure. Mair (1964:58–59) describes the "peace" maintained by the Alur (East African) chiefs: "Brawling and bloodshed in their near neighborhood was regarded as an offense against the respect due to them. . . . The killing of a chief's subject was also regarded as an offense against the chief" (1964:58–59). Thus, the Alur chief had taken to himself the statelike mantle of merging the peace and well-being of the community with his own. If an order he gave was disobeyed "the chief himself would appear on the scene with all his retainers, a band of followers who were *neutral* in the dispute at issue, and powerful enough to give decisive support to the side adjudged by the chief to be in the right" (ibid.: 59, emphasis added).

These "bought persons" are a group "loyal only to the judge and without lineage ties to either side in the dispute" (ibid.: 112). Thus, they stand above contending classes, a neutral representation of the state between the parties. The question then becomes the neutrality of the state. This idea of the state is taken a step further by the personification of the king as god and the source of fertility. Because the protection of the king's life was now vital to community security, an armed guard was created for his protection (Sedov 1978:117).

For more formal and permanent police functions, a review of the African age grade societies is instructive. Together with sex, division of labor based on age is endemic to virtually all societies, and forms an important part of tribal social organization. From an early age boys learn to obey tribal elders (Lowie 1927:82). When such customs are worked into the kind of evolving stratified structure we have described, an incipient police institution is present.

There appear to have been two basic types of age grade societies in operation: one in which the secret societies acted as a check on the power of the chief, and one in which the secret societies were controlled by and acted on behalf of the chief. Neither of these situations, however, appears to be in conflict with the basic thesis offered in this book. To the extent that a particular society is a class society, both the elders controlling the age societies and the chief are members of the elite group. Thus, even if they were in political opposition, the police functions of the age societies were nonetheless operating to protect the interests of the elite group.

It was the second type of chiefdom that led most naturally to coalescence and state formation. When a secret society, such as the Poro society of the Kpelle of Liberia, acted to balance the power of the chief, the disruptive consequences were not conducive to state formation. In contrast to this situation was the well-known and historically documented development of the Zulu state. Shaka, who brought the Zulu state into supreme dominance, and his predecessor Dingiswayo, who solidified and organized the Mthethwa paramount chiefdom, both increasingly employed age societies as police to protect their own interests. Originally, these societies had been age grades not dissimilar to the Poro society of the Kpelle. When a group of young men reached puberty, they underwent a circumcision rite of passage and were formally constituted as a group. Gradually, Bantu chiefs used these age grades increasingly for their own ends until they became rather firmly attached to a chief. Walter (1969:121) describes the situation immediately before Dingiswayo's coalescence of the Mthethwa:

Before Dingiswayo, the military force of each chiefdom was a small "standing army" made up of young bachelors in the warrior age grade. Adolescent boys lived a barracks life in military kraals, serving as aides and herd boys until their age set was organized ceremonially as *iButho*, a new guild or regiment and they were elevated to the status of warriors. Carrying out military and police functions and for certain purposes acting as a labor gang, the warriors constituted the staff, not permanent but assembled according to circumstance, which enforced the chief's will. They fought the battles of the chiefdom, executed judgments by killing people accused of crimes, confiscating their property in the chief's name, and when the supply of the chief's cattle was low, replenished the bovine treasury by making raids on other communities. They cultivated the fields of the chief, built and maintained his kraals, and manufactured his war shields.

At some point that is not historically clear, circumcision rites were abolished, perhaps under Dingiswayo's paramount chieftainship, and chiefs continued to assemble and name sets of young men of warrior age. This stage was a crucial departure, however, because these regiments were not constituted solely by and on behalf of the chiefs. They took on permanent and formalized police functions, clearly in keeping with our central hypothesis. The formation of the Zulu state soon followed.

In addition to the occasional enforcement of a chief's orders, for what other matters are police employed? The various uses to which the police were put can be gathered primarily from scattered references in the literature. Observers, whether anthropologists or not, have not generally recorded detailed descriptions of police forces. As one writer commented after an extensive survey of traditional societies, "the data on the existence of a police force are very scarce. In only four cases was such a force mentioned. In five cases royal servants or guards maintained order . . . ; in most cases the ruler was considered supreme commander, and in most cases he had a bodyguard" (Claessen 1978:560).

There is an occasional allusion to the use of a police or militia to compel labor (Finley 1973:65–66), but as we have indicated earlier, commoners are more apt to be compelled to work by market forces. Police are used to make the market work, not the workers (Pryor 1977:120; Smith 1976:336; Harris 1975:287). But police are used to maintain the mode of production by controlling the freedom of choice of the labor force. One of the distinctions between a stateless and a state society is that "the state is a system specifically designed to restrain" tendencies toward segmentation (Cohen and Service 1978:4). Thus, police can be used to prevent discontented groups from leaving a chief's jurisdiction (Llewellyn and Hoebel 1941:94–96; Skalník 1978:609), or, on a larger scale, "to try and overcome any ethnic differences in the total society" (Skalník 1978:607). In the long term this has meant the crushing of ethnic in favor of state loyalties (Claessen and Skalník 1978c:632).

Inequalities and opposition incident to a class-dominated society lead to struggle among commoners for access to the limited scarce resources remaining after elite appropriation of the surplus; force must often be used to back up elite rights to control these resources; conflict leads to ideological justification of arbiters to settle resulting disputes; arbiters in turn need detectives to search out evidence and police to execute judicial decisions (Pospisil 1971:16, 123; Harris 1975:357–358). For the people's own apparent good, the ruler and his top officials need protection "against attempts at supplantation by pretenders to the supreme power" (Skalník 1978:610). In early states, these hypothetical and real threats generally lead to the creation of a bodyguard for the sovereign (Claessen 1978:563). Thus, we can hypothesize that in its early stage, the police mechanism has been used for regulation of class conflict, as a neutral force, loyal only to the state, without ties to either side in the dispute (Mair 1964). Its function is to permit "a class struggle at most in the economic field, in a so-called legal form" (Engels 1972:228). Having argued that the police mechanism fits within state society as a means by which a ruling class maintains its dominant position, we proceed to review a series of case studies illustrating how such a process unfolds.

4

ETHNOGRAPHIC EXAMPLES

In this chapter we amplify the evolutionary processes outlined in chapters 2 and 3 by exploring a series of ethnographic and historical case studies. We have, of course, chosen illustrative cases for which diachronic data exist in order to examine broad transformations in the social order. We have arranged these case studies in the rough order of the progressive transformations set out at the end of chapter 2, although the reader should be aware that, where historical data are particularly rich, cases may involve several transformations.

RECIPROCITY AND BASIC REDISTRIBUTION

The egalitarian ideology can be illustrated by one of the most structurally simple societies known to anthropologists: the Mbuti tribe (Zaire), where virtually the entire life of the people revolves around the forest (Turnbull 1968, 1983). Here there is essentially no labor specialization other than the division of labor by sex and age. There is a unity of ideological and material life concentrated in the forest. Most matters of social life are communal affairs, and there is no need for judge or jury. According to Turnbull (1968:110),

There was a confusing, seductive informality about everything they did. Whether it was a birth, a wedding, or a funeral, in a Pygmy hunting camp or in a Negro village, there was always an unexpectedly casual, almost carefree attitude. There was, for instance, little apparent specialization: everyone took part in every-thing. . . . There were no chiefs, no formal councils. In each aspect of Pygmy life there might be one or two men or women who were more prominent than others, but usually for good practical reasons. This showed up most clearly of all in the settling of disputes. There was no judge, no jury, no court. . . . Each dispute was settled as it arose, according to its nature.

Thus, a sense of communal responsibility coupled with the intersection of the ideological and material base make more formal policing functions unnecessary:

In fact, Pygmies dislike and avoid personal authority, though they are by no means devoid of a sense of responsibility. It is rather that they think of responsibility as communal. If you ask a father, or a husband, why he allows his son to flirt with a married girl, or his wife to flirt with other men, he will answer, "It is not my affair," and he is right. It is their affair, and the affair of the other men and women, and of their brothers and sisters. He will try to settle it himself, either by argument or by a good beating, but if this fails he brings everyone else into the dispute so that he is absolved of personal responsibility. If you ask a Pygmy why his people have no chiefs, no lawgivers, no councils, or no leaders, he will answer with misleading simplicity, "Because we are the people of the forest." The forest, the great provider, is the one standard by which all deeds and thoughts are judged; it is the chief, the lawgiver, the leader, and the final arbitrator. (Turnbull 1968:125)

Even in such an egalitarian society, however, Godelier (1977) sees the seeds of a developing hierarchical structure:

At the same time, however, these observances—material, political, symbolic and aesthetic, along with the songs and dances which necessarily accompany them— revolve around a real and imaginary being, the Forest; they call upon the Forest and celebrate his watchful presence which brings good health and game in plenty, social harmony, life and it is the Forest which wards off epidemics, famine, discord and death. Religious observance is therefore primarily and totally orientated toward the conditions of reproduction of the Mbuti mode of production and way of life. . . . The phantasmic nature of their social relations is not merely born from the fact that they represent to themselves, inside-out, the observance and conditions for reproducing their way of life, since, in fact, everything occurs as if it were not the hunters who catch game by their skill or technique, but as if it were the gift of an omniscient and benevolent Person. . . . We can therefore understand why, when circumstances permitted, certain men, certain groups came to personify the common good themselves or to gain exclusive access to super-natural powers which were supposed to control the conditions for the reproduction of the universe and society. . . . To stand apart from men and dominate them, to approach the gods and command obedience, are perhaps only two *simultaneous* aspects of the same process—a road and direction leading to class societies and the state. (Godelier 1977:8–9, emphasis in original)

As mentioned in chapter 2, Godelier has conducted an in-depth study of the Baruya of Highland New Guinea (Godelier 1972, 1982a, 1986; Godelier and Strathern 1991). The societies of Highland New Guinea have been viewed as egalitarian, of the "big-man" type (Sahlins 1963), in which men achieve social status largely through manipulation of wealth in elaborate ceremonial exchange. Yet, increasingly, authors are beginning to see fundamental inequalities in such apparently egalitarian societies (see, e.g., Strathern 1982). Godelier (1982a) argues that there are in fact social hierarchies among the Baruya men involving such social statuses as *aoulatta* (great warriors), *koulaka* (Shaman), *kayareumala* (cassowary hunter) and *tsaimaye* (salt maker). Even more fundamental, however, is the domination of men over women:

To sum up, we have already found several systems of differentiation which constitute an intricate social hierarchy. These are, first, the general domination of men over women, a domination instituted in a spectacular fashion by the passage of each individual through collective initiations. In this way the collective domination of men over women is imposed. Second, within each sex another principle works, and adds its effects to the general subordination of women to men. This is the principle of superiority of seniors over juniors. The non-initiated owe respect to initiates, the first-stage initiates to those in other stages, and so on, until the moment when a man, having four or five children and still able to fight, is a great-man, apmwenangelo. Similarly, a non-initiated young girl owes respect to a female initiate and she will become a great-woman when she has given three or four living children to her husband and has demonstrated that she is hard-working and long-suffering. But the principle of superiority of elders is itself put to the service of male domination because, as we have seen, once a boy is initiated, all his older sisters (genealogically) become his juniors (socially). This inequality between the sexes is the fundamental basis of the social order. It is on this basis that other differences are produced which add to it. (Godelier 1982a: 27–28, from translation by C. Robinson)

Women are excluded by men from the very activities that determine access to the forces of production and the acquisition of prestige and influence:

1.   The ownership of real property, but not its use
2.   Owning and producing, and using the most effective tools to work the forest, although women would be perfectly capable of constructing and using these very simple tools
3.   Producing, owning or using arms, engaging in war, in violent combat or in hunting

4. Producing salt and its commercial exchange with tribes
5. The production and use of sacred objects (Godelier 1977: 59–60).

The Baruya cultivate sweet potatoes as their principal crop, the taro for ceremonial purposes, and a cane for the production of salt, used both for ceremonial and exchange purposes (ibid.: 24). Thus, women are denied access to and control of the land they work and the tools with which they work it, thereby limiting their power, influence, and prestige in their lineage, which cooperatively owns its land. They are likewise denied access to the use of arms and forbidden to engage in war outside their tribal boundaries, thereby barring them from acquiring prestige and glory through protection of the community. Neither can they engage in foreign trade, exchanges which bring to the tribe necessary products. Nor are they entitled to have possession of sacred objects, which are the sole way the tribe can communicate with the supernatural forces that determine the tribe's well-being.

Godelier concludes that male-female relations rely on four principles: masculine domination, female consent to this domination, female resistance to the domination, and masculine repression of this resistance (ibid.: 239). Domination is maintained by a combination of violence and ideology. Repression may be either verbal or physical and is habitually exercised by a husband toward his wife. The most severe penalties are reserved for acts by females that directly menace male dominance. For example, a woman is said to have interrogated a young boy about male secret initiation ceremonies. Both the woman and the boy were killed without the right on the part of the family either to assert blood revenge or to obtain compensation, the custom of vengeance being suspended in the name of the general community interest. Likewise, a woman who accidentally or purposely encounters men during their secret ceremonies may be instantly put to death (ibid.: 238).

There are also elaborate ideological and symbolic supports from both males and females for the system of male domination. Baruya myths start with the sun, from which all male power issues. The sun is the father of man and gives light, warmth, and strength. The moon is female and gives cold, darkness, and weakness. In the celestial order, the sun is high and the moon lower. Even though women have a special connection with the moon, they cannot communicate with it because they do not have the necessary sacred objects and magical formulas. Therefore, women can never represent all of society. Only men can do that. Similarly, women are cut off from their ancestors and therefore cannot inherit or pass on property (ibid.: 109–116).

Baruya myths also support male domination and the use of violence for the good of the whole society to maintain that domination. In the past women are said to have had superior powers to those of men. But for legitimate reasons these powers were seized and turned against women. For example, it is forbidden on pain of death for women to see men play flutes at sacred ritual ceremonies. The flutes are said to be the voices that converse with the forest spirits. It is said that it was really the women who had invented the flutes. One day a man hid and saw them playing in the forest. He followed them and stole a flute from a hut where it was hidden. Another myth states that women had invented bows and arrows but, not knowing how to use them, they turned the arrows against themselves. As a result, men took them away, used them correctly, and forbade women to use them.

Thus, these stories inform both sexes that the creativity of women is disorderly, without limits, dangerous, both to themselves and others, so that men are constrained to intervene to put things in order. This intervention, and the violence it implies, is justified as the only means to establish order in society and the universe. Although the female is the source of creativity and fecundity, she and society cannot benefit from it without male intervention. Violence, theft, or assassination is justified to that end. Man has perfected what woman has started just as the sun has intervened to pierce the sexes (Godelier 1977: 117–120).

Here we have a society structured by male domination, but one in which there is no exploitation in that power does not give riches and riches do not give power. Godelier finds that the key reason for the lack of a system of exploitation is that a woman, as part of the marriage system, can only be exchanged for another woman and not for material things (ibid.: 11–12). Thus the system of domination is used to support the system of social relations. Women are not, however, used to produce and maintain a surplus, which could become a basis of inequality and dependence. Such societies Godelier calls "Great Man" societies to distinguish them from "Big Man" societies, in which, indirectly, women can be exchanged for wealth and can be used to produce and maintain a surplus.

In another attempt to analyze male-female relationships in the nonindustrial world, Karen Sacks (1979:6–7) examines the "central relations" of

sisterhood and wifehood. . . . *Sister* is a kind of kinship shorthand for a woman member of a community of owners of the means of production: an equal, an adult among adults, a decision maker. *Wife* is shorthand for a woman's relationship to her spouse. . . . [T]he necessary condition for sister relations to exist was a corporation of owners, a social order based on groups of kinspeople who owned the means to their livelihood. (Emphasis in original)

Using a tri-level typology substantially similar to Hindess and Hirst's, discussed in chapter 2, Sacks (pp. 72–73) organizes her diachronic study of societal levels involving female sisterly relations as follows:

1. The means of production are held in common and are equally accessible to all members of society. All have equal power vis-à-vis the group, and hence the exercise of personal power over the group is almost nonexistent. Real power as a coercive force, however, resides in group consensus because individuals are dependent on the group.

2. *States or classes.* In sharp contrast are societies where a small group or class owns and controls the productive property and has enormous power over those who depend on them for a livelihood.

3. *Corporate kin groups.* Somewhere between these two are societies in which productive property is held by groups of kinspeople. Every individual has access to at least some productive property by virtue of being born into one of these kin-based corporations. Here power exists to the extent that these corporations have unequal amounts of productive property and members within them have unequal access to their corporations' property. (Emphasis in original)

In a communal mode of production, as we have seen in the Mbuti culture, although women may be assigned to different productive responsibilities, this is merely a matter of how work is organized, and thus sexual division of labor need not imply social inequality (ibid.: 113). In such societies all are seen as kin, all have equal access to the means of production, and all have a "productive responsibility—joining others in gathering or hunting" (ibid.: 114).

In keeping with our own analysis, Sacks (1979: 73) shows that sexual division of labor in itself need not promote hierarchical relationships. Only when gender is related to control over the means of production does gender inequality become pronounced:

Although the bases of power are sexually neutral, power itself is exercised with definite regard to sex in that men and women may have unequal or different kinds of access to kin-based property and to private property. Gender underlies but is not synonymous with either men's or women's relations to the means of production; each sex stands in a variety of relations to the means of production; and kinship relations—particularly those of sister and wife—are relations of production and, hence, relations of power.

REDISTRIBUTION AND COMPLEX
REDISTRIBUTION

We have seen how, in a truly egalitarian society like the Mbuti, communal, collective security efforts generally suffice. While seeds of hierarchy may be present, where control of basic resources is open to all, there is no need to protect restricted access. The military societies of the Native Americans of the Great Plains represent an example in which resources were distributed in nature in such a way as to make necessary a police—possibly the most basic example of the police function—to guard resources for the benefit of all.

Llewellyn and Hoebel (1941) describe this function for the Cheyenne tribe. The Cheyennes, numbering at most 4,000, separated into bands, except in summer when they came together for the communal hunts. The Cheyennes were a hunting society in which differences in wealth consisted mainly of horses, clothes, and adornments, and all shared the proceeds of the hunt. Government was by a council of chiefs who had ten-year terms. Each chief chose his own successor. A chief was appointed "because he approached the ideal qualities of leadership—wisdom, courage, kindness, generosity, and even temper" (ibid.: 73).

There were five military societies in which membership was voluntary. Only one such society, the Dog Soldiers, because it constituted a band, remained together during the entire year. The rest of the societies exercised their functions as units only during the summer hunting season. A major function was keeping the peace. They intervened in what would otherwise be private quarrels. But since every private disorder could result in a killing that could bloody the "Sacred Arrows, endangering thereby the well-being of the people . . . it was treated as a crime against the nation" (ibid.: 132; see also Hoebel 1978:40–42). The societies policed behavior of warriors in time of war and during communal bison hunts, supervised the division of meat, settled any resulting disputes, brought laggards to tribal religious ceremonies, and helped the poor and destitute (Grinnel 1956: chap. 5).

Grinnel (1956:218–219) describes how the societies functioned as police:

Camp was broken and two moves were made to that stream. In this new camp the Crazy Dogs, then acting as police, gave orders that no drumming should be done. From this time on the drums were silent. . . . The Crazy Dogs were one of the several soldier societies, of which others were Red Shields, Dog Soldiers, Crooked Lance Soldiers, Kit-Fox Soldiers, Bow String, and Chief Soldiers.

In a large camp, one of these societies was always on duty to enforce the orders of the chiefs and generally to keep order in the camp. Neither the Chief Soldiers nor the Red Shields, both composed of older men, took part in this police work. The principal duty of the other societies was to enforce order. Young men of these societies sometimes became arrogant and endeavored to exert undue influence on the camp, to carry out certain plans that their soldier band had decided on. Under ordinary conditions, when one society had policed the camp for a certain length of time, it went off duty, being relieved by soldiers of another band selected by the chiefs.

The powers of the soldiers were great. They often severely punished men who violated customs or camp rules. Sometimes they whipped men, beat them with their war clubs, or even killed their ponies. Under less provocation they might cut up robes, break lodgepoles, or even destroy lodges. The soldiers took charge of the general hunts and directed the hunters, seeing to it that the rules governing the hunt were observed and that all men had an equal chance to kill game.

The same practice was present among the Dakotas who lived in the upper Mississippi area near present St. Paul, Minnesota. Little Crow, who later became a leader of his people, as a young hunter, with a friend, sought to gain advantage by moving ahead of the main body of hunters. He was first warned by several of the party that his actions would scare off the game. When he ignored the warning, the hunting party formed a soldier's lodge and destroyed the friend's belongings, cut up his mother's tepee, and gave them both stern lectures (Anderson 1986:36–37).

The Dakota, between the 1830s and 1870s, represent a particularly poignant example of the part soldier lodges played in trying to maintain an egalitarian society against incursions of the white settler culture. The federal government supported the settlers' expansion by forcing Native Americans (Amerinds) off their hunting grounds. As white settlers advanced westward, Amerinds were coerced into signing successive treaties, each pushing them off previously agreed-upon reservations. For a paltry sum, these treaties purchased hunting grounds and guaranteed annual cash annuities. The annuities had the effect of making Amerinds dependent for their food and clothing on mostly half-breed traders. Government policy was intended to force Amerinds to take up farming so as to make them into "white men." This policy divided the Amerinds into farmers, who cut their hair and gave up traditional ways, and the so-called blanket Indians, who retained traditional living. By continually breaking its word to the chiefs, the government pursued a policy that also had the effect of weakening the chiefs' influence over their people (Anderson 1986:58–115).

A number of conditions finally led the Dakota to revolt against the settlers. There was much cheating by traders as to the amount owed for supplies. Traders usually claimed that the advances they had made to the Dakota equaled or were greater than the amount of the annuity due them. In addition, a crop failure caused starvation conditions on the reservations, traders refused to make additional advances, and Dakota who demanded supplies for their families were met with insults, the traders telling them they should "eat grass" or "wild potatoes" (ibid.: 122).

From 1857 on, the Dog Soldiers' lodge, principally composed of young warriors from a number of bands, became the focus of a protest movement to maintain traditional ways. Together with other societies such as Bear Dance, the Elk Lodge, the Raw Fish Eaters Lodge, the Dog Liver Eaters Lodge[1] and the Sacred Dance, they "encouraged feasting and dancing and opposed Christianity, the destruction and loss of hunting territory, and the forced adoption of farming" (ibid.: 117).

When three Dakota broke ranks and informed a trader that some lodge soldiers intended to obtain as much credit as possible and then refuse to pay the traders, the Dog Soldiers finally acted. "They were enraged, and finding a horse belonging to one of the [informers], they cut it to pieces, along with all of the man's belongings. Upon discovering who the two others were, they carried them out into the middle of the agency grounds and stripped them naked in public" (ibid.).

At this point, the clash between the two cultures, aggravated by all of the aforementioned grievances, finally led to an almost complete break, and eventually to war.

The actions of the traders went against one of the basic tenets of Dakota culture—the belief in sharing with relatives and friends one's material possessions. The exchanges that occurred at both agencies became a clear example of how traders [most were whites married to Indian women or were half-breeds], now ignored their kinship responsibilities. The trade had become almost completely a business where creditors were "trusted" in relation to their ability to pay, rather than an exchange that was based to any degree upon kinship obligation. . . . In other words, the traders had a responsibility to assist their Dakota relatives that went beyond the profit motive. Their denial of that duty was socially unacceptable, and to the Sioux such action warranted severe punishment. (Ibid.: 129–130)

Regardless of the dramatic acts of these "police," it is important to emphasize that the individuals in military societies, the Cheyennes, for example, remained an integral part of the community social fabric. Almost all mature males were members of such societies. But because there were several military societies within the tribal structure, different men served in that capacity at different times. As a result, almost every member was at one time a member of a police policing the rest and at other times a simple tribal member. Even when on duty, police service was temporary—while the Cheyennes camped together during the hunting season. Moreover, even when acting as police, Cheyennes remained bound by their kin and tribal relations. Cheyennes who overstepped their power while acting as police would have to pay for it on returning to tribal life. In addition, the separate associations acted as checks and balances on each other (Lowie 1927:103–104; see also Llewellyn and Hoebel 1941:130; Krader 1976: 33–35).

After citing numerous incidents of such police activity, William Christie MacLeod (1937) concludes: "Policing of these hunts was of vital *economic* importance [to the Plains Indians] and absolutely essential to prevent failure as a result of the behavior of any individuals who might be selfish enough to scare the herd off by individual action" (ibid.: 186). In fact, MacLeod believed that "It is not possible to conceive of their communal bison hunts being successfully conducted without an adequate police organization" (ibid.: 200). The essential character of the Plains Indian police was that they acted as representatives of the people as a whole:

Their existence reflects, not the development of an organ of control of economically exploited groups within the community developed by exploiting groups; for . . . the Plains peoples represented a condition of considerable economic democracy. The Plains police were, therefore, a rather democratic organization devoted to the maintenance of law and order in the interest of the people as a whole. (Ibid., emphasis added)

Even the punishment function of the military societies was not independent from community well-being. After one offender "had been stopped and beaten by the Bowstring Soldiers for his crimes," a tribal chief happening upon him saw his pitiful condition and stated:

"Now I am going to help you out," . . . after giving him a stiff lecture on proper Cheyenne behavior. "That is what I am here for, because I am a chief of the people. Here are your clothes. Outside are three horses. You may take your choice! Here is a mountain lion skin. I used to wear this in the parades. . . . To these things he also added a six-shooter. (Hoebel 1978:43–44)

Moreover, military societies in their police function were under the "executive and administrative" authority of the Cheyenne Council of Forty-four chiefs[2] (ibid.: 52). Nevertheless, even where, as here, the police function serves the whole community, if the customary way of dealing with such conflicts was to survive, the society would have created in the police function

authoritative declarations on the content of the community's rules of behavior. Whatever technique is used, the result will be the endorsement of a particular standard found in the dominant ideology: . . . the rule would require general participation in the capture of prey. Once the rule has been announced, however, anyone who questions the co-operative hunting practices in the relations of production will be referred not to the customary nature of the behavior but rather to any authoritative determination that governs those activities. (Collins 1982:88)

Such rules represent incipient law, together with an incipient rule-enforcing authority, the essence of the police function.

Although we have posited that the process of transformation from a kinship-based society to state organization may take place as a result of a series of imperceptible changes, John H. Moore (1987:16), writing of the Cheyenne Plains Indians, argues that "nations begin by the conscious and explicit charter of their citizens and develop through periods that sometimes integrate the citizenry and sometimes divide it." Moore follows the Cheyennes from the seventeenth century till they were decimated by federal troops at Sand Creek, Colorado, in 1864. Because such careful diachronic studies of transformation are rare, we will summarize Moore's findings and relate his data to our own.

Moore concludes that during the 1840s to the 1860s, outside factors such as settler incursion, federal raids, and thus the constant necessity to move westward to avoid these threats, forced Cheyenne bands, in order to survive, to change their mode of production from one of hunting and cattle raising (in which their political system depended on chiefs with little decision-making power) to that of raiding settlers (in which the soldier societies became the politically dominant force). In a relatively short interval, therefore, the Cheyennes moved from an egalitarian or ranking society (our designations) to a "tribal nation," "having no classes and no state bureaucracy" (p. 338) but which maintained "ceremonies, laws, and customs that bound the people together," no longer by kinship but by ideology (p. 323). By the use of the concept "tribal nation," Moore attempts to bridge the supposed evolutionary gap between tribes and the more complex nations that have a state structure (p. 16).

At the time of their first contact with whites, the Cheyennes were organized into bands and military societies. Bands were groups of people related by blood or marriage who traveled together for most of the year, their numbers varying according to seasonal needs for hunting or caring for their horses (pp. 106, 323). On the other hand, military societies were more permanent, and were political in the sense that they engaged in relations with other nations as well as between bands and were the only organizations that could declare and conduct war (p. 106; see Hoebel 1978:52–53 and Grinnel 1956:50 for the complex decision-making relationship between the military societies and the council).

Those chiefs who were the "domestic and juristic leaders of the tribe" (elders) formed the Council of Forty-four. Although the council had little power and could not declare war, it did control the trade of buffalo robes with other tribes and with the whites. Chiefs who were elected leaders of their bands often thereafter regarded themselves as part of an elite who could not marry commoners. This elite status allowed them to acquire a monopoly of trade, recognized as such by white traders, who at the beginning of the trading season gave gifts to the chiefs. Failure to give a "customary chief's gift" was regarded by the chief as a grave offense "against the dignity of his nation" (Moore 1987:185; see also Hoebel 1978:51). Trade depended on the chief's ability to control other bunches who brought robes to him for trade. Chiefs often married groups of sisters so as to control the women who produced the robes. "The council chief's status, then, depended on the quality of his trade relations with Anglo traders and his ability to keep peace among the bunches and camps who traded under his sponsorship" (Moore 1987:187). "The chief's authority centered in three functions: trading, peacekeeping, and deciding on the seasonal movements of the bunch. . . . [T]he chief's role as trader both conditioned and determined the other two" (p. 188).

The Cheyenne dual system (peace-war) consisted of a "seasonal pattern of warfare beginning in early summer, when the headsman of the military societies led their warriors against enemy nations, with the council chiefs gradually assuming power in late summer as the bands went their separate ways for grazing, hunting, and trade. . . . The relative ease with which Cheyenne society was transformed onto a war footing in the 1860s, then, can be partly understood in terms of this preexisting dual structure. . . . [T]he so-called Dog Soldiers were merely making permanent an organizational form that was previously only seasonal" (p. 202).

Transition from a trading to a war economy resulted from the westward migrations of whites who drove the bands from their hunting areas; as the whites settled along rivers, their livestock denuded the pastures and thinned the forests for construction and firewood, thereby destroying the resources needed for the sustenance of the trading economy. This slower deterioration was capped by a series of raids by federal soldiers culminating in the Sand Creek Massacre of November 1864 in which the peace faction was decimated. A humiliating peace treaty signed the next year reduced the Council of Chief's reputation among other Cheyennes and resulted in many bands going over to the Dog Soldiers (Moore 1987:193, 197; see also Grinnel 1956:99, 135; Hoebel 1978:109).

The military society thus began to change from a seasonal feature of Cheyenne society to a permanent organization. As a result of the expulsion of a Dog Soldier headsman, Porcupine Bear, who in 1836 murdered a fellow tribesman, this tendency was accelerated. Instead of staying away from the camp for a time and then silently rejoining it some years later as had been the custom, Porcupine Bear set up his own camp with friends and relatives near the main camp. Later, when the main camp attacked the Kiowas,[3] the Dog Soldiers, under Porcupine Bear, successfully led an attack on them (Grinnel 1956:49–57; Hoebel 1978:38 and chap. 12).

This success helped legitimize the bravado of the military societies. In contrast, the Council of Chiefs increasingly accommodated themselves to the white incursions. The Dog Soldiers, on the other hand, reacting to the destruction of the trading economy, filled the gap by turning to raiding whites as their principal occupation. Over time, the Dog Soldiers were joined by other groups: Sioux warriors, who had long been allies of the Cheyennes, Cheyenne braves from other military societies who organized themselves in the same way, and marginal bands that until then had followed the chiefs' bands (Moore 1987:196–197; Hoebel 1978:114).

Thus, the military society had changed from the kind of police organization we discussed earlier, which guaranteed the egalitarian nature of society, to one in which the young men of the band were wild and reckless, engaged in raiding white settlers as their principal occupation, hard to control, and always involved in mischief.[4] In this way, the bands would get the rest of the tribe into trouble. These young men would make a raid, then get out of the way. The troops would pursue them but would frequently stumble across some other band of Cheyennes and punish them for what the Dog Soldiers had done (Moore 1987:198).

These changes in the police function had occurred following significant changes in the social formation. Under the influence of trading with tribes and government annuities, traditional values were disappearing. When tribes were deprived of their lands, treaties usually provided for government annuities. Chiefs, who previously had been judged by their generosity to fellow tribesmen, began to demand that rations be delivered to them for redistribution to the bands, while the bands, considering themselves politically independent, wanted the rations to be directly distributed to them (p. 184). Once the economic organization and the ideology, a product of that egalitarian organization, disappeared for the reasons set forth here, the police function also changed.

There need be no contradiction between Moore's position that transition results from a "conscious" creation of a new tribal nation and the belief that change results from a series of imperceptible changes. In the Cheyenne case, the self-conscious moves of the Dog Soldiers occurred only after a series of precipitating outside events. Their initial attacks were in the interest of the whole tribe and were seen to be so.

John Ehle (1988), in recounting the tragic story of the Cherokees' forced 1838 march from Georgia to Arkansas (the infamous Trail of Tears), likewise provides us with the prehistory of this march. The incursion of white civilization on Cherokee culture initiated a complex series of events that turned a ranked society (again, our designation) into a stratified social structure. The policing mechanism followed this structural change.

The impact of white civilization and its dire results on Native American peoples were foretold by Sweet Medicine, a Cheyenne prophet: "They will keep pushing forward, going all the time. The will tear up the earth, and at last you will do it with them. When you do, you will become crazy, and forget all that I am teaching you" (Matthiessen 1984:12).

Godelier's idea of "certain men" (described in chapter 2), who have the capacity, the inclination, and the opportunity to nimbly skip from one culture to another, dragging their people along with them, fits the story of the Cherokees.

In the 1770s, about 12,000 Cherokees lived in northwest Georgia and the Tennessee valley, fighting off various competing tribes such as the Creeks, Iroquois, Senecas, Chickasaws, and the Catawbas (Ehle 1988:7). Association with whites led to intermarriage, usually a Cherokee woman marrying a white man. Even though these couples frequently continued living in Cherokee towns, the men did not come to the council house; through wills they passed on their wealth to their sons; the Cherokee wives would often take up spinning and, like the white wives, work all day long, together with their daughters and their slaves (p. 36). Whites also influenced the selection of the paramount chiefs by dealing only with the warrior chiefs, frequently through bribes, and ignoring the shamans.

James Vann, "a planter, owner of many slaves, . . . the son of a trader," was one of these "certain men" who turned the traditional way of community land use into a means for capital accumulation (ibid.: 50).

Any Cherokee could assign to himself for his own use land not being used by another Cherokee; he was allowed to develop it. In years past this practice had meant that a family might take a plot for a family garden and, within walking distance, space for a house and a few hog pens. Not so modest were Vann's allotments, which included an entire valley worked by scores of slaves. . . . He had more than a hundred horses and four hundred head of cattle. He owned a store and a tavern. (Ibid.)

Slaves and horses were often stolen from whites. By supplying tools, seed, and instruction, the federal government encouraged this shift to agriculture and the acquisition of riches, a shift away from hunting and war.[5] Although Vann and like men did not usually become Christians, they welcomed Christian missionaries, who brought schooling to their children and the possibility of communicating with whites and learning white ways.

As with the Dakotas, intercourse with whites and the material advance of some leaders led to a split of the Cherokees into traditionals who wanted no contact with whites and those who saw their future tied to white civilization. When the federal government sought to build a road through Cherokee land, Vann sought inn and ferry franchises along the road. Traditionals opposed the road, in part because the vast number of such franchises would be assigned to whites. According to government rationale, whites would be the ones using the road and were therefore entitled to such benefits (Ehle 1988:65). Even the "traditional" chiefs were not outside white influence. While they rejected white customs, many had acquired the taste for wealth and often accepted bribes to "treaty away" Cherokee land (pp. 71, 78).

The ancient blood law of the Cherokees became entangled with this political competition when one man, Doublehead, the leader of the traditionals, killed his wife, Vann's sister-in-law, in a drunken rage (alcohol was acquired from white traders). Vann and other clan relatives assassinated Doublehead, following the Cherokee custom that a Cherokee who sold Cherokee land could be killed without right of the family of the victim to seek revenge[6] (p. 74).

Another Cherokee, named Ridge, eventually took over Vann's leadership role. Ridge was only slightly less wealthy than Vann and had acquired his wealth as had Vann. In 1811, by assembling and leading a band of Cherokees in concert with federal forces, Ridge aided the federal government in forcing the Creeks off their Georgia land, and thereby acquired the title of major (pp. 96–123).

Between 1811 and 1838, when the Cherokees were themselves forced to abandon Georgian land, leaders such as Ridge made frequent visits to Washington to negotiate for their people. During these visits, they were wined and dined by Washington society. Over time many exchanged their customary attire for European clothes, learned English, and saw the advantage of sending their children to missionary schools. Meanwhile, the state of Georgia became increasingly aggressive in demanding their removal West. The state passed laws restricting their rights, arrested their leaders, supported the rights of white squatters on Cherokee land, and sent militia to harass and threaten them. Federal government policy vacillated but gradually changed from encouragement of Cherokee settlement in Georgia to demands that the Cherokees move West. After numerous abortive attempts at negotiating a treaty for the move, Major Ridge succeeded in negotiating one in December 1835, ratified by the U.S. Senate in May 1836. John Ross, the leader of the traditionals (who were mostly full-blooded), opposed the treaty but never suggested any alternative to the inevitable advance of the whites (pp. 295–296).

According to treaty terms, the Cherokees had two years to dispose of their property and clear out. But because of the rift that had developed between the treaty and no treaty factions, no steps were taken during this time to plan for the move. When in 1838 the time was up, the federal government sent General Winfield Scott to forcibly move the Cherokees (p. 330). After about half the Cherokees had been forcibly evicted, Chief John Ross, who had been largely responsible for the failure of the Cherokees to make preparations for the western trek, approached General Scott with an offer to have the Cherokees themselves manage the removal (p. 335). Ross had in mind having his brother direct the operation. As finally negotiated, Ross and his brother were to be paid a certain amount per head for each day of the march. Although the water route to Arkansas was safer and shorter, Ross chose to transport the tribe by land (p. 345).

The march, which became known as the Trail of Tears, took 189 days, during which it is estimated that one-fifth to one-third of the marchers died (pp. 361, 389–392). The wealthier tribal members went by water and suffered no deaths. Moreover, their wealth allowed them to resume the life they had left in Georgia (p. 366). Ross's claims on the federal government for the trip eventually consumed all monies the government had promised to pay the tribe in compensation for their move.

Soon after the immigrants' arrival, a dispute broke out between the new and old settlers. Ross, representing twice the number of the old settlers, challenged the governing constitution and demanded a call for a convention to draft a new constitution. After Ross's failure to take over the council government, several dozen of his followers decided to take things into their own hands by invoking the blood laws that prohibited the unapproved sale of Cherokee land. Their wrath was aimed at Ridge and others who had negotiated the treaty for their removal. Three men from the clan of each accused sat as judges, heard testimony, and judged each guilty. Those found guilty, including Major Ridge, were executed by armed squads. For years thereafter, on each side, revenge murders followed (pp. 372–380). "To the astonishment and dismay of the old settlers among the Cherokees, law and order on all counts broke down; even theft became commonplace, theft of slaves and everything of value. These Cherokee men and women from the East became devourers of their own society" (p. 380).

Thus, during a seventy-year period, Cherokee society was transformed from an essentially ranked society to a stratified structure in which the governing bodies, the customs, and the policing mechanism were equally transformed consistent with the new structure. Aping the white man's customs, "certain men" of the Cherokees used Cherokee customs of free access to land to acquire land so as to produce for exchange rather than for use value as did other Cherokees. Rather than showing generosity in the disposition of their riches, these men used their acquired riches for further accumulation. Riches were translated into prestige (at earlier times such "hogging" could have made the men despised). Prestige led to political power at council meetings. Such power, in turn, gave these men access to the white power structure and more wealth.

Riches for the few promoted internal dissensions and jealousies, and for the first time in Cherokee society the threat of crime, especially theft, made necessary a police mechanism to protect those who had acquired property to protect. "The light horse guard had been created to protect whites and Cherokees from thieves, who were sometimes white, sometimes Cherokee" (p. 76). It was a society primed for theft. Ridge, for example

had crops, slaves, blooded horses, even wagons and a buggy, as well as ornate saddles; his wife had fine clothes, quilts, and blankets, dishes from abroad. They had a smokehouse stocked with bacon and hams, an apple house, a cellar for cider and cabbages and turnips and potatoes. (Ehle 1988:76)

On the other hand, "most thieves were 'poor full-blood Indians' who were hungry, driven to desperation by the virtual disappearance of wild game" (ibid.). One observer remarked that at an earlier time "there had been no thievery in the Cherokee nation itself, except against strangers, but now neighbors stole from neighbors" (ibid.). Thus a police had been created to maintain this imbalance of riches, to punish Cherokees who threatened that balance (ibid.), and to keep order during the long march to the West so that the balance could be maintained (p. 348).

COMPLEX CHIEFDOM/SIMPLE STATE

Having already shown the steps by which a fundamentally egalitarian society develops a policing mechanism, the next step is to illustrate how such a society can be transformed into a class-dominated society. A number of examples of such a transition can be cited. The first of these will be that of the kingdom of Gyaman founded at the end of the seventeenth century and occupying a territory situated at the northeast part of present-day Ivory Coast and northwest Ghana (Terray 1974:320). This society provides an example of an early state organization in which a slave and kinship mode of production exist side by side.

In writing about this society, Terray (1974) sought to test the position of Engels linking the emergence of social classes to that of the state, which in turn resulted in "the first great cleavage of society into an exploiting and an exploited class," masters and slaves (Terray 1974:315, citing Engels). In Gyaman society, judicial, political, and administrative power were in the hands of a warrior aristocracy. The principal means of acquiring wealth was by long-distance trading in gold. Terray shows that the control of the gold trade depended on the labor power of slaves, available only to an aristocracy; that in order to reproduce and defend that order, it was necessary for the aristocracy to maintain an armed presence both outside and inside the society, and that this institutionalization of force to supply the surplus product to support this elite class resulted in the creation of a state society in which there was a continuity of kinship relations as a subordinate rather than a dominant mode of production.

Before these developments, all inhabitants had equal rights to search for and participate in the exchange process, but such equality was more apparent than real once captive slaves entered into the production process. Gold could be obtained in two ways, either by filtering sand that had passed over gold-bearing ground, or by mining. The first method could be accomplished by simple manual labor and in actuality "captives of the king and his chiefs worked side by side with free . . . men and their wives" (Terray 1974:327, 325). On the other hand, work in the mines required skilled labor, working in teams, to accomplish an extremely arduous and dangerous task. In addition, such work was accompanied by financial risk because of the numerous mine shafts that might have to be sunk before the favorable result would be obtained. Thus, this latter work was carried on only with slaves and only "those who possessed a sufficiently numerous reserve supply of captives could profitably engage in this exploitation." Because only kings and chiefs had access to a slave supply, and because mines could only be worked by slaves, it appeared sensible to all that the mines belong to the rulers (ibid.: 328).

The wealth local aristocracies placed in trade thus arose from "the surplus labour extorted from its captives; it was this surplus labour that provided the aristocracy with the products that it introduced into long-distance trade; and if it held a predominant position among the local clients of this trade this was because the aristocracy controlled the greatest share of captive labour, whose activity from Gyaman swelled the flow of long-distance exchange" (ibid.: 329). Looking at the social structure of Gyaman society itself,

the principal factor in the work process was labour-power. It was the only source of disposable energy, apart from donkeys used to carry the loads. . . . Thus, it was command over men—and so the possibility of organising their cooperation on a large scale—that was the key to economic power. In the framework of the kin-based system, this authority belonged to the elders, but the segmental character of the system reduced the number of workers who could be brought under a single head. . . . [Thus,] the subjection of the producer was not able to be accomplished through the appropriation of the material factors of production, as was the case under feudalism with the ground, and in capitalism with machines. Consequently the establishment of bonds of direct personal dependence was the chief means of expanding control over men, and so of access to wealth. Now slavery and captivity were the most effective and rigorous forms of these bonds of personal dependence; this is why the functioning of the entire social formation was organized around them. (Ibid.: 331)

Because the Gyaman social structure was based on slavery, the political apparatus was designed to "create and reproduce the material and social conditions for the exploitation of captives." Thus, all decisions involving the acquisition and control of slaves and other war booty was in the hands of the aristocracy (ibid.: 331–332).

Of particular significance is Terray's analysis of the way such a slave-based mode of production could be maintained side-by-side with a kin-based economy. Terray does not suggest the means by which kin-based society evolved to a society in which the slave mode of production was predominant, but he does show the relations between the two within one society. The amount of surplus extracted from the slaves was such that only the slaves and not the free populations were exploited by the aristocracy; at the same time, the demands on the slaves for a surplus product remained relatively restrained. These results flowed from the fact that the surplus was used (1) only to provide for the "immediate subsistence needs of the dominant class who were consequently relieved by it of any compulsion to productive labour" and (2) to provide products of "con-spicuous consumption" so that the aristocracy might proclaim "its power and social hegemony" (ibid.: 333–334).

Extorting the surplus product was not for the purpose of realizing "a commercial profit." Rather, its purpose was to exchange the gold "for goods that played a part either in the immediate production process—iron, cotton—or in the reproduction process—weapons, captives themselves." As a result, these goods "were sought after because of their own utility," not for purposes of commodity exchange (ibid.: 334).

Thus this pre-eminence of use value explains at one and the same time why the captives were not subjected in . . . Gyaman to an exploitation as intense as the slaves of ancient Rome or of the southern United States, and why Abron . . . slavery did not manifest that tendency to expansion and generalization inherent in ancient or American slavery; it always allowed another mode of production to exist by its side, usually of a domestic or kin-based character, within whose framework the free subjects of the aristocracy in power worked and produced. (Ibid.: 334)

Nevertheless, with the predominance of the slave-based economy came the necessity to institutionalize force (Hindess and Hirst 1975:330 n. 11).

It followed that since the relations of captivity were the dominant element in the social formation, and since military might was the chief instrument of their establishment and reproduction, it was natural for the problems raised by the creation and use of force to be at the very heart of the social formation's functioning. (Terray 1974:332)

Though no longer predominant, the kin-based economy was of great importance in determining the shape of the slave-based economy. Children of slaves were considered free, so that free men felt protected and captives had "the hope of progressive enfranchisement of their children," at the same time reproducing the kin-based system (ibid.: 335).

Thus "the introduction of slave-type relations of production into social formations dominated until then by the kin-based mode of production . . . evoked the formation of a State as the condition of their functioning and reproduction" (Terray 1974:339).

While in Gyaman society the dynamic force in the formation of a class-dominated society was the conversion by the ruling aristocracy of the dominant economic base from kin to slave, in Aztec society, a central-ized elite gradually seduced and coopted local lineage leadership away from their kin-based communities so as to produce a stratified class-dominated state organization.[7]

In the midthirteenth century, Aztec people migrated to the Valley of Mexico. They were organized in *calpulli* (groups of households) politically arranged into clans, with fictive kin relationships. Land was corporately owned but individually cultivated. Separate plots were communally farmed on behalf of *calpulli* leaders, not because the *calpulli* leader could command it, but because it was due by ancestral custom in payment "for the care he took of them, and for his expenditure on the annual meeting held in his house in support of the general welfare" (Adams 1966:92; see also Kurtz 1978:171).

Wealth was unequally distributed; some lineage lines were ranked higher than others with some families receiving more land; those less favored might be forced into slavery or forced to migrate. There appeared to be a complex redistribution system operating through the *calpulli*. Authority of the *calpulli* and of the *tlatoani*, the central overall leader, was limited, in part because of the competition among the *calpulli* leaders. The *calpulli* leaders, apparently concerned with military threats from more centralized states around them, decided to adopt the style of their enemies. This plan was implemented by bringing in as *tlatoani* (literally, "speaker") a foreign noble.

Thereafter, the death of a leader of a rival people that had until then dominated the valley, followed by an internal power struggle, allowed the Aztecs to attain hegemony over the valley and all its riches. With this tribute the *tlatoani* moved to consolidate his power by using the newly found wealth to bring *calpulli* leaders closer to central authority, while at the same time separating them from their own local community power base.

The *tlatoani* set about to develop the *calpulli* into a "self-conscious elite class" by distributing titles of nobility, some lands, and other spoils, by requiring nobles to lodge separately and wear distinctive clothing and jewelry, and by forbidding others to do likewise. He provided elaborate feasts and ceremonies in which only the designated nobles could participate and linked the *calpulli* leaders and the throne by marriage. The *tlatoani* thus defined nobles as those directly receiving tribute from him. All this was conceived to channel the local leader's "immediate self-interest" to the political ends of the *tlatoani*.

The *tlatoani* also required that all administrative business be attended to at the central palace, and he asserted the right to name *calpulli* successors. Over time, the succession had changed from leaders elected by the community to hereditary leaders, and finally, leaders who had to be confirmed by the *tlatoani*. These changes made hereditary succession of lands dependent on acquisition of the office. The *tlatoani*'s control of trade and tribute allowed him to determine the distribution of luxury goods to the nobles (cf. Lenski 1966:220). In sum, he was able to invert the source of the *calpulli* leader's power. Instead of issuing from the *calpulli*, power now came or seemed to come from the *tlatoani*. All this took a number of generations to accomplish. Nevertheless, the *tlatoani* left relatively untouched the political and economic organization of the *calpulli* community. Tribute or surplus, which the *calpulli* leaders were obligated to send to the Aztec state, was collected by the *calpulli* leaders on the same basis as before, through communal labor service accorded by ancient custom (Mandel 1968:32). Thus the unit of responsibility to the Aztec state was not the individual citizen but continued to be the corporate Calpulli unit. Rounds (1979:83–84) sums up the evolution of the Aztec state as follows:

The leaders of the *calpulli*, the political segments of prestate Aztec society, adopted a central ruler as a means of improving their military defense against hostile neighbors. This central dynasty was at first very limited in its internal affairs, which remained largely under the authority of the *calpulli* leaders. However, the entry of [the central leaders] into a career of imperial conquest brought greatly expanded revenues under the control of the dynasty, which was able to use its new wealth to begin consolidation of its power over internal politics. The stratagems employed by the dynasty in its drive toward centralization of power created a distinctive elite ruling class, through which the traditional *calpulli* leaders were coopted as instruments of the state authority. . . . [M]uch of the older *calpulli* political structure still remained intact, as the lower level in the state hierarchy.

This use by a centralized stratified structure of lineage kinship economy to collect surplus in order to sustain an elite class is characteristic of the practice of weak states to use the lineage elite as "hinge figures or brokers linking the lineage territory to state authority" (Fox 1976:100). But equally important as the appearance of the dominant state organization is the continuation of the kinship-based economy, even though in an attenuated form (White 1959:141, 310; Krader 1976:11–12; Fox 1971:157).

Another illustration of how the state put to its own use the kinship-based economy (Schaedel 1978:292 n.5, 308) is Godelier's (1977) description of the transformation of the social relations of Indian communities after they were subjugated by the Incas in the midfifteenth century. Earlier agricultural communities with approximate equality in land ownership were replaced by detaching people from their land and forcing them to produce surplus for the Inca state. This hinging of the local community to the state was accomplished through the double institutionalization of marriage (Diamond 1971:116), that is, the use of marriage by the Inca state to set the date for the male's entrance into state forced labor service:

The *old* kinship relations therefore took on a new function. . . . [M]arriage, as a rite, within a local community became the means of access to a new status, and as a symbol of this status, subjects liable to enforced labour for the Inca State; they therefore became members of a wider community which was quite different from that of the . . . local tribe. . . . [T]he new mode of production took *advantage* of the existing relations of production together with the social and ideological institutions already present in order, eventually to overthrow them. . . . The characteristic feature of this mechanism is that the mode of production positively *maintains* some of the former communal relations, takes advantage of them and utilizes them for its own mode of reproduction; this results in the partial *destruction* of the former communal relations. (Godelier 1977:68, emphasis in original)

Mallon (1983:84–85) describes a patron/clientage relationship in a precapitalist Peruvian economy that acted as a transition point to a capitalist market economy using intermittent force to maintain the relationship. Spanish colonialists employed traditional structures to maintain their power, working through a class of Indian elites to control the labor force. Though rich peasants in the villages had at best a tenuous connection to the old communal traditions of authority, their position of influence did depend on fulfilling certain expectations of generosity and service to the community as a whole. If they financed the community's fiestas, gave aid to individuals in times of need, acted as godparents to neighbors' children (*compadrazgo*), served the village as political authorities, represented the community in court cases or petitions to government, and organized and financed public works, they could expect preferential access to labor and resources. The poorer villagers, if they accepted the "generosity" of the rich, were bound to pay it back in individual or communal work; special grants of usufruct over community lands, pasture, or water; or with a more generalized and vague sense of loyalty and deference that prompted them always to be ready to do a favor, to serve their patrons in whatever way they could.

Medium-sized merchants thus served as mediators with village elites. "In exchange, they received—and made available to *their* patrons—a link to local client networks, through which it was possible to obtain a labor force for the mule trade, haciendas, and mines" (ibid.: 86, emphasis in original). The elites' first choice was to manipulate this traditional relationship, but when this means failed "they did not hesitate to try intimidation and physical violence" (ibid.: 89). "Given the naked exploitation inherent in many of these relationships, their continued effectiveness depended on the ultimate capacity to use force" (ibid.: 90).

A central government must enforce its decrees and supervise any administrative apparatus in place. These tasks may be accomplished by "extensive *travels* through the state on the sovereign's part [and] [t]he use of messengers, envoys, plenipotentiaries . . . ; the employment of spies . . . ; the *forced entertainment* of relatives of regional and/or local functionaries in the capital" (Claessen 1978:584, emphasis in original).

Sacks (1979:chap. 8) provides us with a case study of the transformation from a kinship-based to a class-structured economy. Buganda, on the northern shore of Victoria Nyanza in Uganda, in the seventeenth century was a small client of a neighboring more powerful country. A king of Buganda won some lands from this neighbor and divided the captured lands among his war leaders and other loyal followers. As more land was taken, this group of leaders grew in number compared to clan leaders. By the end of the eighteenth century, the king, in order to consolidate his rule, began killing or imprisoning his brothers and their sons.

In this process relations of production were transformed from direct patrician control over productive means to control by a network of chiefly families of a few of these clans who held hereditary rights to goods and plunder by virtue of their ties to each other through the king. . . . Clans and their component lineages were decorporatized rather than destroyed. Kinship became a basis for establishing vertical, dyadic clientage relations, the central relation of men to productive means. Clans were deprived of their independent base of power by expiration of clan land and installation of appointed officials, together with coaptation, or harnessing clanship to class organization. (Ibid.: 200–201)

By granting special rights such as hereditary positions to certain clans in return for becoming the king's clients, potential clan unity in opposition was breached, rather becoming "transformed into class-centered patronage networks" (ibid.: 201). In the nineteenth century, military expeditions became a way of life, Buganda having the capability to "field a huge army" (ibid.: 202). The spoils of war—women, children, and cattle—were distributed according to the class system (ibid.: 202). "The Buganda rulers relied on their control of armed forces to maintain their rule. The king and district chiefs had their own armed bodyguards even before Mutesa [a 19th century king] was said to have created a standing army. The king also had his own secret police and executioners" (ibid.: 204). Bugandan men were obligated to supply to the king a tax of bark cloth, and labor to build his palaces and roads, carry his firewood, and hunt for him (ibid.: 207).

Sacks sums up the resulting "gender and class relations of production":

Ruler and peasants had diametrically opposed relations of production. The former owned the land and the bulk of the livestock, especially cattle. They determined peasants' land allotments, could evict peasants at will, and could seize their livestock. Peasants obtained access to land by entering into clientage relations in which they provided labor and tax to their patron. Peasant men and women had very different relations to the means of production. Only men's work fulfilled clientage obligations; only men were clients, and thus only men had direct access to land. Women obtained access to land and houses mainly as a wife through her husband and secondarily through any other man who might be her guardian. Women could not inherit land or houses. In the eyes of the Buganda state women were wives, dependents of men, and men were clients. Because the state effectively controlled channels of decision making, dispute settlement, ritual life, and institutionalized social activities, it could enforce wifely dependency. Women were effectively excluded from direct involvement in political and economic processes. (Ibid.: 208–209)

Under this system, people entered into the productive process through clientage arrangements and not by kinship relations (ibid.: 210).

Thus we see how a class-dominated society can develop in a variety of ways. In Gyaman society, a slave-based economy replaced a predominantly kinship-based structure. In Aztec society, a centralized elite gradually gained control over local lineage leaders who became increasingly alienated from their local kin-based communities. In Buganda, enough of the spoils were controlled by a small hereditary elite so that power became concentrated in their hands and a patronage system developed.

This last pattern may not be uncommon. The nature of social stratification in Polynesia has occasioned considerable research (see, e.g., Goldman 1955, 1970; Sahlins 1958; Kirch 1984). As we indicated in chapter 2, there is a relationship between complex production on the high islands and the development of social stratification:

Everywhere in Polynesia, the chief is the agent of general, tribal-wide distribution. The chief derives prestige from his generosity. In turn, his prestige permits him to exercise control over social processes, such as production, upon which his function of distribution rests. Consequently the greater the productivity, the greater the distributive activities of the chief, and the greater his powers. (Sahlins 1958:xi)

Polynesian chiefs employed stewards or managers to oversee the production of commoners. These stewards were typically nobles, close relatives of the paramount chief. Although Polynesian societies never developed the sort of class structure evident in Buganda, as chiefs gained control over extra land through warfare, their powers grew in similar ways as in Buganda.

THE STATE

The English police provide a historical case study of the development of a policing function particularly germane to our theory. An unusually rich corpus of historical materials allows for a long-term and detailed examination of transformations by which the English police emerged. We first sketch a general overview of the period up to the time of the organized police in 1829, and then proceed with a more detailed account.

Anglo-Saxon society in the early part of the first millennium A.D. is described as being organized on principles of kinship, relying on collective security as a means of social control. In this sense, it begins with a structure not unlike many of the societies we described earlier in this chapter. By the year 900, however, tribal social structure had evolved into a series of territorial kingdoms governed by the rules of a budding feudal society. As a means of social control in such a society, all men not owning their own land were required to find a lord who would agree to be responsible for their good conduct or, alternatively, all persons living in the same vicinity had to band together in order to guarantee each other's good conduct. These groups, called tithings, consisted of ten male heads of families organized into hundreds, unified by the hundreds court. The head tithingman is said to be the forerunner of the constable.

With the coming of the Normans in 1066, England was constituted a single kingdom; sheriffs were appointed as royal officers to oversee the organization of tithings. Under the feudal order, the unit of organization became the manor, with the constable emerging as an officer of the manor court as well as the appointed agent of the king to keep his peace. By the middle of the fourteenth century, the constable was subordinated to the justice of the peace, usually a knight who was also the local landlord, owner of the manor. This justice-constable system continued until the formation of the London professional force in 1829.

In setting forth an English model of police development, it is not our purpose to present a thorough study. We seek merely to examine our previously developed hypotheses against generally well-accepted knowledge of English and police history.

As Rivet (1958:33) has observed, "the pre-history of lowland Britain is a long tale of wave after wave of immigrants sometimes surging, sometimes trickling, across the Channel, and the story . . . has thus no clear beginning." Much oversimplifying this history, we can divide it into periods dominated by four different civilizations: Celtic (600 B.C.–43 A.D.); Roman (43 A.D.–410 A.D.); Anglo-Saxon (410 A.D.–1066) and Norman (1066–1154).

Because Roman strategy called for building up and living only in cities and dealing almost exclusively with the native elite, Roman influence effectively ended at the city walls (Trevelyan 1953:43–45). When Anglo-Saxon raids recommenced in the mid-fourth century just as Rome itself was under assault, the Empire, by 410 A.D., was forced to withdraw all its forces. Within a few generations, virtually all Roman culture and influence disappeared (Priestley 1967:72–73; Trevelyan 1953:61,65; Stubbs 1874:65). The earlier Celt culture was pushed west into what is now Wales and had little influence on forming English institutions (Trevelyan 1953:65). Therefore, we can ignore the Roman and Celt periods and begin with the Anglo-Saxon incursions.

Raids by various tribes, which Trevelyan (1953:50) designates Nordic, and others, Anglo-Saxon, occurred from 300 to about 1020 A.D. More than any other group, the Anglo-Saxons gave to the English culture its definitive character. Migrating from northern Germany and the coast of Denmark, they came not as plunderers but in search of better farmland, bringing their families with them (Priestley 1967:127; Whitelock 1968:18–19; Trevelyan 1953:56–57, 68).

Their "form of government was autocratic Kingship, exercised by some member of a royal family supposed to be descended from the gods, although such autocracy was limited by the custom of the tribe, by the temper of the armed tribesmen, and by the personal qualities of the King himself. . . . There were many grades of rank, wealth and freedom among them" (Trevelyan 1953:50). Thus at the time of their arrival, kingship was already associated with "legitimate authority," the "general custom" being "for the man from the royal kin who was fittest to rule to be selected as successor" (Loyn 1984:14–15).

Such difference did not, however, amount to class division or state organization. These inequalities gave the holder no claim to "social and political rights. . . . [L]ike great age, [nobility] entitled a man to a respectful hearing in the tribal councils . . . but it confers no political privilege" (Stubbs 1874:22). In the eighth century, one contemporary writer described the king as a doctor, teacher, and war leader on whose morals and goodness depended the people's fortunes in war, harvest, freedom from plague, and their general prosperity (Loyn 1984:27).

A nobleman's authority over a village community rested on his social rather than his legal dominance, and would be determined in part by sheer physical and material factors. . . . Wealth, size of hall, nearness in kinship to the king or the ealdorman, past prestige as a warrior, judge or royal servant, could determine the degree of authority exercised more so than mere physical force or apparent status (Loyn 1984:49–50).

In this regard, the king was actually quite reminiscent of the early Bugandan king or the Polynesian chief, whose power was directly related to the amount of production controlled and redistributed.

Although slavery existed in Anglo-Saxon England, those slaves were probably acquired in warfare and either traded to states with slave economies such as Rome or put to work on farms (Thompson 1966:192; see also Stubbs 1874:23–25). Tacitus (1942:719), a Roman historian writing of the "Germans" in the first century, observes that "the master is not distinguished from the slave by being brought up with greater delicacy. Both live amid the same flocks and lie on the same ground."

Nevertheless, at the time of their migration, loyalty between tribal members and the chief was personal and no longer tribal. A successful chief attempted to attract to him men from several tribes (Whitelock 1968:29). Tacitus (1942:716–717) shows the ideological strength that had grown around this relationship:

When they go into battle, it is a disgrace for the chief to be surpassed in valor, a disgrace for his followers not to equal the valour of the chief. And it is an infamy and a reproach for life to have survived the chief, and returned from the field. To defend, to protect him, to ascribe one's own brave deed to his renown, is the height of loyalty. The chief fights for victory; his vassals fight for their chief.

Tacitus (1942:716) also describes a society in which there is a division of labor between warriors who war for their chief but do no work and the rest who produce. Although the significance of these economic divisions is limited by the fact that the warriors are apparently able to support themselves on their own exterior plunder, it is clear that there is a social division into producers and nonproducers.

[M]en look to the liberality of their chief for their war-horse and their blood-stained and victorious lance. Feasts and entertainment, which, though inelegant, are plentifully furnished, are their only pay. The means of this bounty come from war and rapine. Nor are they as easily persuaded to plough the earth and to wait for the year's produce as to challenge an enemy and earn the honour of wounds.

Nay, they actually think it tame and stupid to acquire by the sweat of toil what they might win by their blood. (Ibid.)

It is left "to the women, the old men, and the weakest members of the family" to till the land (ibid.). This picture of class division is somewhat softened by the continued importance of the common peasant in the social formation of the Anglo-Saxons at the time of their arrival in Britain. Andreski (1968:64) writes:

The Anglo-Saxons lived in village communities of free peasants. There were the earls, the nobility of birth . . . : they rather resembled the chief of the Bantu tribes of South Africa. The absence of profound social inequalities was undoubtedly connected with the military organization of these tribes, whose armed forces consisted of peasants bringing their own arms. This militia was called the fyrd, and the bulk of it consisted of foot soldiers.

Having established the broad outlines of the Anglo-Saxon social structure at the time of Anglo-Saxons' arrival in Britain, we are now ready to examine in more detail the development of class structure and the modifications of the police function growing out of that structure.

By the sixth century the Anglo-Saxons had consolidated their military gains sufficiently to establish kingdoms in the western half of England, while the rest of the island remained in Celtic hands. Significantly, although the Anglo-Saxons had a king in their homeland, he ruled no kingdom. This military adventure, therefore, must have had a profound effect on any incipient aspects of societal stratification. Stubbs (1874:36–37) suggests that such "state of society in which the causes are at work" contains the germs of a later feudal structure:

the principle of common tenure and cultivation . . . , the villages themselves, their relation to the [territorial division] and the fact that they were centers or subdivisions for the administration of justice. . . . [W]e have the nobleman, we have the warlike magistrate with his [retainers], whose services he must find some way of rewarding, and whose energies he must even in peace find some way of employing. The rich man too has his great house and court, and his family of slaves or dependents, who may be only less than free in that they cultivate the land that belongs to another. (Ibid.)

Given such a ready social mix, the leader "has but to conquer and colonize a new territory, and reward his followers on a plan that will keep them faithful as well as free, and feudalism springs into existence" (ibid.: 37). "Springs" perhaps is not the word, but the invasion of England, providing the available territorial spoils for distribution, supplied the basis for setting this mechanism in motion.

Stubbs (1874:76,79) speculates that subsequent to the invasion, the following events may have occurred:

[T]he successful leader of a large colony or a victorious host, having conquered and exterminated the natives, must have proceeded to divide their land according to a fixed scheme. The principle of this allotment he would find in the organization of the host. That host was the people in arms, divided into hundreds of warriors, sustained and united by the principle of kindred. . . . [T]hese allotments varied according to the numbers of the kindred, the portion assigned to a single family or house being a hide of land; . . . besides these the nobles or other great men received grants of estates . . . ; and . . . the surplus land remained the common property of the nation.

This surplus would later be distributed in part to the monasteries and in part retained by the king (ibid.: 79). According to Stubbs, that mode of allotment may arguably be traced back to a communal system of land tenure known as the mark, "held by the community, the absolute ownership of which resides in the community itself, or in the tribe or nation of which the community forms a part" (ibid.: 53). It is by virtue of a person's status as a freeman of that community that he is entitled to his share of land, but his claim is in use, not in ownership. Conversely, the possession of the land "is the attestation, type, and embodiment of his freedom and political rights" (ibid.: 55).

Such status entitled the freeman to be a member of and participate in the decisions of the assembly of that political unit. As rights in private property were asserted and inequalities of ownership developed, these distinctions were perpetuated in rank and class differentiations. The inequality in the allotment of land both affirmed and concretized these distinctions, providing at the same time the rationale for different allotments. By enlarging the number of retainers attached to his household, the nobleman thus became entitled to a larger share (ibid.: 78,80).

The ancient communal concept of land as the common property from which issued all rights maintained its constitutional importance, albeit in a specially restricted form. Stubbs (1874: 80,85) explains how rights attached to the possession of land radiated out to all aspects of society:

The question of the primary allotment leads directly to that of the primitive tenure. The possession of land was, even whilst the idea of nationality was mainly a personal one, the badge, if not the basis, of all political and constitutional right. On it depended, when the personal ideal yielded to the territorial, the rights and obligations, the rank, value, and credibility of the member of the body politic; it became the basis as well as the tangible expression of his status.

The dependent class thus includes a great variety of relations; the *comitatus* or personal following of the King or ealdorman; all freemen hired as household servants or field labourers; the rent-paying tenants of other men's lands; and the hereditary dependents who have personal rights, the [slaves] and the freedmen: the landless, the homeless, the kinless, must all seek a lord whose protection is to be secured by voluntary service, who is responsible for their appearance in the law courts, and who in some cases exercises over them an authority which is scarcely less than legal jurisdiction. (See also Hindess and Hirst 1975:235–236)

Stubbs (1874:87–98) suggests that in the primitive Saxon community the tie of kindred was synonymous with communal ownership of land, that as this community went through transformation to private and unequal ownership, the original kindred community became a township consisting of "the body of tenants of a lord who regulates them or allows them to regulate themselves on principles derived from" the original communal organization (ibid.: 91). Church parishes were often coterminous with townships. Tithes paid to the church gave the name of tithing to the township as a unit of local administration. The term *hundred* had been used by Saxon tribes to designate a tribal unit of one hundred families. As territorial ties replaced personal ones, the hundred became territorial and the tithing signified one-tenth of a hundred. Simultaneously, the hundred also designated the jurisdiction of the hundred court, while the tithing represented the transfer of the communal police function to a part of a hierarchical landlord-dominated system.

Once English kings in the seventh century were converted to Christianity, the church developed a reciprocal power exchange with the evolving state. As the king's decrees became written down, only the church could provide literate persons to draft them, while only the king could provide legal and military protection to church property and personnel. The church in turn could provide the king with legitimacy (Loyn 1984:44–45).

Folk right or custom was still dominant, but by the eighth century, the king "together with a great assembly of the chief men of the kingdom" by degree sought to "clarify" and to set down the "true law" (Loyn 1984:42–43). As part of this process, a number of laws, principles, and ideological homilies grew up to replace the kin principles of mutual aid for collective security. Primary responsibility for a man under the jurisdiction of a lord no longer rested with the man's kin but with the lord; the duty to the lord came first. Vendetta, for example, could not be carried out against a man who had killed in defense of his lord; and one who entered the priesthood thereby terminated ties with his kindred (Whitelock 1968:37–43; Loyn 1984:77).

Indeed, throughout the Middle Ages the relationship of lord and man was regarded as a sort of kinship, never as purely mercenary. The lord must not protect a man from the law, but see that justice was done upon him, or else himself pay compensation to the plaintiff and a fine to the king. (Harding 1966:19)

What the state had done was to "seize," to double institutionalize, in Bohannan's (1968) apt phrase, the kindred social control mechanism. The further introduction of the view of frankpledge, the use of collective security mechanisms to inform the king's officer, the sheriff, of the alleged offenses of kindred, all had the effect of turning men's loyalty away from kindred toward the feudal order of lords and kings (Pollock and Maitland 1968:32). This trend toward stratification was hastened by the Viking raids at the end of the eighth century:

Under the impact of the Norsemen's raids the military organization altered. The heavily armed horsemen were found much more effective than the fyrd [peasants on foot]. Naturally, ordinary peasants could not afford the equipment of a heavily armed horseman. So, a professional force became indispensable. It consisted of thegns: the nobility of service which grew out of king's retainers. They were endowed with land, and rapidly developed into a privileged stratum. Finally, the society came to be divided into the warriors and the peasants who toiled for them. Even before the Norman conquest England was covered by manors, where the serfs lived under the jurisdiction of their lords. (Andreski 1968:65; see also Loyn 1984:32)

Melville Lee (1971) describes a two-tiered system of collective responsibility during the reign of King Alfred (871–899). The object of the system was to place every subject in some arrangement of collective security. To the thegn, the resident owner of considerable real property, the king looked to secure to him all members of the thegn's household. If any person broke the "law," his overlord, the thegn, had the responsibility to bring him to justice. According to Stubbs (1874:85), one immediate result was to reconstitute the community into

those who have land of their own, and those who have not. Of the former the law can take immediate cognisance, they have a tangible stake in the community through which the law can enforce its obligations. Of the latter it can take cognisance only mediately, through some person whom the law can touch, and they are therefore compelled to put themselves in dependence on someone with whom it can deal as answerable for their forthcoming.

The landless freeman thereafter had to find a guarantee for his good behavior. If he was unable to attach himself to some thegn, he was compelled to combine with others so that their aggregate goods should provide sufficient bail for the shortcomings of any member of the group. Those who could not or would not find such security were forbidden to possess cattle, and were no longer under the protection of the law. Freemen, who had no freehold, were banded together into tithings consisting of the adult male members of ten homesteads. The members elected one of their number to be the headborough, or chief pledge or surety, who thus became their representative and was responsible both to the community and to higher authority for the good behavior of each person (Lee 1971:3–4; Critchley 1967:2; Jeffery 1957:657; Reith 1975:26).

Apparently because of concern by large landowners about cattle theft, under King Athelstan (924–939), an ordinance grouped freemen into tithings and hundreds, each tithing to have one tithingman in charge of the other nine. A hundredman was to be appointed, who, with the senior tithingmen, was to be responsible for collection of dues from the subordinate tithingmen. There were to be ten tithings in a hundred. Failure to enter a tithing incurred the loss of the right to claim blood price in case of injury or death.

Thus surety, or *borh*, represented an initial transformation from an earlier time when tribal custom engaged reciprocal duties of mutual aid and blood feud to that of feudal oaths of homage and protection. The tithing organization represented the replacement of this latter obligation of the feudal lords by fictive self-help tithings. The tithing, rather than the lord, then became the unit of responsibility of an evolving state organization— part of a hierarchal organization that had to answer to the king's representative, the sheriff, for wrongdoing of one of its members.

By the time of the Conquest, two yearly meetings of the hundred court were held at which the sheriff examined the tithingmen about theft and the presentation of offenders; and collected the dues coming to him for these inspections. It could be said that the "shiring process" provided 1066 England with "a general pattern of ordered territorial government" (Loyn 1984:147–148,154–155). In practice, this process was often controlled by the local lord, who, by royal charter, was granted powers "to supervise good witness, exact tolls, and hang a thief" (ibid.: 163). Thus at the time of the Conquest, English local government was in place, controlled by three powers: the king, the Christian bishops who composed the king's laws, and the local lord who administered the laws through a structure created by the bishops. All had the common interest of protecting their large landholdings (ibid.: 162–163,171; Corrigan and Sayer 1985:20).

In about 950, the Hundred Ordinance decreed that the hundred was to meet every four weeks, and in case of theft, was to follow the trail of the thief. If recovered, the value of the stolen property was to be given to the victim, and the offender's property was to be seized and divided between the hundred and the lord. Failure to participate or the breach of rules could result in fine or outlawry. Particularly concerned about cattle theft, voluntary peace guilds had before the ordinance grouped freemen into companies of ten to guarantee the behavior of the group (Loyn 1984:142). Later legislation during Edgar's reign (959–975) placed other responsibilities on the hundreds: to report suspicious movements of cattle, to flog the offending herdsman, and to see that trading was legitimate. Laws thereafter extended the hundred's court jurisdiction and required it as a place of first resort before appeal could be taken to the king (ibid.: 143).

The shire reeve or sheriff had responsibility to the king to preserve the King's Peace in the shire (a unit of about 120 hundreds), and to muster, in case of emergency, the *posse comitatus*, the whole available civil force of the shire (ibid.: 137). All members of the community were also under the obligation to respond by hue and cry in pursuit of a felon (Critchley 1967:23). Crime, which did not exist under customary society, now was defined by the king or his courts under the concept of a common law for the kingdom—that is, a law common to all England, created by the king's judges, who traveled from parish to parish converting local variations in custom to a common brew. A further centralizing development involved the frankpledge system, which consisted of men, usually twelve in number, responsible to others in the group for the appearance of each other in court, "a highly developed, kin police system, *without a kin basis*" (Reith 1975:27, emphasis added).

As feudalism and Christianity changed the organization of Saxon society, the blood feud was superseded by a system of compensation. The collective responsibility of the kin was gradually weakened and was absorbed by other groups. Between 700 and 1066, lords and bishops replaced the kinship group as the recipients of the *wer* and the *wite*. The *wer* was now determined by the amount of land owned by a man and by his feudal rank, rather than by his rank in the family (Jeffery 1957:655–656; Loyn 1984:48). By the beginning of the eleventh century, the basis of authoritarian kinship had been established. One contemporary Benedictine scholar described this transition in the following words: "No man can make himself king, but the people has the choice to select as king whom they please; but after he is consecrated as king he then has dominion over the people, and they cannot shake his yoke from their necks" (Loyn 1984:84).

By time of the Norman invasion, the election of the king had become merely a ritual act as part of the consecration ceremony (ibid.: 85). The church ("one belief, one *cristendom*, one king") became the transition mechanism for the transfer of the concept of community from kin to king and from kin law to territoriality. Wulfstan, Archbishop of York, called on all to

love and honour one God and earnestly hold to one Christian faith (*cristendom*) and eschew completely all heathen belief. And let us be faithful to our one king and lord . . . and protect life and land together as best we may, and ask in our inmost heart the help of God Almighty. (Quoted in ibid.: 88)

Christian kingship, according to Wulfstan, was not only a "spiritual" office—but a velvet glove encasing an iron fist.

The object of its proper exercise was the achievement of spiritual welfare in the community. The means of achievement involved consultation with the wise, listening to the good, and the exercise of force in the basic matter of exacting compensation. Royal authority in itself should be enough to ensure that the evil-doer paid-up, but if not, royal power should be so strong that justice could be done against the will . . . of the evil-doer. (Ibid.: 86)

The Norman invaders of 1066 accepted the Saxon legal system in its entirety but took over and centralized the administration of the laws (ibid.: 179; Trevelyan 1953:127). William promptly seized the lands of all who stood against him, then required all landowners to buy their lands back from him, thereby establishing the principle that all land originated from the king. This maneuver also had the effect of increasingly concentrating economic and political power in a few hands. It has been estimated that about "a quarter of the landed wealth of England in 1086 was held by no more than twelve men, most of whom were bound to the king by close bonds of blood or personal loyalty or both" (Loyn 1984: 179). Only about 180, almost all of whom were Normans, held land worth over 100 pounds a year (ibid.: 179–180). Sheriffs became the most powerful royal officers of the shire, and supervised the hundreds by holding a hundreds court (ibid.: 196). By the end of the twelfth century, the unit of responsibility had become the feudal manor. The hundreds courts gave way to local manorial courts or court *leet*. Officers were annually elected by the court leet to serve their turn as assistant to the lord on the manor in regulating the affairs of the manor community. The constable became the principal representative of the manor for making presentments to the court leet (Critchley 1967:3–4; Lee 1971:17).

Trevelyan (1953:127) concludes that the rule that "every man must have a lord" was a means of maintaining order when

the old clans and kinships, long decadent, were ceasing altogether to function in the sphere of justice and police. Since a man's relations were no longer answerable for him, his lord must answer for him instead. The lord, whether thegn or prelate, performed in each locality many of the functions, judicial, military and economic, performed by the clan in more primitive societies, and by the State in the modern world. (Ibid.)

Thus by the end of the thirteenth century, the constable had lost his connection to the tithing. He became at the same time the annually appointed or elected representative of the manor in making presentments to the court leet as well as an officer of the Crown as keeper of the King's Peace (Critchley 1967:5; Reith 1975:28). No longer a member and an integral part of an independent community, he now became subject to a competitive struggle for his services between the landlord and the Crown (Kent 1986:15–23).

As a regulator of class conflict, the role of the police in England is well documented. We mention only a few of the more obvious instances of statutes requiring police control of the working class. From the twelfth century onward, the police had a special function with reference to vagabonds, vagrants, and the "sturdy, unworking poor." The Assize of Clarendon of 1166 required sheriffs to enforce restrictions against "entertainers of strangers and the harbourers of vagabonds" (Lee 1971:25). A statute of Edward III (1327–1377) ordered town bailiffs "to make enquiry every week of all persons lodging in the suburbs, in order that neither vagrants, nor 'people against the peace' might find shelter" (ibid.: 33). During the reign of Edward VI (1547–1553) a statute required a laborer to obtain a testimonial from the constable before he could leave his parish or township. Constables were empowered to compel laborers to work on farms where labor was scarce, to wake them up in time for work, and to urge them not to take too long at their meals. These laws were in addition to many other obligations placed on constables for the control of "rogues and idle persons" (ibid.: 116–117; see also Critchley 1967:12; Dalton 1975:59–63; Kent 1986:30).

Under this system, the constable became subordinated first to the lord of the manor, and eventually to the justice of the peace (frequently the lord of the manor). As feudalism ended, capitalism developed as an economic system, and the nation-state formed (Corrigan and Sayer 1985:15–28). Thus, in gross, the origin of the English police, in its modern form and function, can be said to be consistent and coincident with the origin of the English state and with the model we have developed.

Likewise, the process of the growth of English feudal society meant the separation of the community into thegns and serfs. The process whereby the constable was a "neutral between disputants" was begun at the point where the kindred organizations were replaced by the later tithing and the constable–justice of the peace relationship. With the passage of the Justices of the Peace Act of 1361, the Crown recognized a hierarchical relationship between the constable and the justice of the peace, usually the largest landowner in the district. This same English system was extended to eighteenth century colonial America (Wood 1992:79–80), enduring until the organization of the professional police in 1829. The social and economic status of the justice as the landlord and the constable as his unpaid inferior infused the relationship and determined the enduring socioeconomic position of the constable or police officer to this day (Critchley 1967:8–9; Robinson 1978).

The case studies described here show how a number of different types of societies developed the policing mechanism, essentially to protect the resources of an emerging elite class. In the following chapter, we proceed to review the cross-cultural evidence for this proposition.

NOTES

1. Whites recognized the function of these lodges, calling them "police" (Anderson 1986:117).

2. The history and social structure of the Cheyennes are discussed in more detail later. Hoebel (1978:69) suggests why there should be seasonal variation of rules as to individual hunting practices and therefore a difference in the use of the military societies as police:

When buffalo are scarce, anyone may hunt where and as he pleases. When they are plentiful the restrictions of the communal hunt come into force. The reasons for this are clear and simple: while scattered buffalo in small herds cannot be efficiently hunted by large groups, the massive early-summer herds . . . are best attacked by a closely working cooperative group.

3. As the Cheyennes moved south out of the Black Hills country in search of horses, they came in contact with the Kiowas, who had previously been chased out of the Black Hills by the Dakotas. Grinnel (1956:38) suggests that the warfare engaged in by the two tribes between 1826 and 1840 "very likely arose from the need for horses, which they obtained chiefly from the south, and it is likely that the horse was one important cause for the southward movement of all these tribes."

4. Because the Cheyennes had no formal controls, sorties by individual Indians were not unusual (Grinnel 1956:55, 71, 87, 92, 97, 182–185). Contradictory traditional values guaranteed such violations. On the one hand, young men were to heed their elders' admonitions. On the other hand, their own prestige depended on exhibitions of individual bravery in battle against the enemy. Such apparent contradictions were reconciled by the fact that instances of individual bravery were to take place only after a decision of the military societies to do battle. Once the Cheyennes reorganized so that the Council of Chiefs no longer restrained the younger men, the policing mechanism became an uncontrolled and uncontrollable independent force.

5. Beginning in 1792, federal agents were sent to persuade Cherokee men to take up farming and women to plant cotton and learn spinning (Matthiesson 1984:55–56).

6. Vann had become the wealthiest of Cherokees; he also became paranoid, believing others were stealing from him. While drunk, he savagely beat his wife, burned at the stake a young slave girl he suspected of stealing from him, killed a white man, wounded another, and refused to listen to those who counselled him about his conduct. Finally his own clan members became exasperated with him. He thereby met the same fate of tribal execution that he had earlier meted out (Ehle 1988).

7. The material on the Aztec state substantially follows Adams (1966), Rounds (1979), and Wolf (1959).

5

CROSS-CULTURAL TEST

To this point in our analysis we have drawn mainly upon evidence from societies whose development from a kinship-based system to a state system could be historically traced, at least at some particular critical transformation point. We have used this evidence to develop our propositions, which interrelate types of economic and political organization with the presence of certain types of police functions in society. If our theory is correct, given any society with a particular type of economic and political development, we should be able to predict the corresponding police function. Thus, if we examine a sample of societies at a single point in time, we should have a synchronic test of our theory. Before we proceed to our own test, it is instructive to review some of the previous studies that have examined elements of our theory.

LITERATURE REVIEW

Schwartz and Miller (1964:160), in an early cross-cultural study, sought to determine factors in the evolution of legal organizations. They concluded that "elements of legal organization emerge in a sequence, such that each constitutes a necessary condition for the next." Defining police as a "specialized force used partially or wholly for norm enforcement," they found that of the fifty-one societies studied, twenty had police. For the most part, these societies were characterized by sufficient economic complexity to use money. The presence of full-time priests, teachers, and government officials indicated a considerable degree of specialization. They concluded that police are found "only in association with a substantial degree of division of labor" (ibid., p. 166) and that mediation and the development of damages as compensation for injury almost always precede the police institution.

They hypothesized that before a police could develop, a "cultural foundation" must be laid to

include a determination to avoid disputes, an appreciation of the value of third-party intervention, and the development of a set of norms both for preventive purposes and as a basis for allocating blame and punishment when disputes arise. Compensation by damages and the use of mediators might well contribute to the development of such a cultural foundation as well as reflecting its growth. (Ibid.: 166–169)

Schwartz and Miller (1964:160) found that a high percentage (85 percent) of societies that developed specialized police also utilized damages and mediation. This finding and those indicating norms for the assessment of blame and punishment, use of lawyers and other legal mechanisms, and the value of third-party intervention, affirm the point made by Engels that one of the functions of police is to aid the state in reducing class struggle to legal form, that is, the legalization of social life (Black 1976), one aspect of which is to act as a "neutral party" as between the disputants.

There have been two relatively recent attempts not only to review and to restate theories of the evolution of the state, but to operationalize and test the theories once formed: Haas (1982) and Newman (1983). Such attempts are obviously of great importance to us, and therefore we will set forth their work at some length.

Haas (1982:15) attempts to combine archeological evidence of state formation with cross-cultural anthropological studies to find a satisfactory evolutionary theory of the state. All these theories, he finds, have a common feature: "a ruling body controlling production or procurement of basic resources and exercising economic power over its population."

The ubiquity of this economic power base in all the theories provides a starting point for constructing a broad framework for looking at the evolution of states in terms of power. Beginning with the economic power base, certain predictions can be made about the development of subsequent power bases, and the interaction of these bases in the process of governing a population. (Ibid.: 15)

Most major theories of the state resolve themselves into conflict and integrative models. In testing these theories against available archeological evidence, Haas selects four geographical areas where there is evidence of pristine societies of the kind suggested by Fried (1967): Mesopotamia,

China, Mesoamerica, and Andean South America. Haas finds that there is a paucity of evidence to adequately test these theories, largely because archeologists have not been primarily interested in state formation and therefore have not sought to collect these kinds of data. For us, however, what is of interest is Haas's operationalization of Fried's concept of stratification. Haas sees two "central issues" in accomplishing this task: "to define and distinguish basic resources" and "to determine how to recognize archaeologically differential access to those resources" (Haas 1982:91). He thereafter reduces stratification to five "types of basic consumer items": "food, tools for acquiring or producing food, tools for preparing food, protective devices for coping with the physical environment, protective devices for coping with an aggressive social environment" (ibid.: 92).

As a guiding principle, he states:

Theoretically, stratification can be inferred if *any* of the necessary or adaptively advantageous goods or products are found to be distributed differentially in a society. However, it is probable that stratification based on unequal access to one type of resource will be accompanied by unequal access to other types as well. In other words, there should be a pattern of differential access, not just an isolated instance. (Ibid.: 93, emphasis in original)

Haas concludes that there is adequate evidence to find that stratification does exist. He next asks if "qualitative differences in access to resources and standards of living will lead to conflict between social groups" (ibid.: 106).

The residences of the privileged group would be safeguarded against possible aggressive measures which might be taken by the unprivileged group in attempting to equalize the distribution of resources. Types of specific safeguards would include defensive walls surrounding the residences, or location of the residences in naturally defensible or inaccessible positions. (Ibid.: 107)

Haas posits that the researcher should look for evidence of "separation, isolation, and internally oriented defense mechanisms," as well as evidence of revolution or rebellion (ibid.: 111). He also discusses the "application of forceful coercive sanctions in support of a system of stratification" and notes that it "may be manifested either in direct physical violence or . . . in the withholding of certain necessary goods and services." Moreover, it need not be "omnipresent, nor will it be the only means used to govern the population" (ibid.: 115).

Because, as mentioned earlier, archeologists have not collected evidence of the type needed, it is impossible to "definitively confirm or refute" either the conflict or integration position (ibid.: 127). Nevertheless, Haas concludes that both positions have merits and that "while the major thrust of the conflict and integration models represents a complete opposition, a significant synthesis can be effected by introducing major integration elements directly into a broadened conflict model" (ibid.: 129).

Haas (1982:150) also reviews "alternative routes to statehood" and concludes that there are three theories offered to explain the development of pristine states: (1) under conditions of circumscribed and intensified warfare, (2) when material conditions demand extensive importation or exchange of basic resources, and (3) when a society initiates irrigation agriculture on a large scale.

The author next focuses on the "analysis of the processes of state formation and development in terms of the exercise of *power* by rulers over their population" (ibid.: 156, emphasis in original). Power is defined by Haas "as the ability of an actor, A, to get another actor(s), B, to do something B would not otherwise do, through the application, threat, or promise of sanction" (ibid.: 157). In operationalizing the concept, Haas extrapolates nine variables either from the literature or his own research: a power base, a means of exerting power, the scope of power being exerted, the amount of power being exerted, extension of power, the costs to the power holder of exerting power (power costs), the costs to the respondent of refusing to comply with the demands of the power holder (refusal costs), the costs to the respondent of complying with the demands of the power holder (compliance costs), and the gains to the respondent in complying with the power holder's demands (ibid.: 158).

Taking into consideration his study of power relationships, Haas defines the state "as a stratified society in which a governing body exercises control over the production or procurement of basic resources, and thus necessarily exercises coercive power over the remainder of the population" (ibid.: 172). He then sets forth a step-by-step evolutionary hypothesis somewhat similar to the one we have developed:

1. From the different theories of state formation, it can be inferred that the evolutionary process of stratification provides the leaders of a complex society with a new form of economic power based on control over the production or procurement of basic resources. This new economic power base enables them to apply coercive sanctions as a means of gaining the compliance of the population.

2. Differences in the type of resources controlled by the leaders of different states produce differences in the scope and amount of power they may exercise. Specifically, control of basic subsistence resources provides greater power than control of basic nonsubsistence resources.

3. The initial economic power base also allows the leaders to accumulate additional economic bases of power when environmental circumstances permit.

4. Development of the initial economic power base provides the leaders with the potential and need for developing a police force as an independent physical power base.

5. To protect their economic power base from external threat, the leaders of a state society need to support a military force, which provides them with another form of physical power base. The police force and the military force may be one and the same.

6. To legitimize their exercise of power and thus decrease the costs of exerting power, the leaders may also be expected to initiate or exploit an existing ideological power base. This ideological base is derived from control over religious symbols and iconography.

7. An additional function of the ideological power base is to balance the physical strength of the military and police forces. By attempting to legitimize their superior position in the eyes of the population, leaders holding ideological power can use the physical plurality of the population as a balance against the physical strength of the military and police. In other words, ideology can be expected to be used in an attempt to prevent a coup d'etat. (Ibid.: 173–174)

Thus for Haas, state societal members "no longer have equal access to . . . the means of production of subsistence resources" (ibid.: 175, order of sentence inverted).

It is this differential access that makes the new economic power base of the leaders in an emergent stratified society markedly different from the power base of leaders in prestratified societies. The critical difference lies in the ability of the state leaders to withhold basic resources as a coercive means of enforcing their demands on the population. (Ibid.: 175)

Haas notes, as we have, that "without increased access to basic resources, [leaders] cannot support a specialized police force as a physical means of compelling obedience. Consequently, the possible refusal costs to a respondent population in a prestratified society do not normally include the loss of life, liberty, or the pursuit of reproduction" (ibid.: 175). Haas further observes that a police force as a physical base does not stem from its inherent physical strength, since a population will always have physical superiority in terms of sheer numbers. Rather, its power is derived from its superior organization, technology, and/or specialization. A police force can focus superior physical strength on selected portions of a population, and thus effectively threaten an entire population with physical sanctions. (Ibid.: 177, citation omitted)

Police forces, he observes, may also emerge as a result of external use of an army. Having two forces, one to serve an external and the other to serve the internal security function, would be costly. Early states, therefore, would be expected to combine the two functions in one force (ibid.: 179).

In another cross-cultural study of legal institutions, Newman's study parallels our research. Specifically, her work (1983:4) is a test of "a materialist theory of comparative legal institutions," that is, one "concerned with the nature of material production in societies and the internal distribution of the fruits of labor." She argues "that legal systems play a vital role in regulating labor, allocating economic surplus, controlling land and water rights, and other vital aspects of economic life."

In sum, Newman suggests that

there are underlying strains in the social relations of production, patterned inequalities in access to crucial resources, which are surfacing as disputes and which are addressed by prescriptive legal rules. It is in this sense that law should be viewed as regulating the social relations of production. . . . Thus, if the tensions generated within particular modes of production can be isolated, recurrent disputes and substantive rules should be interpretable as manifestations of these tensions. (Ibid.: 137–138)

After reviewing major theories of legal evolution, Newman (ibid.: 49) concludes that there have been few recent attempts to do comparative evolutionary studies, and that those that have been done have had no theoretical paradigm other than "traditional functionalism . . . : Dispute settlement takes the form it does because it is necessary to sustain a social order that is undifferentiated, multiplex, and integrated on the basis of a kinship structure." Nevertheless, she concludes, the many recent specific evolutionary studies have prepared the groundwork not only to formulate a theory but to test it once formulated.

In order to do this testing, Newman (ibid.: 52) constructs a typology of legal institutions:

The existence of a third party or "hearing body"

A social requirement to use the third party

The authoritativeness of third-party "decisions"

The centralization of decision making

Multiple levels of jurisdiction or appeal

These are not to be taken as unrelated steps but, on the contrary, can be expected to be interrelated so that only certain combinations occur. A society that is centralized probably would have multiple levels of jurisdiction (ibid.)

Newman (ibid.: 53) next "ranks eight institutional types in terms of increasing complexity using the five dimensions":

Type 1 represents the simplest form of legal institution, which lacks any involvement of third parties in dispute resolution. It corresponds to societies that have only self- or kin-based redress mechanisms for resolving conflicts; these mechanisms are labeled "self-redress systems."

Type 2 describes societies in which third-party involvement is available but is not normatively defined as necessary. Third parties give "advice" rather than authoritative decisions; as such, these systems are labeled "advisor systems."

Type 3 describes a situation when self-redress has become socially unacceptable as a solution of first resort. Disputants are supposed to approach certain third parties for a solution to a dispute. However, these third parties lack authoritativeness; that is, they cannot make decisions that are socially binding upon the disputants. Instead, they can only aim at a compromise, which may either be accepted or rejected by the disputants (though social pressure may be brought to bear upon litigants to accept). Into this category fall various types of mediators and go-betweens, hence the label "mediator systems."

Type 4 requires disputants to turn to a third party and, for the first time, the third party may render decisions or verdicts that are socially defined as binding upon the disputants (whether or not they agree). . . . [T]his system involved *adjudication* rather than mediation. The simplest form of adjudication institution may be termed an "elders' council."

Type 5 is another type of authoritative council that has a more restricted membership than elders' councils. As such, decision-making power is more centralized than in type 4. This second type of council system is labeled "restricted councils."

Type 6 describes systems where authoritative decision making has become further centralized and is in the hands of one person. This type is labeled a "chieftainship." . . . My use of the term "chieftainship" is limited to contexts where the ethnographic evidence confirms that the chief can give authoritative verdicts. . . .

> Type 7 describes authoritative chieftainships with multiple levels of jurisdiction and/or appeal. Such societies are often referred to as "paramount chieftainships." . . .

> Type 8, the most complex institution . . . is that known as a "state-level" legal system. It is distinguished from paramount chieftainships by a higher concentration of legal authority. (Ibid.: 53, 55)

For each of these categories, Newman identifies the basic structure of the institution and discusses the allocation of authority and the recruitment of personnel. Each of the eight types of legal systems is characterized by a particular arrangement of five underlying dimensions of legal complexity: the presence or absence of a third party, a social requirement to utilize this third party, the authoritativeness of third-party decisions, the degree to which legal authority is centralized in the hands of the few, and the presence or absence of multiple levels of jurisdiction or appeal (ibid.: 98).

Using Murdock's (1967) coding scheme, Newman (1983:111) then sets out to show "that these systems of dispute settlement are systematically linked to particular modes of production" (ibid.: 103), grouping "preindustrial societies into seven basic categories according to the level of their forces of production: (1) hunting and gathering, (2) fishing, (3) pastoral, (4) incipient agriculture, (5) extensive agriculture, (6) intensive dry agriculture, and (7) intensive wet agriculture." Using the Tuden and Marshall (1972:442–3) codes for the "Standard Cross-Cultural Sample," Newman (1983:113) "constructed an index that represents the various ways in which individuals, families, or classes obtained the surplus products of others, including (1) controlling the labor or products of slaves or unfree dependents; (2) obtaining contributions, taxes, or labor of free citizens; (3) securing rents and/or other incomes from large landholdings; (4) levying tribute or taxes against a conquered or subject people; (5) gaining profits from investments in industry, business, or other capitalistic enterprises; and finally (6) extending loans or credit." She also operationalizes stratification using Murdock's five-step "class stratification" variable: (1) absence of significant class distinctions, (2) wealth distinctions, (3) elite stratification, (4) dual stratification, and (5) complete stratification (ibid.: 114), thereafter reworking Murdock's stratification variable into three levels:

1. Societies that have neither significant wealth differences nor class distinctions among freemen.

2. Societies that do have significant wealth differences between individuals, but in which these have not "crystallized into distinct and hereditary social classes."

3. Societies with distinct and/or hereditary social classes. (Ibid.: 115)

After having operationalized the variables, she then sets forth the hypotheses to be tested:

Hypothesis 1. The greater the degree of development of the forces of production, the greater the degree of social stratification.

Hypothesis 2. The greater the opportunities for some individuals to control the surplus labor of others, the greater the degree of social stratification in a society. (The larger our index of exploitive social relations, the greater the degree of stratification.)

Hypothesis 3. The more stratified a society, the more complex its legal institutions.

Hypothesis 4. Holding stratification constant (i.e., within each given level of stratification), the more developed the forces of production in a society, the more complex its legal institutions.

Hypothesis 5. Holding the forces of production constant (i.e., within each subsistence type), the more stratified a society, the more complex its legal institutions.

Hypothesis 6. The greater the development of the forces of production, social relations of production, and social stratification, the more complex a society's legal institutions. (ibid.: 116–117)

In order to test these hypotheses, Newman (1983:138) examines "each of the six subsistence types (or forces of production) . . . one at a time." Societies within each subsistence type are classified according to their social relations of production, grouping together those societies with the same modes of production. Disputes that constantly reappear in these modes of production "should be interpretable as manifestations of these tensions."

Having carried out this analysis, Newman (1983:204) concludes that

the degrees of development of the forces of production, "exploitive" social relations of production, and social stratification are strong independent predictors of legal complexity, defined according to my fivefold variable. Moreover, I determined that the social relations of production are imprinted on the substantive, prescriptive rules of preindustrial legal orders. Strains that these relations produce surface as patterns of recurrent disputes.

In sum, one cannot simply take any dimension of social life and argue that the more complex that dimension, the more complex the law. All aspects of social reality are *not* equally effective in predicting levels of legal development. Even within the model developed here, it is the *interaction* among three distinct dimensions—the forces and social relations of production, and social stratification—that seems to best explain the variance in legal complexity, and by inference, the likelihood of a police function. (Ibid.: 205, emphasis in original)

Newman sees the dynamics of social inequality to be dependent on unequal access to limited means of production; in turn, such unequal access triggers social inequalities: some families use this unequal access to make others work for them, setting the stage for class stratification (ibid.: 205).

With reference to even the simplest societies, distribution of women's labor power, for example, may be a source of dispute. Once there is corporate kin property, problems involving violation of these usufruct rights arise among family groups. In societies where inequalities include use of labor of nonfamily members, there is "growth of such phenomena as rent, interest on debts, wage labor, and the like," over all of which there may be disputes and around which property law develops. Finally, with the emergence of a class society, there is a "marked increase in the complexity and authority of legal institutions," with matters earlier under the aegis of kin groups now under central control. Second, "differential rights and privileges of the classes" are institutionalized (ibid.: 207–208).

The comparative, cross-cultural studies reviewed here have provided reviews and/or tests of parts of our model, and have informed our discussion. Each has examined elements of the police function as embedded in a broader nexus of relationships. We proceed now to more direct tests of elements of our theory, using the cross-cultural method.

CROSS-CULTURAL TEST

As stated in the introductory chapter, there are two basic paradigms for testing anthropological theories of social and cultural change. The first involves diachronic analysis by examining particular case studies through time; the second involves synchronic analysis by examining a sample of societies at a moment in each of their histories. There are clear advantages and disadvantages to each approach.

The diachronic case study approach is hampered by the lack of detailed, objectively collected data on a range of societies over a long time period in their development. While the processes in which we are interested may take place quite rapidly, they may also take hundreds of years to unfold. However, modern, objective ethnological field research is less than one hundred years old. Many of the case studies that we have described are based on uneven historical information from a variety of sources. These sources are often biased in favor of cultures with a written, historical tradition or toward those with a long colonial history. Neither of these situations is typical of the pristine emergence of a specialized police function that we would like to examine. In other cases, social change has been so rapid that it can be examined through time by a single ethnographic researcher. This, too, is probably not typical. In short, the diachronic case study approach, while yielding rich information on the dialectical processes that occur between variables through time, can be criticized for sampling bias.

We have developed and refined our theory primarily on the basis of such detailed case studies. However, a synchronic cross-cultural analysis allows for another type of test. In this approach, a more objective sample is drawn from the entire range of societies known to anthropologists. This sample is examined for associations between and among particular variables. In our case, we wish to examine the extent to which our dependent variable, the police function, is associated with such things as the existence of social classes and other forms of social stratification, the nature of private property, and so forth.

The main weakness of the synchronic, cross-cultural approach is that an association found between two variables says nothing about the process through which they have come to be related. If an association between a specialized police function and the existence of social classes is found, for example, we cannot say either that the emergence of social classes led to a "need" for police or that the emergence of specialized police precipitated the development of a class structure. We know only that they are related, possibly through other intervening variables. For example, they may both merely be characteristics of complex societies with other prime moving variables.

Thus, while the diachronic and the synchronic analysis each has its weaknesses and strengths, the combination of these two research paradigms provides a powerful analytic tool. The diachronic approach provides useful data on the interplay among variables but may not be cross-culturally valid because of sampling bias. The synchronic approach provides a more objective sample but little detail on the causal relationships among variables. A theory derived from the first research paradigm should be supported by data from the second. In this chapter, we intend to provide such a test of our theory.

Our first problem in this analysis was to operationalize our dependent variable, the police function. We began by searching the literature for previously existing codes that captured the structure of the police function. The code we initially found most valuable was established by Tuden and Marshall (1972). It organizes the degree of specialization and institutionalization of police functions along a five-point ordinal scale: where police functions (1) are not specialized or institutionalized at any level of political integration, (2) display only incipient specialization, (3) are assumed by retainers of chiefs, (4) are assumed by military organizations, and (5) are specialized and institutionalized at some level of political integration. The Tuden and Marshall codes were developed for some 186 societies of the world selected for representativeness and independence (Murdock and White 1969). Data concerning the function of police were available for 181 of these societies. In addition, Tuden and Marshall coded twelve other variables concerning political organization.

We decided to use these codes in order to explore some of the bivariate associations developed in previous chapters. Even though these categories of police function do not precisely correspond to our own, they are sufficiently close for these purposes. The Tuden and Marshall code has the advantage of having been developed for a representative sample of the world's societies and, insofar as possible, guards against sampling bias. Its code of police function shows that most (nearly 70 percent) of the societies studied had no specialized police function. A considerable number (23 percent) had a specialized police function, leaving only about 8 percent with the transitional forms in which we are particularly interested (see Table 1).

Our four basic propositions (stated in chapter 1) together with the material developed in chapters 2 and 3 would lead us to make certain predictions about these police functions. Proposition 1 would suggest that we should generally find unspecialized police functions associated with simpler social organizations, such as stateless societies or petty chiefdoms, and specialized police functions associated with state societies. Proposition 2 predicts that unspecialized police functions should be associated with generally egalitarian societies and specialized police functions with societies having a class structure, particularly where the ruling class has control of basic resources. Other propositions suggest that specialized police functions should also be present in societies having political apparatus controlled by the ruling class and in labor-intensive economies. We proceed to test each of these predictions.

Table 1
Degree of Specialization and Institutionalization of Police Functions

Degree of Specialization and Institutionalization	Number of Societies	Percentage
Police functions are not specialized or institutionalized at any level of political integration, with the maintenance of law and order left exclusively to informal mechanisms of social control, private retaliation, or sorcery.	125	69.1
Police functions display only incipient specialization, as when groups with other functions are assigned police functions in emergencies.	4	2.2 (Palauns, Gros Ventre, Omaha, Pawnee)
Police functions are assumed by the retainers of chiefs.	4	2.2 (Suku, Tikopia, Natchez, Warrau)
Police functions are assumed by the military organizations.	6	3.3 (Azanda, Fur, Konso, Babylonians, Zuni, Haitians)
Police functions are specialized and institutionalized on at least some level or levels of political integration.	42	23.2
TOTALS	181	100.0

Source: Tuden and Marshall 1972: 441, 444-451.

Hypothesis 1: Specialized police functions are associated with societies politically organized as states.

In order to test this association, we used Tuden and Marshall's (1972:438) code on "Levels of Sovereignty" in a society. Following their categories, we have distinguished among petty chiefdoms, small states, and large states as representing increasing levels of complexity. *Petty chiefdoms* are illustrated by "a petty paramount chief ruling a district composed of a number of local communities." They are defined as societies in which effective sovereignty transcends the local community at a single level. *Small states* are illustrated by "a small state comprising a number of administrative districts under subordinate functionaries" and thus having two levels of sovereignty transcending the local community.[1] *Large states* are illustrated by "administrative provinces which are further subdivided into lesser administrative districts" and have at least three levels of sovereignty transcending the local community.

A contingency table consisting of type of police function as one variable and level of political sovereignty as another variable would provide a cross-cultural test for proposition 1. That is, we would expect that increasing levels of political complexity would be associated with increasing specialization of the police function. Such a table (Table 2) was prepared using the total sample available in Tuden and Marshall (1972).

It is apparent that, in broad outline, proposition 1 is supported by these data. The presence of a specialized police function is associated with state organization of society. State societies generally have specialized police functions, whereas stateless societies generally do not.

Hypothesis 2: Societies having a class structure will generally have specialized and institutionalized police.

In order to test this hypothesis, we used Murdock's (1967:165) code for class stratification. Although Murdock's code was not originally rank ordered, we have created an ordinal scale of stratification in order to test whether increasing levels of social stratification are indeed associated with increasing specialization and institutionalization of the police function. Thus, (paraphrasing Murdock) we consider five levels of class structure: (1) the absence of significant class distinctions among freemen (although slavery might be present), (2) wealth distinctions not crystallized into distinct and hereditary social classes, (3) the existence of a single elite class with superior status based on resource control, (4) the existence of a hereditary aristocratic class, and (5) complex stratification, consisting of a number of social classes based on specialization of labor. Again, we prepared a contingency table (Table 3) to examine the association.

Hypothesis 3: Societies in which control of the means of production is communal or kin based will not require specialized and institutionalized police.

In examining the previous hypothesis, we have shown that increasingly complex class structure is associated with increasing institutionalization of the police function. In chapters 2 and 3, we indicated that communal or kin-based security arrangements in stateless societies do not require a specialized police to protect differential access to resources. Only when the ruling elite perceives a need to protect its control over basic resources do such structures become necessary. In order to test this hypothesis, we

Table 2
Specialized Police Functions Generally Characterize State-Level Societies

Police Functions	Stateless Societies	Petty Chiefdoms	Political Sovereignty Small States	Large States	Totals
not specialized or institutionalized	90	20	8	6	124
incipient specialization	3	0	0	1	4
assumed by retainers of chiefs	0	3	0	1	4
assumed by the military organization	1	1	0	4	6
specialized and institutionalized	4	5	6	27	42
Totals	98	29	14	39	180

Kendall's Tau C=0.42, p<.001
Gamma=0.82

Table 3
Class Structure

Police Functions	None Among free persons	Wealth Distinctions	Elite Class	Aristocratic Class	Complex Stratification	Totals
not specialized or institutionalized	63	34	2	21	3	123
incipient specialization	2	0	0	2	0	4
assumed by retainers of chiefs	1	0	1	2	0	4
assumed by the military organization	1	1	0	2	2	6
specialized and institutionalized	7	9	0	7	19	42
Totals	74	44	3	34	24	179

Kendall's Tau B=0.40, p<.001
Gamma=0.61

Table 4
Control of Production

Police Functions	Communal	Kin Corporate	Class-based or Incipient Class-based	Totals
not specialized or institutionalized	24	12	60	96
incipient specialization	1	1	2	4
assumed by retainers of chiefs	1	0	3	4
assumed by the military organization	0	1	5	6
specialized and institutionalized	0	2	35	37
Totals	26	16	105	147

Kendall's Tau $C = 0.20$, $p < .001$
Gamma $= 0.64$

utilized codes developed by Hendrix and Hossain (1988:444–445) on the basis of categories devised by Karen Sacks (1979). Three types of societies were distinguished. *Communal* societies are basically egalitarian, lacking differential access to resources. *Kin corporate* societies are those in which there is little socioeconomic inequality, the control of the mode of production being based on kin corporations. *Class-based or incipient class-based* societies are those in which the means of production are concentrated in the hands of a few and social differentiation is based on the relationship to productive means. Table 4 presents the results of this analysis.

It is particularly instructive to note that only seven of the seventy- four communal or kin corporate societies in this sample have specialized or institutionalized police.

Hypothesis 4: The more labor-intensive the economic base, the more specialized and institutionalized the police function.

Table 5
Subsistence Base

Police Functions	Gathering Fishing Hunting Pastoral	Incipient Agriculture	Extensive Agriculture	Intensive Agriculture	Totals
not specialized or institutionalized	56	17	31	19	123
incipient specialization	1	2	1	0	4
assumed by retainers of chiefs	1	2	1	0	4
assumed by the military organization	0	0	1	5	6
specialized and institutionalized	0	2	11	29	42
Totals	58	23	45	53	179

Kendall's Tau C=0.37, p<.001
Gamma=0.74

Previously we argued that the existence of surplus in and of itself was not a sufficient condition to produce social complexity, because many egalitarian societies had (or had the means to produce) surplus. Where surplus was produced by a labor-intensive economy, however, the ruling class tended to institutionalize the police function to protect its control over this surplus. Thus we would expect to find specialized police associated with labor-intensive economies.

In order to test this assertion, we utilized codes developed by Hendrix and Hossain (1988:444–445), based on Murdock's (1967:154–155, 163) codes for subsistence. We collapsed certain of Hendrix and Hossain's categories to produce four basic types of economies: (1) gathering, fishing, hunting, or pastoral, (2) incipient agriculture, (3) extensive agriculture, and (4) intensive agriculture. We then cross-tabulated this modified code with our dependent variable. Table 5 supports hypothesis 4.

We have presented evidence suggesting that the specialized police function is most commonly associated with societies politically organized as states, where there is a class structure, and where control of the means of production in a labor-intensive economy is in the hands of the ruling elite. Yet this strong association between specialized police and state societies is not necessarily obvious; there is no a priori reason why stateless societies cannot develop a formal police function. Similarly, when control of resources is in the hands of an elite class, they do not *need* to develop a formal police function in order to protect differential access to resources; indeed, 60 of the 105 such societies had no specialized police. But the fact is, elite classes often do institutionalize police for just such a reason, which is why virtually all of the societies with institutionalized police also have a ruling class controlling the means of production. Given the associations that we have already established, however, it would not be surprising if the formalized, modern police function were also associated with complex judicial and administrative apparatus, dense populations, taxation, and the use of general purpose money, because these variables are known to be associated with state-level societies. In fact, we tested all these bivariate relationships (and more) using various codes found in the Tuden and Marshall (1972) or Murdock (1967) studies and found them all to be positively associated with our dependent variable at $p < .01$ using the appropriate Kendall's Tau statistic. There were two, however, that seemed to us to be somewhat less obvious and worthy of separate presentation. The first involved private (movable) property.

Hypothesis 5: Societies having a specialized police function will tend to have inheritance of private property.

If we are correct that the ruling class uses a police to protect its wealth to the detriment of a peasant class, we would also expect that it would protect that wealth by having formal rules of inheritance for private property. We would not, however, necessarily expect the converse to follow. That is, societies having rules of inheritance would not necessarily need institutionalized police, because the items inherited would not necessarily be of great value. To test this hypothesis, we again modified one of Murdock's (1967:167) codes for inheritance of movable property. Murdock was interested primarily in the type of inheritance pattern found in a particular society. We are not concerned with the means of transmission of property, however, but rather in whether it is inherited. Conse-

Table 6
Transfer of Movable Private Property

Police Functions	No Inheritance of Movable Private Property	Inheritance of Movable Private Property	Totals
not specialized or institutionalized	52	50	102
incipient specialization	2	2	4
assumed by retainers of chiefs	1	2	3
assumed by the military organization	0	6	6
specialized and institutionalized	3	31	34
Totals	58	91	149

Kendall's Tau C=0.35
Gamma=0.74

quently, we have collapsed all of his types of inheritance into a single category, retaining only the distinction between societies that have inheritance of movable property and those that do not, the latter category also including the destruction, burial, or giving away of movable property. Results are presented in Table 6. Again, the hypothesis is supported.

A final bivariate relationship is perhaps not surprising, but informative. If the ruling elite has a political apparatus governing its restricted access to resources, we would expect it to exercise some control over that apparatus.

Hypothesis 6: Societies having a specialized police function will tend to have hereditary or other formalized control over succession to local political office.

We tested this hypothesis using a modified version of Murdock's (1967:166–167) code on succession to the office of local head man (or the equivalent). We collapsed and reordered his categories to produce four types of succession: (1) there is no head man or equivalent and consequently no succession, (2) succession is by informal consensus, (3) succession is hereditary, and (4) succession is nonhereditary but occurs through some mode of formal consensus.

Although Murdock's codes (and consequently our categories) do not precisely capture our independent variable in the way we would like, results nevertheless support the hypothesis.

We regard the foregoing analyses as fairly strong support for our overall theory. The nature of the police function is statistically associated with a variety of factors in the manner that the theory would predict. We decided to use multivariate analysis as an exploratory technique to help us further probe the complex interrelationships among these and other variables. After considering options, we decided to employ discriminant analysis (Nie et al. 1975) to examine the relationship between our dependent variable, the police function, and the whole range of independent variables at our disposal. Discriminant analysis is a technique used to "statistically distinguish" between two or more groups of cases (Nie et al. 1975:435). In this instance, our groups were societies having different forms of the police function. We sought to identify a small set of discriminating variables that distinguished, predicted, or explained observed differences in police functions.

Employing such a technique is not without problems. The formal theory of discriminant analysis makes certain assumptions about the nature of variables: they should be normally distributed, for example, and not all of our independent variables were. However, we feel that this particular technique was most appropriate for our investigations because we believe that the linear combinations of independent variables produced by discriminant analysis most closely approximates our research model. Since we use the technique for exploration rather than confirmation, we felt that some of the formal mathematical assumptions could be relaxed. For as Nie and colleagues (1975:435) state, "The statistical theory of discriminant analysis assumes that the discriminating variables have a multivariate normal distribution and that they have equal variance-covariance matrices within each group. In practice, the technique is very robust and these assumptions need not be strongly adhered to."

One final problem deserves special mention. Discriminant analysis requires listwise deletion of cases. Thus, if information for only one analysis variable of a case is missing, the entire case will be deleted from

Table 7
Succession to Local Political Office

Police Functions	No Headman or Equivalent	Informal Consensus	Hereditary	Nonhereditary Formal Consensus	Totals
not specialized or institutionalized	20	16	50	8	94
incipient specialization	0	0	2	0	2
assumed by retainers of chiefs	0	1	3	0	4
assumed by the military organization	0	0	3	2	5
specialized and institutionalized	0	5	14	13	32
Totals	20	22	72	23	137

Kendall's Tau C=0.25, p<.001
Gamma=0.59

the analysis. We therefore considered a set of codes developed by Ross (1983) that focus specifically on various aspects of political decision making. Ross organizes the nature of the enforcement function in society along a three-point ordinal scale: where (1) enforcement is limited and/or carried out by the whole society, (2) enforcement is by nonspecialized leaders, and (3) there are enforcement specialists. The Tuden and Marshall codes that we used above were developed for some 186 societies of the world selected for representativeness and independence (Murdock and White 1969). The Ross codes were developed for 36 variables related to political decision making and consist of a subsample of 90 of the 186 societies in the Murdock and White sample. The Ross subsample was selected in such a way as to favor the inclusion of these groups for which relatively rich data on political life were available. Thus, while it might be argued that the Ross sample is less representative, it has the advantage of more detailed data on many of the variables of specific interest to us and thus was potentially more useful for multivariate analysis.

We began this analysis by cross-tabulating the Tuden and Marshall codes with the Ross codes—with surprising results. The codes conflicted on 19 of the 88 cultures examined by both sets of researchers. Table 8 illustrates the discrepancy between the Tuden and Marshall code as having a noninstitutionalized police function, and Ross codes as having a specialized police function. Furthermore, Table 9 illustrates the Ross codes as possessing a noninstitutionalized police function, and Tuden and Marshall code as being institutionalized.

We had further difficulty in comparing Tuden and Marshall's codes with those of Ross because of differences in the manner in which they created their typologies. As previously mentioned, Tuden and Marshall organized the degree of specialization and institutionalization of police functions along a five-point ordinal scale, whereas Ross used a three-point scale. As a result, it was not possible to directly compare codes for 23 of the remaining 69 cultures. Table 10 indicates these societies. Finally, there were forty-six cultures in which Ross's codes were in agreement with those of Tuden and Marshall. These are given in Table 11.

In an effort to resolve these differences, entries for societies represented in the Human Relations Area Files (HRAF) were checked. First, several of the police entries in the HRAF were from different periods in time than were the works referred to in developing the political codes of Tuden and Marshall's (1972) sample. Because we were interested in a synchronic test of variable relatedness, those police function entries that were not from the same time period as the political variable entries were excluded. Second, there was the problem of cultures that had a specialized police

Table 8
Cultures that Tuden and Marshall Coded as Having No Institutionalized Police Function, and Ross Coded as Having an Institutionalized Police Function

Lozi	Trobriands
Nyakyusa	Mbau Fijiams
Ganda (Baganda)	Yapese
Mende	Ofugao
Shilluk	Eyak
Kwala	Aymara
Albania	Shautie
Burusho	

n = 15

Table 9
Cultures that Ross Coded as Having Noninstitutionalized Police Function, and Tuden and Marshall Coded as Having an Institutionalized Police Function

Irish	Lepcha
Kurd	Araucaina

n = 4

Table 10
Cultures for which Direct Comparison Could Not Be Made Between the Codes of Ross and Those of Tuden and Marshall

Kikuyu (Waluguru)	Tikopia
Tiu (Munshi)	Samoans
Tallensi	Marshallese
Azande	Ainu
Somali	Yokut
Rif (Riffians)	Grosventre (Atsina)
Gond	Pawnee
Santal	Goajiro
Lakner (Mara)	Warrau Waroa
Lamet	Timbiria
Iban (Sea Dyayak)	Toradja
Kapauku	

n = 23

Table 11
Cultures for which There is Agreement Between Tuden and Marshall and Ross

Bushmen (Kung)	Maori
Suku (Pindi)	Koreans
Mbuti (Banbuti)	Gilyak
Dahomeans (Fon)	Ingalik
Banbar (Bammana)	Copper Eskimo
Huasa	Ojibwa (Saulteaux)
Otoro	Slave (Etchareoltime)
Masai	Bellacoola
Amhara	Yurok
Teda	Klamath
Egyptians	Huron (Wendot)
Basseri	Commanche
Kazak	Chiricaua Apache
Vietnam	Havasupi
Semang	Papago
Andamans	Aztec (Tenocha)
Bali	Mosquito (Miskito)
Tiwi	Cuna Ltule
Orokaiva	Carib
Manus	Mundurucu
Caypa	Jivaro (Xibaro)
Nambicuara	Aweikoma (Shokleng)
Abipon (Mepene)	Yahgan (Yamana)

n = 46

force as the result of foreign occupation. Consistent with our attempt to consider pristine states, these cultures have been excluded from the sample. Lastly, cultures for which data were missing were, of course, eliminated. This led to a substantially smaller sample (n = 40), but one that we believe is more precise with regard to police function.

Based on our information from the HRAF, we constructed our own code for the police function consistent with the findings discussed in chapters 2 and 3. This code consisted of societies in which the police function is (1) nonspecialized and informal, (2) temporarily assumed for specific purposes, (3) held by certain retainers, or (4) specialized and institutionalized.

We first performed a stepwise discriminant analysis (Wilks' method) using as dependent variables Tuden and Marshall's (1972), Ross's (1983), and our own code to produce three separate analyses. As independent variables, we used the codes previously discussed in our bivariate analyses together with many other codes available from Murdock (1967) and elsewhere for a total of 67 independent variables. The purpose of this step was twofold: (1) to determine if variables (other than those hypothesized) had significant independent effects on the police function and should be included in subsequent analyses, and (2) to see whether our code produced a discriminant function comparable to the other codes even though the sample size was much smaller. We requested that only one function be derived to find the single best discriminating continuum. Results of these analyses were too detailed to present in full here. Nevertheless, we felt that all three analyses were reasonably consistent (see Table 12), giving us confidence in our own police function code even with its correspondingly . smaller sample size.

Furthermore, we found no compelling reason to include in subsequent analyses any but the following six variables (previously discussed):

1. Levels of effective political sovereignty [PLEVELS] (Tuden and Marshall 1972:438)
2. Class stratification [CLASTYPE] (Murdock 1967:165 as modified, see earlier discussion)
3. Control over mode of production [MODEPROD] (Hendrix and Hossain 1988:444–445)
4. Subsistence base [SUBECON] (Hendrix and Hossain 1988:444–445) as modified, see earlier discussion)
5. Transfer of movable property [STAYRULE] (Murdock 1967:167 as modified, see earlier discussion)
6. Succession to local political office [SUCCESSOR] (Murdock 1967:166–167 as modified, see earlier discussion)

We then produced another discriminant analysis using our own police function code as dependent variable with these six variables as independent variables. Results are presented in Table 13.

The variable entered at the first step measured levels of effective political sovereignty. This was not surprising, since the Gamma measure of association for Table 2 was particularly high. As we have previously argued, stateless societies are characterized by nonspecialized and informal police functions, while state societies generally have specialized and institutionalized police. While by now this finding seems rather obvious and almost tautological, it is important to note that under the null hypothesis, it is theoretically possible for stateless societies to have formal policing

Table 12
Comparison of Stepwise Discriminant Analyses Figures for One Function, All Independent Variables

Police Function Code	Eigenvalue	Percent of Variance	Canonical Correlation	Initial Wilks' Lambda	Number of Steps	Number of Cases
Tuden and Marshall	2.34	60.7	.84	.09	30	179
Ross	5.42	72.8	.92	.05	34	88
This Research	657.63	73.1	1.00	.00	34	40

Table 13
Stepwise Discriminant Analysis: Summary Table

	Step 1	Step 2	Step 3
Action Entered Removed	Plevels	Modeprod	Subecon
Vars In	1	2	3
Wilks' Lambda	.59092	.52684	.43069
Sig.	.0003	.0008	.0005
Label	Levels of Effective Political Sovereignty	Control Over Mode of Production	Subsistence Base

Structure Matrix:

Pooled within-groups Correlations Between Discriminating Variables and Canonical Discriminant Functions

(Variables ordered by size of Correlation within function)

	Func 1
Subecon	0.82767
Plevels	0.80479
Stayrule	0.41344
Modeprod	0.38518
Clastype	0.33928
Successor	0.03466

Canonical Discriminant Functions

	Function 0	Function 1*	Function 2	Function 3
Eigenvalue		1.06862	0.12239	0.00002
Percent of Variance		89.72	10.28	0.00
Cumulative Percent		89.72	100.00	100.00
Canonical Correlation		0.7187396	.3302200	0.0043175
After Function	0	1	2	
Wilk's Lambda	0.4306914	0.8909382	0.9999814	
Chi-Squared	29.904	4.0995	0.66176E-03	
D.F.	9	4	1	
Significance	0.0005	0.3927	0.9795	

*Marks the one (1) canonical discriminant function remaining in the analysis.

Standardized Canonical Discriminant Function Coefficients

	Func 1
Plevels	0.59904
Modeprod	-0.00988
Subecon	0.63033

mechanisms or for state societies to lack them—but they almost never do in practice.

What interested us most is the variable entered at the next step—control over mode of production. As we saw in Table 4, formal and institutional-ized police occur almost exclusively in societies with class-based control of the means of production.Thus, while societal organization is a good predictor of the police function by itself, when coupled with control of production, it becomes an excellent predictor.

Because, as we stated earlier in this chapter, diachronic, historical approaches, and synchronic, cross-cultural approaches each have their strengths and weaknesses, we do not put our faith entirely on one or the other. We are most encouraged by the fact that our analysis of the particulars of case studies presented in chapters 2 and 3 is consistent with the quantitative analysis presented here. In tandem, we believe that strong evidence is provided in support of our propositions. The formal police function is associated with state societies having a class structure in which control of the means of production is vested in the hands of the elite. In the next chapter we explore some of the consequences of these findings for contemporary police-community relations.

NOTE

1. One analysis found that small states have "three-tier administrative appa-ratus" consisting of "general functionaries" normally found at a regional level; less frequently, general functionaries at internal and local levels; and "specialist functionaries" found at the top level, with both the sovereign's family members and priests influencing top political decision making (Claessen 1978:579–584).

6

IMPLICATIONS FOR MODERN POLICE AND POLICE-COMMUNITY RELATIONS

At the very start of this book, we summarized the notion of police history and function found in much traditional English and American literature on the police. Those notions were that: (1) the police institution in England has deep historical roots and is said to have experienced a slow but continual development from ancient to modern times; (2) the police institution originates with the people, depends on them for support, and, in effect, the people are the police and the police are the people; (3) the community is divided into a majority of good, law-abiding people and a minority of lawbreakers; and (4) one function of the police is to protect this virtuous majority from that criminal minority. In attempting to show how the police institution developed out of a class-structured society, we have at the same time shown how a police ideological history has developed side by side with the structure it was meant to portray (Robinson 1979). For the dominant class, this idyllic picture of history gives the best answer to the charge that the police represent a class-dominated system. It asserts that, on the contrary, from its very beginnings, the police function sprang from the body of the people and that this integral identity with the community has never changed or, under current community policing theory (to be discussed in this chapter), has been temporarily submerged and can be restored by a joint police-community effort.

Here is certainly all that we have asserted stood on its head. The police is said to have delivered us out of a hypothetical chaos. Collective security is conferred from above. This reversal of history was not accomplished by deceit. Rather, police historians took up the story of the beginnings of the English police, in the case of one author (Reith 1975) about the year 600, and in the case of another author (Critchley 1967), about the year 900 A.D., at a time when the kindred fabric of the Anglo-Saxon community was already in the process of disintegration.[1] Classes had already been formed; landed and private property were unequally distributed; the police mechanism, formerly a product of custom, was now largely determined by the edict of local kings who used the remains of the tithing-kindred system for maintaining the King's Peace against the incursions of those highwaymen, vagrants, rebels or broken men who were unable or refused to find a lord within that increasingly stratified society. It was this minority of lawbreakers who would not keep the peace, thereby endangering the survival of the feudal order. It is the benefactors of this order that needed to protect themselves by using the ready-made collective security system of old.

DIFFERENCES IN POLICE FUNCTION BETWEEN KINDRED AND STATE-ORGANIZED SOCIETY

We have suggested that the collective security organization, described by Critchley (1967) and Lee (1971) as that in existence shortly before the Norman invasion, seems to represent a vestige and re-adaptation by the king of an earlier true kin structure. It was the Normans who arguably turned or began to turn a stratified society into a nation-state. Based upon this analysis, what differences in police function may be posited between a kindred and a state-organized society? Why was there little need for a specialized police function in the former and a necessity in the latter?

In an egalitarian society there are traditional mechanisms that are called into play for the occasional wrongdoer. Just as the wrongdoing is occasional and spontaneous, so is the response. "Crimes" in such a society are nonexistent. A crime can be designated only by a political structure (Jeudwine 1917:84–86). Breaches of customary behavior are wrongs against the collectivity and are punished by customary responses whose predominant purpose is to maintain harmony within that collectivity.

The egalitarian society should not be confused with romantic notions of a society without conflict. In a kindred-organized society, ideological relations (Hindess and Hirst 1975) and custom (Diamond 1971) rather than law dominate. Conflict there is, but it is between individuals responsible to their kinship groups (Llewellyn and Hoebel 1941:293–294), not between classes—one class trying to protect its riches and the other trying to gain a larger share (Sahlins 1972:98). The "law of blood" is a "law of prevention and a law of termination" of bloody conflict, "not a law of violence" (Reid 1970:92). The absence of classes allows conflict to be resolved on an individual basis—or, if not resolved, coerced individuals and their families may just segment.

The sense of kindred is dependent on the material condition that each individual is an essential part of a functioning community. Community living results in a series of reciprocally related customs and traditions that are self-evidently related to the community style of life and are self-enforcing. As Sahlins says, "Peacekeeping is not a sporadic inter-societal event, it is a continuous process going on within society itself" (1972:187; see also Diamond 1971:134, 141 n.50). Basic resources and access to these resources are communal, and therefore all persons have a stake in their preservation and in retaining open access to them. A breach of the custom of free access will bring down a sanction on the violator, who is part of that community. In most cases, the communal desire for free access to resources does not require the development of a formalized police function; the community polices itself. Occasionally, as we have shown, social situations are such that police functions must be temporarily established in order to protect communal resources on behalf of the entire group.

However, some stateless social formations contain within themselves an internal coercive network of traditions, rituals, and customs accruing to leaders that may induce certain individuals to turn a simple distribution network to their own advantage. Developments may include the expansion by certain men of concepts of community ownership to that of individual ownership and accumulation of goods and their subsequent acquisition of prestige, the dependence of some persons on these prestigious big-men, the exchange of labor for security and personal safety, the accompanying demand for loyalty and allegiance, the temporary and then permanent acquisition of authority, the settling of groups in one place and the holding and tilling of land, the disproportionate distribution of former communal land to favored loyal retainers, the development of the patron-client relationship, the capture and use of slaves to develop and enlarge personal accumulation of property. Such developments may be accompanied by the proliferation of political forms to protect these acquisitions, incurring, in some cases, the parallel deterioration of the kinship group as a political-economic unit, and in others, the seizure and preservation of the kinship-based economy as an alternative means of appropriation of surplus labor.

The customary response to wrongs from within the community may then be slowly replaced by sanctions (laws) imposed from "above" and without a developing class system (Diamond 1971:115). The model of laws and lawbreakers that replaces a simple bargaining model of conflict management is decidedly to the advantage of an emerging elite. Laws compatible with their own ends can easily be created. Prestige, which initially raises certain men first to the position of temporary mediators, eventually becomes a permanent part of the offices of chiefs to make them permanent arbitrators and guarantors of the peace. These developments may be accompanied by the conversion of communal to "private" property, perhaps resulting from placing a prestigious person, the elders, or a chief, in charge of the protection of some basic communal resource such as a river or waterhole. The notion arises or is promoted that he or his clan has a special "right" to this resource; that in holding it, he is holding it "in trust" for the whole tribe (Balandier 1970:118–119). A "trespass" on that land or resource then becomes a "wrong" eventually so defined by the king. A parallel developing ideology provides the "ruler with a rational explanation of what he, the ruler, had already done" (Parkinson 1958:9).

As we have previously argued, the police function emerges when there is the perceived need by the chief or some bureaucratic clique to protect for themselves limited access to basic resources. However, there is a transitional stage before the state is fully formed when other forms of coercion besides an organized police are used to maintain this class society. A good example of the use of a combination of authority, patronage, and paternalism is the American colonial elites that

enabled the great Virginia planters to mobilize their "interests" and to maintain law and order over the local communities without the aid of police forces. The leading Virginia gentry were the vestrymen of their parishes and the layleaders of the Anglican church, so that the sacredness of religion and the patronage of poor relief further enhanced the hierarchy of authority.... Everywhere it was the same: those who had the property and power to exert the influence in any way—whether by lending money, doing favors, or supplying employment—created obligations or dependencies that could be turned into political authority. (Wood 1992:89)

Once such a class system develops, a police agency becomes a logical institution to aid in maintaining this equilibrium of inequality.

POLICE ASSERTION OF THEIR OWN INTERESTS

But it does not follow that because the ruling class determines to use the police as their instrument to maintain inequalities, the police may be described as a mere instrument in the hands of a capitalist class. Such a designation confuses the desires and needs of the ruling class (that is, that the police be just such an instrument) with the desires, needs, history, and material working conditions of the police themselves, who often assert interests antagonistic to those of the ruling class (Robinson 1978). Even the use of the appellation the *police* to cover three different entities—the working police officer, management, *and* the police institution—hides the real and separate interests of these three, and particularly those of the police officer.

Like the state, the police agency takes on a cloak of neutrality. But the working police officer is anything but neutral.[2] Problems police administrators historically have found with the line police officer—lack of professionalism, corruption, insubordination, laziness, low productivity—are likewise characteristically found by employers of all workers. Together, these qualities are best understood as a police counterculture in which police workers attempt to assert their right to control their conditions of work (Manning 1979).

Moreover, police continue to be affected by their double and split loyalty—loyalty to their ethnic and working-class identity, and loyalty to the state, imposed on police officers by virtue of their government employment (Robinson 1978). This schizophrenic portrait is exemplified by the metaphoric depiction of the officer as at once a "philosopher, guide and friend" (Cumming, Cumming, and Edell 1965) and as a soldier in an army of occupation of the same ghetto community. Using history as a tool, we have tried to show that the roots of this conflict lay in the destruction of the original collective security system of kinship-based society by the usurping state organization. That system of collective security resided in the very nature of the particular social formation. In destroying the integral nature of that society but at the same time saving the collective security structure for its own use, the evolving state created an institution with at least a toe still dipped in its democratic past.

WHO IS TO CONTROL THE POLICE?

We are now ready to take on the question we raised at the beginning of this book: Who do the police represent? Who is to control the police—the state or the community? If control is to be exercised by the community, how is that possible within a state structure? Is the community a unity or a multitude of interests—and if a multitude, how is the public interest to be determined? The ideology suggested by police historians has no difficulty with such questions. The police are the people and the people are the police. The state, being a democratic state, represents not one segment but *all* the people. The people already control the police.

But to those who do not accept this view of the police (and there have been many since the collision of the police with blacks and other minorities during the 1960s), the answer has been to propose various police reforms.

These have included talk sessions between police and communities to establish better communications, the addition of minority officers to the police, the suggestion of civilian review boards to police the police, team policing, and, most recently, community policing. One of the earliest attempts at community control of the police took place in Berkeley, California.[3] There, in 1971, a proposal for community control of the police was placed before Berkeley voters and defeated by a two-to-one margin. The proposal called for the city of Berkeley, for police purposes, to be divided into three districts consisting of the three city neighborhoods: the black, the campus youth, and the middle-class Northside Hill communities. This attempt at community control has been criticized as being

based on a narrow conception of power, limiting struggles to the "local" and failing to confront the interlocking, national bases of economic power. [Focusing on the concept of community] tends to dismiss or replace the concept of class. . . . Secondly, there is an assumption . . . that it is possible to capture a piece of the bourgeois state and convert it into an instrument of popular control. This view of the state . . . assumes either neutrality of the state or the possibility of legislating it out of the hands of the ruling class. (Center for Research on Criminal Justice 1977:190)

Perhaps a more serious and less abstract defect was the approach the reformers took to the police officers. They treated the line officers as the enemy.[4] Police as individuals were merged with their state function. They were seen as mere agents of an "enemy" state, not as workers. Police, however, are as much subjects of that state as are the community people (Robinson 1978). Because of their failure to treat police as workers, reformers merely represented the replacement of one employer with another from the police worker's standpoint. And this time it was an employer who threatened to impose strict controls over their working conditions in exchange for little opportunity to control or participate in the control of those conditions. Community control of the police, under such a plan, represents dubious control over the police workers and little or no control over the employer—the city—and other segments of society that ultimately determine the conditions under which both the community and the police operate.

There are additional reasons why, in today's society, community control of the police is unlikely to work. We have seen that historically only two kinds of communities controlled their policing mechanisms—both in stateless societies. One was a society in which social controls were the result of reciprocal relations interwoven with custom that sanctioned individuals who violated those reciprocal relations. The other was a society that temporarily employed a police force to maintain its egalitarian structure, its equal access to basic resources.

Contemporary communities, on the other hand, are dominated by law rather than custom. They are not united by kindred-reciprocal relations. Instead, they consist of atomized and isolated individuals. There is little sense that each individual has a value to the community. On the contrary, individuals are in competition with their neighbors for scarce resources. Therefore, individuals are at the same time both "surplus" and potentially harmful to their neighbors. Sanctions for breaking laws and customs are not automatic. To be effective, violators must be caught, punished and rehabilitated, and few are. There is, in sum, neither custom nor law effectively restraining violators. Expressed another way, noncriminal individuals in the community often have the same antidemocratic values as those for which the police are criticized.

One would expect, therefore, that if the community did gain control of its police, various divisions within that community (different age, sex, race, ethnic, income, and property ownership levels) would attempt to use the police in the same way the state did—to gain and then protect limited access to basic scarce resources. Such a result appears inevitable for a police force policing an inegalitarian society. Community police actions, of course, would be taken in the public interest, of which each group would claim to be the sole representative. Moreover, even assuming that the community had control of its police, the community would have control of little that would answer to its problems, as black mayors of cities such as Newark, Detroit, Cleveland, Los Angeles, Philadelphia, and Chicago have found. More recently, there has been another elite-backed attempt to reconstruct history and to build on the admitted failure of the past—a movement dubbed "community policing."

COMMUNITY POLICING

Community policing, touted as "the first major reform movement in policing since the 1930's," or "perhaps the most significant police effort to identify, label, and implement a new organizational strategy"[5] (Steele 1987:5) is a joint product of Harvard University's John F. Kennedy School of Government's Executive Session on Policing and Michigan State University's School of Criminal Justice, and has been financed by grants from the C. S. Mott and Guggenheim Foundations, and the National Institute of Justice (Steele 1987:5; Trojanowicz and Bucqueroux 1990:vii,3). The movement sports a "Community Policing Newsletter" published by the National Neighborhood Foot Patrol Center (later renamed the National Center for Community Policing) of Michigan State University, and an ever-increasing mountain of descriptive, self-congratulatory memoranda, studies, and reports published by one or both of the founding institutions.

As part of this flood of literature, the National Institute of Justice and the Kennedy School of Government authored a number of publications under the rubric "Perspectives on Policing," setting forth the description, history, and philosophy of community policing. The words inset on each National Institute of Justice publication set forth its structure and origin:

This is one in a series of reports originally developed with some of the leading figures in American policing[6] during their periodic meetings at Harvard University's John F. Kennedy School of Government. The reports are published so that Americans interested in the improvement and the future of policing can share in the information and perspectives that were part of extensive debates at the School's Executive Session on Policing. (Kelling and Moore 1988:1)

In 1979, the C. S. Mott Foundation funded an experimental foot patrol program in fourteen Flint, Michigan, neighborhoods, at the same time financing a four-year evaluation to be conducted by Dr. Robert Trojanowicz of Michigan State University. Under Trojanowicz's direction, the National Neighborhood Foot Patrol Center was created, and nearly 500 people were trained in it over this four-year period. Although initially funded by the Mott Foundation, the city of Flint eventually approved a special tax to pay for the experiment. A report commissioned by the Flint city government, however, recommended that the program be terminated when funding expired in 1988.[7]

Dr. Marilyn Steele, officer of the C. S. Mott Foundation, sums up the "Harvard approach" as a "focus on the police elite, involving police chiefs who tend to have great influence on their peers" (Steele 1987:6). Like Reith and company before them, community policing proponents have created a capsule history and philosophy for its support. Thus, according to its exponents, and despite its own history of creation, community policing is not merely an "elite" product of Harvard's Executive Session on Policing issuing down from above. Rather, it represents a retaking of control of the police by the community—a restatement of the English police philosophy that the police are the people and the people are the police (Trojanowicz and Bucqueroux 1990:45).

Two of the movement's chief proponents (Trojanowicz and Bucqueroux 1990:xiii) restate this idea as the first of their stated "Ten Principles of Community Policing":

Community policing is both a philosophy and an organizational strategy that allows the police and community residents to work closely together in new ways to solve the problems of crime, physical and social disorder, and neighborhood decay. The philosophy rests on the belief that law-abiding people in the community deserve input into the police process, in exchange for their participation and support.

According to one commentator on community policing, its essential components are: "(1) community-based crime prevention, (2) proactive servicing as opposed to emergency response, (3) public participation in the planning and supervision of police operations, and (4) shifting of command responsibility to lower rank levels" (Bayley 1988:226). Community policing, sometimes also referred to as "neighborhood-oriented policing," is said to include

a sense of trust between police and citizens. . . . The central premise of community policing is that the public should play a more active and coordinated part in enhancing safety. . . . [T]he public should be seen as "coproducers" with the police of safety and order. Community policing thus imposes a new responsibility on the police, namely, to devise appropriate ways of associating the public with law enforcement and the maintenance of order. (Skolnick and Bayley 1988:3–4; see also Mastrofski 1988:56; Alpert and Dunham 1988:25)

For the proponents, the major analytic concept is community. They point to the idyllic period a decade after World War II when "residents shared a common geography and a common culture, as well as elements of mutual interdependence" (Trojanowicz and Moore 1988:3). As "industrialization" drove people from farms to cities (ibid.), "community" began to become synonymous with "neighborhood," when applied to areas within cities (ibid.:4). "[M]any major cities were still dominated by clear-cut, virtually self-contained, ethnic neighborhoods" (ibid.:4).

"[T]he glue that held communities together flowed from the communication between community residents that took place during those daily activities" (ibid.:6). But beginning in the 1950s, "three major technological changes—mass transportation, mass communication and mass media—have played a great role in the divorce between geography and community" (ibid.:7). To the above triumvirate of causes can be added a "profound shift in the country's economy," characterized by the replacement of higher-paying factory jobs with lower-paying service jobs, budget cuts to city schools, reduced housing supply, and an increasing gap between rich and poor. People no longer define themselves in terms of geographic location (neighborhoods) but in terms of interest, that is, careers (ibid.:9–11; see also Trojanowicz et al. 1987:10).

These various factors combined to cause the modern problem in communities of "crime, disorder, and fear of crime." Far from being a disaster, these factors represent a kind of phoenix out of which the new community police can arise.

The point in this comparison [before and after the decline of community] is not to point any finger of blame concerning the apparent growing inequity between rich and poor in this culture,[8] but to examine the dynamics that play a role in shaping the new kinds of community, today's politics must serve. . . . Most community relations programs were based on the traditional definition of community, the idea that there was a cohesive group within a specific geographical area that could be persuaded through an educational effort that the police are "good guys." . . . [C]ommunity relations programs failed because they did not address the issues—crime, disorder, and fear of crime—that provide modern communities and the police with a mutual community of interest that can allow for meaningful interaction. (Trojanowicz and Moore 1988:13)

Bearing this analysis in mind, police history can be divided into "three different eras" based on an "apparent dominance of a particular strategy of policing" (Kelling and Moore 1988:2).

The political era, so named because of the close ties between police and politics, dated from the introduction of police into municipalities during the 1840's, continued through the Progressive period, and ended during the early 1900's. The reform era developed in reaction to the political. It took hold during the 1930's, thrived during the 1950's and 1960's, began to erode during the late 1970's. The reform era now seems to be giving way to an era emphasizing community problem solving. (Ibid.)

These "strategies" had certain characteristics, both good and bad, related to the communities in which they operated. The political era was characterized by the police being "integrated into neighborhoods and enjoy[ing] the support of citizens—at least the support of the dominant and political interests of the area; [they] assisted immigrants in establishing themselves in communities and finding jobs." On the debit side, the "closeness to political leaders, and a decentralized organizational structure, with its inability to provide supervision of officers, gave rise to police corruption" (ibid.:4; see Walker 1984 for a critique of this reading of police history).

From the 1930s through the 1960s, a series of reforms, such as civil service, police commissions, life tenure for police chiefs (to be revoked only for cause), and prohibition of officers living in the beats they patrolled, all had for their purpose an end to "the close ties between local political leaders and police" (Kelling and Moore 1988:5). Thus, in the reform era—again, according to community policing proponents—"policing a city became a legal and technical matter left to the discretion of professional police executives under the guidance of law." Their function was narrowed "to crime control and criminal apprehension. . . . Activities that drew the police into solving other kinds of community problems and relied on other kinds of responses were identified as 'social work' " (ibid.:5–6). "Success lay in being able to control crime effectively without having to depend on others," including the community they were policing (Sparrow, Moore, and Kennedy 1990:113).

This era was dominated by two organizational principles adopted by police management: "division of labor and unity of control," requiring that tasks be broken into specialized components and based on the belief that workers could be "best managed by a *pyramid of control*, with all authority finally resting in one central office" (Kelling and Moore 1988:6, emphasis in original). Special units (vice, juvenile, drugs) were created under central commands. The proper relationship between police and citizens was redefined to be impartial, professionally neutral, and impersonal. The proper role of the citizen was to be an impassive recipient of professional services (ibid.:6; Payne and Trojanowicz 1985:5).

Nevertheless, a number of factors from the 1960s began to raise questions about this strategy: crime began to increase; in the 1970s, research tended to show that preventive patrol and other crime control methods were ineffective; fear of crime rose and citizens abandoned entire neighborhoods; many minority citizens believed their treatment by police to be inequitable and inadequate; the civil rights and antiwar movements questioned police legitimacy; research challenged the impersonal view of police by showing the frequent use by police of discretion and the small amount of time police spent on law-enforcing activities. In addition, line officers were not treated in practice like professionals but were limited to routinized and standardized work, city fiscal difficulties resulted in reduced departmental size, and police acquired competition "from private security and the community crime control movement" (Kelling and Moore 1988:8–9; see also Payne and Trojanowicz 1985:5–6).

"[R]eform strategy" was a successful strategy for the police during the relatively stable period of the 1940s and 1950s. Police were able to sell a relatively narrow service line and maintain dominance in the crime control market [but] the reform strategy was unable to adjust to the changing social circumstances of the 1960s and 1970s [civil rights, migration of minorities into cities, increases in crime and fear of crime, etc.]. (Kelling and Moore 1988:9)

This literature also provides a rationale for the police to ignore the root causes of crime:

While it may be useful to examine what some call the root causes of crime (e.g., social injustice, unequal economic opportunity, poor schooling, weak family structures, or mental illness), such things are relatively unimportant from a police perspective since the police exercise little influence over them. The police operate on the surface of social life. They must handle incidents, situations, and people as they are now—not societies or people as they might have been. For these reasons, the immediately precipitating causes of serious crime are far more important to the police than are broader questions about the root causes of crime.[9] Four precipitating causes of crime seem relevant to policing: (1) dangerous people; (2) criminogenic situations; (3) alcohol and drug use; and (4) frustrating relationships. (Moore, Trojanowicz, and Kelling 1988:4)

Yet recent research has shown that reactive policing cannot control these types of crime. For example, "the Kansas City Preventive Patrol Study found that levels of serious crime were not significantly influenced by doubling the number of cars patrolling the streets"; further, the probability of making an arrest for serious crimes was most affected by the "quality of the information" supplied by victims and witnesses, not by follow-up police investigation (ibid.: 6; see also Trojanowicz and Carter 1988:9–11). Nevertheless,

the police [did not] understand that a partnership with the community could be constructed only from the material of daily encounters with the public. . . . Second, . . . [t]hey tended to limit their responsibilities to applying the law to incidents to which they were summoned. (Moore, Trojanowicz, and Kelling 1988:7–8)

Such a role had a protective function for the police:

It protected police organizations from criticisms that they were lawless and out of control. . . . [T]hey merely enforced the laws. . . . They could blame the other parts of the criminal justice system for their failure to deter and incapacitate the offenders whom the police had arrested. (Ibid.: 8)

Building on these social changes in the community, on the research showing the ineffectiveness of reform strategy, and on the inability of the police to solve problems they faced in the 1980s, the concept and practice of community policing, its advocates argue, is in the process of replacing reform policing. Harking back to the proponent's earlier concept of community, community policing, they believe, can create a new form of community out of the ravages of the old.

[C]rime, disorder and fear of crime can help create a community of interest within a geographic community. Enhancing and emphasizing this particular *community of interest* within a specific *geographic community* can provide the impetus for residents to work with a community policing officer to create a positive *sense of community* in the fullest sense of the term. . . . The community of interest created by crime, disorder and fear of crime becomes the goal to allow community policing officers an entry into the geographic community. Then together the officers and the residents can develop new structures and tactics designed to improve the overall quality of life, allowing a renewed community spirit to build and flourish. (Trojanowicz and Moore 1988:1–2, emphasis in original)

Thus, the essence of community policing is the rediscovery by police management of the need for community participation in crime control:

More than anything else, the police are rediscovering that ordinary people and communities are the first line of defense in controlling crime and fear. The police cannot succeed without an effective partnership with the communities they serve. Without the eyes and ears of residents to extend the scope of police surveillance, the reach of police control is pathetically thin. Citizens' vigilance and willingness to come forward are an integral part of police operations. If that piece of the machinery is not working well, the police, for all their sophistication and equipment, are rendered ineffective. (Sparrow, Moore, and Kennedy 1990:46)

COMMUNITY POLICING—A CRITIQUE

Perhaps the most trenchant criticism of community policing comes from a minority view expressed by two members of the Kennedy school's Executive Session on Policing: Hubert Williams, president of the Police Foundation, and Patrick V. Murphy, professor at John Jay College of Criminal Justice and former president of the foundation (Williams and Murphy 1990). They charge that the majority's "interpretation of the changing role of police in America" is "disturbingly incomplete" in that "it fails to take account of how slavery, segregation, discrimination, and racism have affected the development of American police departments."

Moreover, they "remain silent on the important role that minorities have played in the past, and will play in the future, in affecting and improving the quality of policing in America" (ibid.: 1). Williams and Murphy further conclude that whereas the majority

attempted to explain the evolution of policing in terms of strategic choices made by police executives who were developing a professional ideology, we see policing as powerfully conditioned by broad social forces and attitudes—including a long history of racism. The [majority] see police departments as largely autonomous; we see them as barometers of the society in which they operate. (Ibid.: 2)

Williams and Murphy also point out that the majority's analysis "fails to recognize that members of those minority communities received virtually none of the benefits of policing that were directed to those with more political clout" and "that [the majority] account is based largely on an analysis of policing in cities of the northeastern United States," reflecting a "twentieth-century bias toward northern urban, white conditions" (ibid.: 2–3). More important, with reference to the contemporary relevance of community policing to these same northern urban cities, they conclude:

A recent assessment by the Commission on the Cities found that, despite a brief period of improvement, the conditions that produced the dissolution of ghetto communities are actually getting worse. . . . Furthermore, although the police are better prepared to deal with the residents of the inner city than they were twenty years ago, they are far from having totally bridged the chasm that had separated them from minorities—especially blacks—for over 200 years. There are still too few black officers, at all levels. Racism still persists. . . . Regardless of rules and guidelines, inappropriate behavior on the streets still occurs. . . . And empirical studies have shown that community-oriented approaches that are effective in most neighborhoods work less well, or not at all, in areas inhabited by low-income blacks and other minority groups. (Ibid.: 12)

In addition to criticism from within the movement itself, community policing, perhaps because of its exaggerated claims—made well in advance of its having given any evidence of the worth of such claims—has been attacked from many sides. Some of these criticisms can be summarized as follows:

1. Regardless of the program or structure of police departments, according to "accumulating evidence," police have little effect on the crime rate. Rather, "most of the variation in crime rates can be explained in terms of structural factors in society such as unemployment, education, age distribution, and

ethnic homogeneity" (Bayley 1988:228; see also Sparrow, Moore, and Kennedy 1990:151). Under present conditions of gang and drug-related crime in urban areas, the police are "incapable of protecting them" (Neely 1990:13, 71–76).

2. While the idea of police and citizens as partners is an attractive idea, it is the police department that remains in control of information gathering, of initiation of action (as a proactive department), and that approves or disapproves any initiatives by citizen groups (Mastrofski 1988:52). Moreover, the internal command structure and police culture of departments remain unchanged, regardless of what happens at the street level of the community policing officer (ibid.: 60; see also Sparrow, Moore, and Kennedy 1990:51–57, 148–149). "[R]estructuring of relations among police officers may be more difficult than the restructuring of relations between officers and the citizenry" (Bittner 1990:15. See also Clairmont 1991:477; Skogan 1990:123–124).

3. The fundamental assumptions of community policing are based largely on myths of ideal communities, difficult to define, meaning different things to different people.[10] "To urge that a community be crime-free, or that the public is dissatisfied with current practices, does not provide an alternative program. . . . Or, to put it another way, community police is a solution in search of a problem" (Manning 1988:35; see also Klockars 1988:248). Thus, the ideal of "community" is used to obviate the necessity of entering into the complex economic, political, and organizational analysis necessary to understand and influence the community-police relationship in a real community (Duffee 1990:128–132).

4. According to community policing theory, "communities are to be consulted, surveyed, organized, and negotiated with, in order that their interests, needs and concerns are incorporated into neighborhood police priorities and strategies. This vision of a more active, democratic, and politicized community, however, begs the question of who legitimately represents that community" (Murphy 1988b:186). Rather than finding a value consensus, it is more likely that the police will key into the politically or culturally dominant group, which will direct their notions of social control at their neighbors (Bouza 1990:20, 32; Police Foundation 1981:23–124; Skogan 1990:109,132). Such a belief is heightened "by their concern for crimes poor people specialize in and their neglect of crimes committed exclusively by well-to-do individuals," thereby giving "the appearance of acting in a class-biased manner that owing to the distribution of wealth in the United States, is also apt to include elements of racial bias" (Bittner 1990:22–23). Moreover, research tends to show that there is no necessary correlation between the perceptions of problems held by those most active in the neighborhood with the perception held by most people in that neighborhood (Mastrofski 1988:51).

5. "A key element of the community service strategy is the notion that to accomplish safer, more orderly communities, police must acknowledge that they share that responsibility with the citizenry—that indeed without close

cooperation these objectives can never be realized. This notion of police-community reciprocity or coproduction has the ring of a coequal partnership between police and public, but in practice its programs manifest a markedly asymmetrical relationship.[11] Coproduction in practice means citizens do what police think is best" (Mastrofski 1988:56; See also Klockars 1988:248); and in practice, "in their encounters with citizens, police officers seek to establish a position of dominance as soon as possible and to maintain it" (Bittner 1990:26).

6. Those few community policing programs that have been evaluated tend to show that such programs have little or no measurable impact on the crime rate or that they have more positive impact on middle-class than on lower-class communities (Skogan 1990:107–109). What they do accomplish is to show the public that the police are trying to protect them, and therefore may increase the public's sense of security and reduce their fear of crime (Brodeur 1991:312; Bennett 1990:167; Mastrofski 1988:57; Bayley 1988:227; Alpert and Dunham 1988:25; Police Foundation 1981:122–123). Other similar initiatives give similar results: the "large majority" of block watch programs did not work to reduce crime (Lewis, Grant, and Rosenbaum 1988:99, 133); Guardian Angels reduce fear of crime but not crime itself (Neely 1990:156).

7. The word "resources" is banished from the community policing vocabulary. Not only is the police an institution that fails to distribute or redistribute resources as one of its functions; one of its important functions is to maintain the present maldistribution of resources.

Thus, while community policing has mixed ratings on one of its intended purposes, that of reducing crime, as a public relations device, intended or not, it has been a howling success. As one major study of foot patrol concluded, a conclusion applicable to community policing as a whole, "Although people seem to be only modestly aware of the levels of motor patrol . . . , they seem to be acutely aware of the presence of foot control" (Police Foundation 1981:122).

Other critics take the more sinister view that the movement provides a means for the informal state to extend its social control and to blur the distinction between formal and informal social control systems (Cohen 1985:68–69, 83; Hofrichter 1987:73–74, 82–83).

Besides general image building, all this is directed to obtaining greater citizen cooperation in the form of reporting and informal surveillance. . . . [A] much more formalized type of enlistment of private citizens into police work has been taking place. . . . With overload on the formal criminal justice system and the perception among victims and potential victims that the state is "letting them down," new forms of private and vigilante justice—fanned by racialism and community tensions—have developed. Whether they see themselves as "by-passing" or as "helping" the police, these activities are easily blurred with the formal system (Cohen 1985:68–69). . . . [The state] rationalizes this [control] by appealing to a vision of what the real family, school or community looked like once or should look like now—and these institutions are then changed further rather than restored to their pristine state. (Ibid.: 83)

More fundamentally, community policing advocates and others who advocate auxiliary police or vigilantes such as the Guardian Angels[12] either misunderstand or perhaps unconsciously adopt a mechanism that aligns them with the state in an effort to use the formal controls of the state to institutionalize, that is, incorporate the informal controls of the community into the state control apparatus. Many of the poverty-stricken communities about which these writers are concerned have been deprived of their access to basic resources. As a community, they are unable to feed, house, and nurture (educate, heal, and protect) their residents. Many of their young men have turned into predators, most often victimizing others in their own community in their individual search for survival.

Moreover, emphasis of the CP movement on "public" police completely ignores private security arrangements, which, by 1990, approximately doubled expenditures for public police, and go unmentioned in community policing rhetoric. Such a public-private police dichotomy effectively reflects the economic structure in which those Americans with nearly limitless access to riches wall themselves off from their less fortunate compatriots. Policing is thus used in the classic sense we have described: The poorest Americans are left with neither security nor justice. This dilemma is well expressed by a National Institute of Justice representative (Phillips 1993:141):

Something has really changed in this country. I'd say we are moving from a system of justice to a system where people are purchasing security, which is different from justice, because justice is a value that benefits all of society. Private security partitions off security to just a few.

Far from being the radical departure from "reform" policing, community policing is merely the reformulation of the same structural formulation—that of the neighborhood versus the police, so that the police appear to be both the "enemy" and the savior. In other words, the police remain as the buffer, the blame-taker, between the neighborhood and the real policy-maker—the state (Robinson 1975).

Crime prevention activities that attack issues of inequality, police brutality and social injustice might be closer to the needs of the community members than block watches, security surveys and property marking programs, which can do little to change the number of jobs in the community, the quality of education and the amount of power which community members possess. By deflecting the community organization towards the victimization type programs, the argument can be made that such activities are deflecting the group from goals that are in the true interests of the community. (Lewis, Grant, and Rosenbaum 1988:20)

Moreover, the concept of community, as understood by community policing advocates, is corrupted by their division of the community into the good (law-abiding citizens) and the evil (street criminals). Similar metaphorical imagery was used by Reith (1975) and in reference to seventeenth-century England, in which the

politically marginal were a disordering agent akin to disease, parasite or pathology. . . . All their actions were necessarily tinged with their twin qualities of dangerousness and devalued social status. . . . Large segments of that penumbral group were expected to be hanged as a matter of course. (Rock 1983:210)

While many of these young men are not just thought to be dangerous but are dangerous in their own right, they remain the sons and grandsons of people in the community, in a milieu without jobs or hope of jobs other than as muggers, thieves, pimps, hustlers, or drug dealers. So while the very essence of community is unity, redemption, and reconciliation, the central idea of community policing is to split kin from kin. "Criminals" are dehumanized into a *category* to be expunged.

Furthermore, the idea of community becoming "lost" is a familiar but mistaken reading of history:

While almost every period in American history has been described by one scholar or another as the watershed when community was lost,[13] there have been few periods in which it has been restored. . . . A moving analysis of what is wrong with ourselves and society is not the same thing as a strategy to change it. This is precisely the problem with community approaches to social reform in criminology. . . . [T]he critique is built on a notion that communal man is hiding within economic man and that he will respond to the call to restore himself through community. . . . To hope that in the area of crime prevention we will start to act differently and that those actions will pay off in increased solidarity and security is to underestimate the overall impact of the very system which is seen as being so destructive.[14] (Lewis, Grant, and Rosenbaum 1988:136, 125–126)

State policies today have the effect of creating groups in increasing numbers that must be excluded socially for the state to continue to exist economically—those on welfare, the homeless, those without health insurance, the jobless, and those designated the criminal class. As those excluded from the economic cycle of the capitalist state become more numerous and detached from their communities, the police will have to be called on more and more to control these groups. In other words, the police, as a state agency, will become increasingly the principal agent of the dominant class to maintain an unequal distribution of wealth. Under such circumstances, it is difficult to see how the police can function as an agent of that same community for the well-being of the entire community.

As Duffee (1990:137) has stated:

Making changes in any particular criminal justice agency must be done in light of information about the specific functions of that agency in that specific [political and social] setting. . . . [I]f we are to make effective changes in some level or type of social order, we must begin outside the criminal justice system with redesign of basic living and working arrangements.

That is, while it is all to the good to try to reform the police if the real object is to provide a safe community, "only if a community decides to take responsibility for its own safety can the police be truly effective" (Osborne and Gaebler 1992:64). "Community police" is placing the police horse before the community cart. There is good reason, therefore, that police reformers call their reform community policing and not community police.

We now turn to our proposal for a redesign of basic living and working arrangements that will tend to produce a kind of community out of which a community police will issue whose purpose and function will be to see that community resources are distributed equitably.

NOTES

1. Critchley (1967:1), the leading author treating this early period, begins his book as follows:

The origins of the English police *system* are to be found in tribal laws and customs of the Danish and Anglo-Saxon invaders. . . . The nearest equivalent to the modern policeman is the Saxon tythingman, otherwise borsholder or headborough. *Above* him was a hundred man and then the shire reeve or sheriff. Collective *fines levied* on a community as *punishment* included fightwitt, grithbryce, and frithbrec; and territorial divisions in which policing operated were variously known as hundreds, wapentakes, rapes, and lathes. (Emphasis added)

Note that the system as described by Critchley is already hierarchical and punitive.

2. There is considerable historical and contemporary documentation (police activity in racially motivated riots, recent busing policies, policing of ghetto areas) to indicate that working police are influenced by ethnic and class backgrounds in their policing. See generally Robinson 1977.

3. In the 1960s, there was one other attempt at community control of the police, in which the Black Panther Party "demanded that the public have a direct voice in hiring, disciplining, and firing officers, and in day-to-day management issues" (Skogan 1990:124).

4. The conversion of the police into a scapegoat for more pervasive societal ills is a common ploy of various groups (Robinson 1975).

5. David H. Bayley (1988), a friendly critic, describes community policing as "the new philosophy of professional law enforcement in the world's industrial democracies. . . . Community policing has emerged as the major strategic alternative to traditional practices that are now widely regarded as having failed" (p. 225). "Community policing does not represent a small, technical shift in policing. . . . It is the most fundamental change in policing since the rise of police professionalism" (p. 236). See also Skolnick and Bayley 1988:1; Murphy 1988a:393; and Trojanowicz and Bucqueroux 1990:3. According to a recent report, over 300 departments, among which are Los Angeles and New York City, have "some form of Community Policing" (Trojanowicz and Bucqueroux 1990:4). For its influence in Canada, see Brodeur 1991:285. From this and other articles in this collection, it is evident that the same criticisms of community policing in the United States are said to be applicable to the Canadian version.

6. For example, Lee P. Brown, formerly Chief, Houston Police Department; Susan R. Estrich, Professor, School of Law, Harvard University; Daryl F. Gates, formerly Chief, Los Angeles Police Department; Herman Goldstein, Professor, School of Law, University of Wisconsin; Francis X. Hartman, Executive Director, Program in Criminal Justice Policy and Management, John F. Kennedy School of Government, Harvard University; George L. Kelling, Professor, School of Criminal Justice, Northeastern University; Robert B. Kliesmet, President, International Union of Police Associations, AFL–CIO; Edwin Meese III, former Attorney General of the United States; Patrick Murphy, Professor of Political Science, John Jay College of Criminal Justice; Sir Kenneth Newman, former Commissioner, Scotland Yard; Robert Trojanowicz, Professor and Director, School of Criminal Justice, Michigan State University; James Q. Wilson, Graduate School of Management, Harvard University. In addition, there were police chiefs representing Peoria; Baltimore; Long Beach, California; Boston; Philadelphia; New York; as well as the mayors or former mayors of St. Paul, Minnesota, and Fresno, California; and representatives of the National Institute of Justice, the F.B.I., the Police Foundation, and the Vera Institute of Justice. The Bureau of Justice Assistance, a subdivision of the U.S. Department of Justice, has created the Innovative Neighborhood-Oriented Policing program, whose "projects are designed to develop innovative community policing programs that target demand reduction at the neighborhood levels in small cities and rural areas" (National Institute of Justice 1991:19).

7. The history of the experiment is found at Trojanowicz and Bucqueroux 1990:195–228.

8. Thus, capitalist accumulation either as a cause of community deterioration or as a drag on community future prosperity can be ignored.

9. The advocates of this argument—important to its proponents because it attempts to narrow the police function so that it can fit within their view of community policing—never does assign responsibility for those "root" causes. The police are thus placed in the uncomfortable position akin to the Dutch boy with his thumb in the dike. While one is conceding areas over which the police "exercise little influence," recent research, presented below, shows such a conclusion applies as well to "crime," leaving the exact function of the police in doubt. The same rationale as proposed for community policing has been made by advocates of block watch programs: "The block watch would allow them [community participants] to do something not about the causes of crime but about its *effects* by reducing 'opportunities' for victimization" (Lewis, Grant, and Rosenbaum 1988:44, emphasis in original).

10. Nearly every article on community policing begins with an attempt to define it. See, for example, Leighton 1991:487.

11. A good barometer of the ability of most police departments to coproduce with citizens are citizen's police complaints departments, which, according to one review, "have the opportunity to be dedicated 'ears' for the police, but few have adopted that role energetically" (Sparrow, Moore, and Kennedy 1990:167). Summing up, these same commentators state: "Current practices in complaints, community relations, and press offices provide little evidence of police commitment to genuine openness and effective accountability. [These offices] are instead being used as a shield behind which the remainder of the organization can operate as usual" (ibid.: 170).

12. Auxiliaries are recruited, trained, equipped, and under supervision of the police department, but they serve as unpaid and unarmed volunteers. In New York City, for example, at any one time there have been up to 9,000 auxiliary police officers (Greenberg 1984:148). Guardian Angels and other vigilantes, on the other hand, are privately financed and trained, wear distinctive uniforms, and have only the powers of private citizens (ibid.; Neely 1990). Recent revelations about the Guardian Angels show the dangers inherent in such groups when they are unattached to other community institutions. "Curtis Sliwa," the founder and leader of the Guardian Angels, "has admitted that six of his group's early crime-fighting exploits were actually faked and former and present associates contend that even more of the group's activities were publicity stunts" (Gonzalez 1992:1).

13. In the early nineteenth century, Emerson saw "community" replaced by an "age of severance, of disassociation, of freedom, of analysis, of detachment. Every man for himself," the destruction of all societal "ties and ligaments" (Wood 1992:365).

14. Robert Bellah and his associates see a contradiction in the American psyche. In a study of the way middle-class Americans viewed their society, the

authors concluded that "Americans" searched for a "spontaneous," "harmonious," and "idealized" community, in "a wish to transform the roughness of utilitarian dealings in the marketplace, the courts, and government administration into neighborly conciliation. But this nostalgia is belied by the strong focus of American individualism on economic success. The rules of the competitive market, not the practices of the town meeting or the fellowship of the church, are the real arbiters of living" (Bellah et al. 1986:251).

7

WHAT CAN BE DONE

We have concluded that the police function is a product of the societal structure of which it is a part. Simply stated, where the structure of that society is classless and egalitarian, that is, where there is more or less an equal right and opportunity for all societal members to share in access to and use of basic resources, then the police has as its function to see that individuals who attempt to interfere with that free and equal access are prevented from doing so. Where, however, a society is class-based, that society must have a state structure to maintain that unequal access to basic resources. A police is the element of that state structure that has for its function the maintenance of that inequality by force.

Recent examples of propertied classes using police to patrol inner-city minority areas, to control worker efforts at unionization, to suppress protests against government policies to fight unpopular wars, or to maintain repressive regimes such as the southern slavocracy are legion and need no citation. In detailing the development of the English police in chapter 4, we have noted earlier examples.

There is also little question that our (U.S.) society fails to supply equal access to use of basic resources.[1] How, then, is it possible to have a community police in a society that by definition "must" produce a police in its own image? Or, to put the question in an operative mode, how do we extract the principles from egalitarian societies and apply them to our nonegalitarian society in such a way as to produce an egalitarian police?

We have concluded that the possibility of producing an egalitarian police from an inegalitarian society would have about the same chance as expecting a swan to emerge from a hen's egg. Yet, having examined as many societal attempts to deal with this problem as we have, we believe that we should make an attempt to apply what we have learned to at least imagining a society in which such a police would be possible rather than leave the reader with the unsatisfactory conclusion that nothing can be done until society, at some distant moment, is restructured to our satisfaction.

Let us start our quest by abstracting the principles that underlie present conceptions of community policing, as discussed in chapter 6. These ideas apply not merely to community policing but to a number of other community programs that began to appear in the 1960s, lost support in the 1970s, and were reborn in altered form in the 1980s, including proposals for community health, corrections, schools, financial institutions, and others.[2] These proposals had all or most of the following characteristics:

1. Problems are seen through the perspective of individuals rather than through the prism of class, and in terms of the locality rather than the whole society, the nation.
2. Where efforts are made, as they usually are in neighborhoods that have a scarcity of resources, no part of the plan calls for a redistribution of resources from those with greater to those with lesser resources.[3]
3. The inspiration and initial proliferation of the idea originates from an academic and professional elite rather than from below, the community itself.
4. The core idea is the proposed sharing of responsibility but not power with the "community."
5. The end result of the reform is to maintain and affirm the hierarchy of power.
6. The newly recognized connection of the institution with the community results in the renewed legitimation of dominant institutions.
7. To the extent that there are reforms and changes, such reform is limited to local institutions, in our case, the local police. The result is that any reform is restricted to the fragment of power targeted.

These core ideas can be contrasted with those we found to be characteristic of the police in simple, egalitarian societies:

1. The police institution remains part of and serves the entire social unit or community; security is organized on a collective basis.
2. The police are not specialists. Different persons serve at different times; all able-bodied persons serve at one time or another, and service is therefore temporary. Upon completion of the temporary policing function, the individual returns to the community.
3. The main obligation of the police is to the community.

4. Community (kinship) obligations dominate over aspirations toward personal acquisition, profit, and prestige.

5. The community is organized on the basis of redistribution, as much as possible to attain equal access to basic resources. Therefore, the values of caring, sharing, reciprocity, respect, generosity, and cooperation to attain these goals is encouraged in activity among residents and taught to the young.

6. In principle, community resources belong to (are owned by) the community in common, or by its users.

7. In instances in which community rules or values are violated by individuals, punishment will be governed by informal sanctions, with redemption and return to good standing in the community the overarching value.

8. Institutions in the community (schools, parks, health and social services, legal clinics and dispute resolution centers, halfway houses, community centers, public housing, and police stations) are controlled by community residents, who select personnel, set policies, determine how those policies are to be implemented, and amend those policies from time to time.

The core value of an egalitarian society is to promote survival of the social unit. It is understood by all that survival of the unit is dependent on the performance of each individual, each of whom has an assigned role to contribute for the common good. Conversely, individuals understand that their survival depends on the successful survival of the social unit. Thus the survival of the social unit and that of the individual are united and not in contradiction.

In our national debates, problems involving access of much of our population to basic resources have often been replaced by symbolic issues such as character, family values, trust, revocation of gay rights, patriotism, capital punishment, abortion, and the like. To the extent that these access problems are addressed at all, they tend to be dealt with as individual issues: health, housing, crime, education, child or female abuse, welfare, and so forth. Plans and policies fail to focus upon communities or neighborhoods as a unit, political or social, and certainly fail to focus the nation as an economic whole.[4]

In trying to find a way out of this conundrum for the police function, it will first be useful to inquire historically how our communities became transformed from the relatively stable ethnic enclaves of the 1950s to the crime-ridden, disorganized neighborhoods we find in many inner cities today (Fischer 1982:263). We will then look at some attempts to recreate survival-centered communities, and finally, from these examples we will distill principles that may be applied to today's neighborhoods to produce a police institution whose function is to maintain approximately equal access to basic resources.

HISTORICAL SOURCES OF INNER-CITY VIOLENCE AND CRIME PROBLEMS

In the late nineteenth and early twentieth centuries, industries were often built near transportation facilities—rivers, harbors, and rail depots—areas that for that very reason became less attractive as residential areas. Beginning in the 1930s, and increasingly in ensuing years, as southern agriculture became mechanized, aided by federal government research and crop support legislation, large numbers of southern black and white tenant farmers and sharecroppers were displaced. Plentiful industrial entry-level jobs beckoned from northern cities. Having the oldest housing and therefore the cheapest rent, the deteriorating neighborhoods in industrial areas became magnets for newly arriving black immigrants, who could take jobs in factories near where they lived. Incoming blacks, denied access to adjacent white areas, had little choice.

In the 1950s, a federal $100 billion highway construction program linked city to city and city to suburbs. Such construction encouraged factory owners to leave their aging inner-city factories and move to the suburbs, where they found cheaper land, a skilled nonunion labor force, and local governments eager to zone according to their needs. Whites, aided by federally financed home mortgages, which were generally denied to blacks, fled the aging cities by these same routes.

Manufacturers, seeking cheaper nonunion labor, took profit-seeking businesses first to the suburbs, then to the South, and finally out of the country entirely, thereby depleting inner cities of lower-level jobs and leaving in their wake wells of unemployment, desolation, and hopelessness filled by gangs violently competing for turf to sell drugs. In Los Angeles, the Watts riot of 1965, and the South Central riot of 1992 can, in part, be attributed to these societal changes.

The seeds of the rebellion are inherent in the restructured economy and the massive job loss between 1978 and 1989, when about 200,000 jobs disappeared from the Los Angeles economy, most of them centered in South Central Los Angeles. . . .

These were high-paying, highly unionized jobs in manufacturing, jobs that were the lifeblood of the communities in South Central Los Angeles, providing stable employment and livable wages that allowed people to maintain stable families. (Mydans 1992:10)

As in other such areas following job loss, small businesses collapsed, housing deteriorated, and city services, including schools and health services, declined. Those who could moved away, leading to further deterioration of the inner-city economy. In South Central Los Angeles, the school dropout rate is reported to be between 60 and 80 percent, leaving a population of mostly "young males who are neither at work nor in school" (ibid).

In recent years, Hispanics and Koreans have moved into the neighborhood. Even when construction jobs became available, as some money found its way into the area after the riots, the available jobs were insufficient to meet the demand, complicated as it was by racial changes in neighborhood composition. All wanted a cut of the limited pie[5] (ibid.).

ATTEMPTS OF OTHER GROUPS TO ADDRESS TOTAL SOCIETAL NEEDS

We now turn to two groups, Native Americans and the Amish, to illustrate the societal values adhered to by those groups and the social control mechanisms consistent with their social formations.

Native American Values and Enforcement Methods

In a series of interviews with elders of the Cree, Blackfoot, Blood, and Slavey groups from Alberta, Canada, those interviewed continually referred to "respect" as the concept that was necessary for survival: "We were put here by the Great Spirit to love the country and live with it and work to survive—so that people would love each other and work with each other and so they will survive and live in harmony with the country" (Nielsen 1982:3). An elder further declared that

if a guy or a woman didn't have anything to eat at home, . . . or got sick or had problems getting this or that, they helped each other, fed each other, shared with the others. . . . Sometimes, when I was a girl, other girls and me used to go out picking berries, so one of the girls wouldn't have her pail filled up so we use to help her fill up the pail so that all of us would take the same amount of berries home. . . . Wrongdoing occurred when people did not show respect—when they stole someone's horse or wife, when they fought with or tried to harm someone, when they got jealous or were impolite. All these acts, directly or indirectly, affected the survival of the group because they destroyed the harmony and therefore the working effectiveness of the unit. (Ibid.:4–5)

Another writer, an anthropologist who studied Native Americans in the post–Civil War period, after they had been herded on reservations, described their social control mechanisms and how these affected individual behavior:

Offenses against property were insignificant because Indian society stressed cooperation and sharing. Hunger drove no one to steal where sharing was a cardinal virtue. And the very scarcity of personal possessions would make a stolen article too conspicuous to be used in a tightly knit society where everyone was constantly on view. Therefore theft was virtually unknown, although some Indians had bad reputations for borrowing without first seeking the owner's permission. . . . It was a very serious offense when one thoughtless individual frightened away game, causing the entire tribe to enter the winter short of meat, hides for new tepees, and robes to protect them from the fierce northers. (Hagan 1980:12–13)

Where kinship was an important binding force, shame could be used as a deterrent. In Alberta, troublesome young men were controlled by such a threat:

In those days they used to go and get the Grandmother's skirt and they put it on him. . . . He was told this was the way he would look—if he beat his wife or if you're lazy and good for nothing and if they don't do nothing. . . . There was always one old lady's dress handy for that purpose. Let me tell you—the young men did not want to put this dress on. (Nielsen 1982:6–7)

Among the Kiowas, "such embarrassment and ridicule" was heaped on a repeated rapist that "he reportedly soon died."

Tribal women laid an ambush and baited the trap with a beautiful young girl. When he took the bait, they suddenly appeared and overpowered him. As others held him helpless on the ground, each woman in turn raised her skirt and sat on his face. . . . [T]he loss of status . . . was perhaps more chastening than the threat of the electric chair in more sophisticated societies. (Hagan 1980:17)

We have discussed in chapter 2 punishments meted out by Native American soldier societies as well as the redemptive aspects often accompanying these punishments. In chapter 4, we have shown how white society, with values emphasizing acquisition and profit, overwhelmed Native American society (the Cherokees), initially creating "certain men," who were enthralled by these values and who were then able to corrupt the entire tribe (Hagan 1980:20–24).

The Amish as a Society Dedicated to Survival

The Amish derive from the sixteenth-century Anabaptists and came to this country from Germany and Switzerland between 1727 and 1790, and again between 1815 and 1865. They were persecuted in Europe because of the way they interpreted the Bible:

Membership in the Christian church should be voluntary, initiated by adult rather than infant baptism, . . . the church should be separate from the state, and . . . Christian believers should practice the teaching and example of Jesus in a disciplined and separated community. Emphasis was placed on simple rather than ostentatious living, regeneration of character, and caring and sharing with the poor. They insisted on loving their enemies and would not fight in or support war. (Hostetler 1992:4)

The core values of the Amish can be summarized as follows:

1. Central to their belief is the biblical story of creation in which "they and their children acquired a sinful (or carnal) nature." In "the gift of God's son" to the world, they believe they have received "an undeserved gift" for which "they must therefore prove themselves worthy, faithful, grateful and humble," and feel obligated to form "a community incarnated with the attributes of godliness. . . . The individual is implored to choose humility rather than pride, and love for the believing community rather than love for self" (ibid.: 8, 9).

2. Individuals must separate themselves from the "blind, perverted world;" be "in the world but not of it. . . . What must be guarded against is the love of physical comforts, the love of material things, and the lust for power" (ibid.). The emphasis is on community versus the individualism of the outside world.

3. Baptism is an adult ceremony signifying a covenant with God and the corporate community.

4. After baptism the individual takes on a moral responsibility for keeping church rules, rules that are unwritten but are repeated orally after church services, to which each is asked to assent.

5. "Obdurate and erring" members are excommunicated and, if not repentant, are shunned by other community members (ibid.:11). Shunned members may not associate with, buy, sell, or eat with other members, and if husband or wife, marital relations are suspended until the person is allowed to rejoin the community.

6. For the Amish nature is a garden, with human beings the caretakers. Manual labor is good. Therefore, farming, carpentry, masonry, and other means of working in harmony with nature are preferred. The city is viewed "as the center of leisure, nonproductive spending, and often, wickedness. . . . The

farm economy incorporates the elements of hard work, cooperative family labor, crop and livestock productivity, and extreme thrift" (ibid.:13).

All Amish are considered equal and most live in small units, so all know and continually mingle with each other. "Recreation consists primarily of meaningful social experiences, group solidarity" such as "barn-raisings, woodcuttings, husking bees, quiltings, preparations for church services, weddings, and funerals (including casket-making), all combined work and recreation" (Hostetler 1980:16).

Social control among the Amish is exercised by a sense of conscience instilled during the socialization process; informal talk or gossip; admonishment by the deacon or a preacher; admonishment by a delegation, usually of two ordained men; being asked not to take part in the communion; and excommunication and shunning until a change of attitude is shown or, if no sign of obedience is given, shunning for life (ibid.:354–355; see also Turnbull 1984:77).

Over the years, there have been numerous divisions among Amish groups concerning their adherence to the rigid beliefs required by the doctrine. These have been dealt with either by groups segmenting and continuing under their own variation of belief or, in the case of individuals, leaving or being expelled by the community. These separations have allowed the church to retain most of its adherents unchanged in a changing world.

Nevertheless, in instances in which the Amish have lived adjacent to non-Amish and have multiplied to the extent that they no longer live in small communities and therefore do not know each other, social order problems have arisen somewhat as in non-Amish communities, although in a milder form. Reportedly, youths who have worked outside the community have occasionally been involved in shoplifting and passing bad checks, but not in forcible crimes (Hostetler 1980:340). In large communities, Amish teenagers have also formed "gangs" that have sponsored hoedowns, or barn dances, on Sunday nights where there was music and beer drinking. In some cases, police have been called and arrests made for drunkenness. In such cases, parents have lost control of their children (ibid.:345–349).

CREATING A NEW COMMUNITY MODEL

According to our analysis, the insidious and unique relationship of the police to the state consists of a cadre, neutral in itself in one sense, but a mere instrument in the hands of the state in another. This relationship can be altered only by changing the community's relationship to the state. Before the community seeks to control its police, it must seek to control itself. The community must be able to restructure itself in such a way that it emphasizes the elements of kinship and reciprocity among its inhabitants, a feeling that every resident is a needed contributor, and an understanding of mutual obligations that upon breach will incur informal correction by and in the community. Upon fulfillment, resulting benefits may be appreciated by neighbors through reciprocal exchange, enhanced prestige, opportunities for leadership, the chance to be thought wise and to be a Big Person (Turnbull 1984).

Any knowledgeable and thoughtful reader will realize that when commentators are writing about community-police relations, they are not concerned with all communities. Few if any are troubled by community-police relations in upper-class or upper-middle-class neighborhoods. The focus, often unstated, is on neighborhoods peopled by the poor of one or more minorities, high percentages of female-headed households, and young unemployed adults who are perhaps engaged in drug sales, gang turf wars, easy accessibility to guns, and hence much violence and death. The near–carbon copies of this situation found in almost all northern cities makes it unlikely that these conditions happened by chance. On the contrary, one of us has suggested that federal and state governments, by following some policies and failing to follow others, inevitably brought this situation into being (Robinson 1993).

We have seen that in Amish and certain Native American societies their economic base was the central factor in encouraging social cohesion—in terms of some Native Americans, hunting and gathering, and in the case of the Amish, farming. We must then begin our quest for a community police by reconstituting the neighborhood as a viable economic and social unit.

As the agricultural revolution proceeded, and farm labor was no longer needed, those millions of people displaced from the land were forced to enter the employment relation, dependent on an employer for their livelihood. No longer were they able to survive by relying solely on their own labor. The movement into industrial jobs before World War I had allowed millions of immigrants of various ethnic groups to gain a foothold in the economy, and therefore to rise to more secure positions. But after World War II, for reasons already stated, industries left ethnic neighborhoods. Entry-level jobs disappeared, leaving large numbers of minority youths, in particular, without access to job markets. Jobs, in turn, supplying earnings sufficient to support a family unit, have been shown in a multitude of studies to be the single most significant variable in maintaining family stability (Robinson 1993).

In suggesting what it will take to create a viable community and a police evolving from that community, we are unconcerned whether our creation is politically probable, or even whether all of the component parts of our scheme are compatible. Rather, it is our object to create a model that is in harmony with a police that is responsive to the needs of a community that itself functions for the benefit of its residents.

Few communities in the United States are able to subsist as self-suffi-cient units; most cannot return to hunting and gathering of Native Ameri-can or to the farm economies of small Amish communities. Therefore, from the perspective of the survival of the nation, we propose that the United States be seen as a single unit, or community.

Under this reconstitution of society, federal and state governments would have the function of collecting and then redistributing tax revenues with the object of providing all citizens with approximately equal access to basic resources. How to dispense these resources would be decided at the community level, controlled by citizen boards elected by neighbor-hood residents. We realize that it is fanciful to expect a class-dominated society, where the wealth of the top 1 percent of the population equals that of the middle 20 percent (Phillips 1993:25), to agree to such a redistribu-tion just as it is fanciful to believe that such a society will produce a community police. Nevertheless, there is no other organization in society that can assume this function (Rueschemeyer and Evans 1985:54–55).

One of the major problems of today's communities is ethnic rivalries, as illustrated by the South Central Los Angeles neighborhood described earlier. When such a problem was faced by the Iroquois League of chiefs from different tribes, the problem of mediating their diverse interest was accomplished by "the principle of unanimity."

Unanimity was not merely an idea; it was a necessity. Communities were small and lacked any duly instituted police force to deal with potentially divisive actions. Lacking that "coercive force" to prevent dissenters from simply moving out of the community and hence greatly weakening the ability to defend itself, considerable effort was devoted to finding consensus. Among North American Indians generally this consensus was sought in council, each man of the village being free in council to express his opinion, and through these various expressions of concern the council as a whole sought the thread of agreement—for all well knew the dire consequences of division. Of necessity, orators were valued not merely for their ability to persuade listeners by rhetoric, but also for their ability to state the issues clearly and by this means move the council toward the unanimity required. (Tooker 1988:315; see also Champagne 1992:28–30)

Because this principle of unanimity generates pressures on the participants in the council to seek agreement among themselves before taking action, no recourse to force was necessary, and as the league had no police force, none was possible.

The requirement of unanimity did not preclude—in fact—it necessitated leadership. The Hopi and other nineteenth century Native American tribes provided models of leadership emphasizing "consensus decision making, egalitarianism, decentralized noncoercive authority relations, and accountability of leadership" (Champagne 1992:30). Although the Hopi may have had a ranking differentiation, there were no differences in access to basic resources. Individual distinctions did arise as to those who excelled in craft production or trade. Those who acquired positions of authority bore "the responsibility for maintaining the spiritual well-being of the community and can be blamed if they fail. . . . Hierarchy, thus was a device for allocating spiritual responsibility and assuring that all necessary protective roles were filled" (Schlegel 1992:381).

The Hopi balanced two "cultural themes: communality, the goal of community harmony even at the expense of the individual, and individuality, the freedom of individual choice to act and to advance" (ibid.:392). Nevertheless, priority was given to an individual's duties and responsibilities to the community. Individual efforts that raised persons to be "important people" in the eyes of their neighbors, were "justified . . . to promote the well-being of all"[6] (ibid.).

In order to promote such qualities, our national government would guarantee to all Americans access to basic resources, namely: to adequate housing, health care, infant day care, and education to the extent of the individual's ability.[7] Each person would also be entitled to work, primarily in the private sector, but in the event that work was not then available, opportunities in government projects would be offered.[8] These might include variations of Peace Corps and Vista jobs: working together with international youth on various projects to help other nations and to repair cultural treasures, archeological projects, aiding older people unable to care for their own homes, helping out in disaster zones. The object would be to expose our youth to other cultures and to other economic opportunities, particularly to agriculture.[9]

Every person would be assigned some task related to community betterment. The neighborhood population would be surveyed to determine what skills are available. These skills would be used in reciprocal work exchanges, providing various home improvement, child, and health care services. Parents would coach their children at home and as school aides (Osborne and Gaebler 1992:55). Vacant lots would be used for gardens;

painters, carpenters, plasterers, and masons would repair buildings and artists would decorate them with murals; resident stage companies would mount plays to represent the ethnic diversity and the Big People in the neighborhood's past; and local news gazettes would broadcast neighborhood problems and triumphs and provide a forum for community exchange of views. Musicians, dancers, magicians, and peddlers would populate the sidewalks. As with the Amish, construction repairs, songfests, festivals, holidays, food fairs, and dances would be community events.

Community work should express a " 'civic-religious conception of justice'—'as a calling, contributing to the common good and responding to the needs of others as their needs becomes understood' through public discussion about the economic and social relationships among different groups" (Bellah et al. 1986:218). With work now available, residents would be more ready to patronize neighborhood businesses.

Among neighborhood residents there must be a proper mix of cooperation and competition. Competition between community residents would generally be discouraged in favor of cooperative behavior. But cooperation among community residents to enhance their own communities so as to compete with other communities for community excellence would be encouraged: which had the best athletes, the best teams, the best festivals, the best newspapers, or which can provide their residents with the best and most comprehensive services (Osborne and Gaebler 1992:79–80).

Corporate entities would be invited to invest in the neighborhood with the proviso that community residents have a financial interest in the corporation and be able to name members to the corporation's board of directors. The corporation must be accountable to the community as a quid pro quo for any tax or other incentives provided to it (Bukowczyk 1984:75–76). Mutual aid societies of residents would be fostered (Light 1972). Federal and state governments would provide loan guarantees to community banks to give loans to small businesses such as street vendors and to residents who wished to become doctors, dentists, lawyers, accountants, and other professionals on condition that they promised to return to live and practice in these same communities.[10]

And these Big Persons, having been spotlighted because of their qualities of generosity and compassion, their community-seeking propensities, their skills in bringing people together, and thus their ability creatively and constructively to help in solving community problems, could dedicate their time as temporary leaders to receiving and redistributing fairly community wealth and access to it. Neighborhood residents who had the fortune to rise above others in wealth would hold annual potlatches to help redistribute the bounty.[11]

"Democracy means participating in the election and running of the unit of political authority that most affects one's daily life" (Patterson 1991:374). Using this idea as the community's operating principle, the various community institutions—schools, libraries, legal services, health and day care centers, banks, halfway houses—would be governed by boards elected by residents of their jurisdictional unit. Each would have funds originating with the federal or state governments to provide outreach programs whose object would be to prevent illness; inform children of and expose them to a multiethnic and multiracial society through field trips to other neighborhoods, to farms and Native American reservations, and to sports such as sailing and skiing; and to encourage them to work on community projects during their weekends and holidays.[12] People who were elderly, ill, orphaned, disabled, homeless, or for other reasons unable to take care of their own needs would be a community concern.

All this activity together would not create an egalitarian society in which all residents have equal access to basic resources. But it would result in a society in which all have access, in some degree, equal or not, to such resources. Such access is the necessary prerequisite to develop among residents the appreciation and encouragement of the virtues of generosity, sharing, and cooperation toward common ends, a sense of community attachment, and if not a constraint on community over self, at least a weighing of the two in the individual's decision (Turnbull 1984). People are more likely to know and appreciate their neighbors when they are experienced in the many roles played: as resident, fellow project worker, school board member, grocery store owner, father or mother of the boy who fixed their fence.

In sum, this would be a community that was ready to choose a police in its own image.

A COMMUNITY POLICE THAT SERVES THE ENTIRE COMMUNITY

A devastating critique of the English version of community policing reform in policing inner cities is equally applicable to U.S. attempts:

Most officers live outside the areas they police, and strangers are always less influential in community action than insiders. Some inner city residents who develop a feeling of community with one another do so on the basis of deviant behavior which the police will want to suppress. . . . If the residents of an area do manage to develop some joint identity, a sense of community, they will tend to reinforce it by trying to change strangers in their midst (as with the pressure to conform in rural village communities). Policing as an outside force would be subject to this kind of pressure which would undoubtedly be resisted, thus reinforcing the notion of the police as outsiders. (Irving et al. 1989:194)

In the United States (as in most other complex societies) the police have two separate and distinct roles: as law enforcers and as peacekeepers. While the former role is popularized and stressed, the latter role actually comprises most of the city police officer's time. During the 1960s, the separate nature of these two roles was often noted (e.g., Banton 1964; Goldstein 1967; President's Commission on Law Enforcement and Administration of Justice 1967; Wilson 1968). Furthermore, it was clear that the conflicting nature of these roles created considerable stress both for uniformed officers and for the community members policed. Recruits entered police departments with idealistic notions of crime fighting and became quickly disenchanted with ordinary day-to-day uniformed social work (Bittner 1967:699–700; Edwards 1968:5; Skolnick 1968:17; Wilson 1968:68). At that time, various proposals to separate these police functions were put forward (e.g., Bard 1969; Bard and Berkowitz 1967; Family Crisis Intervention Unit n.d.; Vera Institute of Justice 1969; Von Rosensteil 1971).

These proposals generally involved the establishment of two separate policing roles: (1) the professional law enforcement officer who, exercising a minimum of discretion, apprehends offenders who are then processed through the traditional criminal justice system, and (2) the peace officer who maintains order by exercising discretion in settling disputes and civil problems, channeling them to neighborhood conflict resolution centers when possible. A few experiments based on these proposals were even successfully tried on a limited scale (e.g., Family Crisis Intervention Unit n.d.; St. Louis Metropolitan Police Department n.d.; Vera Institute of Justice 1969), but no serious attempt to implement this scheme on a large scale has yet been made.

In kin-based societies, as we have pointed out, only the second of these policing roles exists. Furthermore, the individuals who fill these peacekeeping positions are genuine members of the community, and often serve on a temporary basis. There is no need for the professional specialist. Yet, in our complex, class-based society, which arguably "needs" professional specialists, these specialists not only perform their necessary functions but also handle a wide range of problems that communities have traditionally managed by other means.

We would argue that even in our complex society, for many types of community problems and disputes, the professional law enforcer is neither necessary nor desirable. One clear example is in the area of domestic disputes, which police particularly dislike handling (see, e.g., Scaglion 1973:65–66) and which result in considerable citizen dissatisfaction (e.g., Scaglion 1973:32). It was in these sorts of situations that the Family Crisis Intervention Unit was designed to intervene in place of ordinary uniformed officers. We believe that if the law-enforcing and peacekeeping roles of modern police were separated, the peace-keeping role could be developed and modified according to some of the models we have explored in this volume.

Nevertheless, these reforms would not of themselves produce a community police. A police cannot be a community police unless the institution and the officers are of and in that community. Using the soldier societies of Native Americans as our model, police would be selected by a police board elected by community residents, would *be* community residents, and would serve during a period (perhaps one year) when they would be excused from their regular jobs for such service. To the extent possible, all able-bodied adults would serve as police. Police would be trained in the community by a small staff of permanent "professional" officers who would be elected by the community from time to time.[13] Through projects researching their own neighborhoods, all officers would learn the neighborhood's history, including its political, social, and economic structure.[14] As in England, officers would have weapons available to them at the community police station but would not carry any on their beats.

In a recent study of "how neighbors settle disputes," Robert Ellickson (1991:280, 282, 286) concluded that formal "law," that is, legalized coercion,

is not central to the maintenance of social order. . . . [c]lose-knittedness enables victims of social transgressions to discipline deviants by means of simple self-help measures such as negative gossip and mild physical reprisals. Under these circumstances, informal social controls are likely to support law. . . . [L]aws that serve to distribute power more broadly and equally are likely to bolster informal-control systems.

Following the above principle and the organization of the police themselves, offenses would be divided into less dangerous and more dangerous offenses. Those that relate to relatively minor violations of property rights, such as shoplifting, simple theft, assaults not involving serious injury, and disputes between landlord and tenants as well as various youth offenses such as vandalism, loud noise, rowdy behavior, and so forth, would, for the first offense, be brought to the attention of parents, or in the case of adults, to the attention of dispute resolution centers (Harrington 1985; Hofrichter 1987). More serious offenses involving force and offenses repeated by an individual would be referred to a permanent professional police force (somewhat similar to the one we have now) that would act with reference to the community, as the National Guard acts with reference to the state. That is, the professional police would enter the community only when invited in by the community police.

Community police would recapture some of the functions they embraced in the nineteenth century, all of which would aid access of poorer residents to basic resources and tend to redress the inequality between large-property owners and small- or non-property owners. They would report housing code, garbage, and toxic waste violations; find temporary housing to aid the homeless; return intoxicated persons to their homes; and steer residents to appropriate work and social services.

The community police would form an integrated community norm-enforcing group together with health, school, and church officials. They themselves, having engaged in cooperative working projects with many of the persons they came in contact with, would be in a better position to understand others' problems and motives. Such cooperation would be facilitated by a community center where police, health and legal clinics, and employment and youth advisors would be housed.

Every encouragement would be given to the offending person to reintegrate into the community (Turnbull 1984). This policy would also be available for those who initially were turned over to the outside police and court system because it was believed to be beyond the capacity of the community police system to help them.

Such a police, instead of dividing residents into criminals and noncriminals, would see everyone as valuable to the survival of the community and would make an effort to see that each person had the access to basic resources needed to lead a useful and harmonious existence. To the extent that such a police was successful in that task, it would truly be a community police.

If this chapter seems to be a mixture of magic, fantasy, and chimera, it is because the Big Men in our society have made it so. It is just as chimerical to believe that the conditions of our inner cities "just happened" or that they were caused by the reforms of the 1960s, as was alleged at one time during the 1992 presidential campaign, or that nothing can be done about them, as it is to propose our model for community policing. Our choice remains to hold either to the fantasy that the police institution is somehow independent from the injustices and inequalities of our society and that it can aid the deprived population only by imprisoning some of its sons and daughters or to admit that the police, like our other institutions, can only be the reflection of the inequities of our society.

NOTES

1. Although in "Western European countries, . . . basic physical and material needs are met either by the market mechanism or by the different kinds of social policies and programs of the welfare state" (Badura 1986:55), this has not been true in the United States, where the state takes no responsibility for child or health care, housing or equal educational opportunity. To take one example, housing, in New York City, "the median rent of a two-bedroom apartment is $600—about twice welfare's housing allowance for a family of three" (Martin 1992:A13). One-quarter of the city's population lives below the poverty line, and half of the residents do not earn enough to pay for housing. "So they make do. They combine welfare, jobs in the underground economy, whatever" (ibid.). Another study showed that 69 percent of Chicago's poor spent at least half their incomes on housing costs *(Chicago Tribune*, November 28, 1992, Sec. 1, p. 28).

2. The community policing movement was preceded by the community crime prevention of the 1970s and early 1980s, which was itself inspired by the 1967 President's Crime Commission report that in turn gave birth to the Law Enforcement Assistance Administration (LEAA), and in 1977, the LEAA's Community Anti-Crime Programs. With the flowering of neighborhood organizations in the 1960s, a great variety of crime prevention programs were produced, including: citizen patrols, crime reporting, block-watch programs, home security surveys, property marking, police-community councils, plans for changing the physical environment such as increased street lighting, and foot patrol. These eventually inspired the community police movement (Rosenbaum 1986:11–12,19). A careful evaluation of these various programs concluded that such crime prevention efforts were unlikely to work in low-income, high-crime areas because:

Given the peculiar history of racial and ethnic relationships in American cities, and especially the social and cultural distance between black residents and city police, such joint efforts might be particularly difficult to mount. . . . To the extent that the neighborhoods in greatest need cannot be served in the immediate future; the incidence of crime is not likely to be reduced significantly as a result of community crime prevention efforts. (Ibid.:307–308)

3. One of the issues during the 1992 presidential campaign was candidate Clinton's proposal for a tax on the rich, who had assertedly gained by reduction in their taxes under the Reagan-Bush administrations. President Bush attacked such taxing of the rich (those earning over $200,000 a year) as "redistribution of wealth," in his eyes, a carnal sin.

4. During President-elect Clinton's speech following his victory, he did indicate a comprehension of the nation as a "community": [W]e need more than

new laws, new promises, or new programs. We need a new spirit of community, a sense that we're all in this together. If we have no sense of community, the American dream will continue to wither. Our destiny is bound up with the destiny of every American (Clinton 1992:B3). But since then, almost all debate carried on through the media has been about the "economy." As more and more people drop out of our formal economy while remaining members of our larger society, this debate and its resulting policy determinations have little meaning for the excluded ones—that is, the homeless, the jobless, the underskilled and those employed but paid under the poverty level. See Phillips 1993; Schwarz and Volgy 1992; Ropers 1991; and Jones 1992.

5. Although following the Watts riot of 1965 substantial aid was promised to rebuild and provide jobs for areas such as South Central Los Angeles, and again after Tom Bradley was elected mayor in 1973, aid went instead to rebuild downtown areas, supported by "bankers, corporate executives, law firms, real-estate developers, and labor leaders," on the theory that "what is good for downtown is good for everybody" (Curran 1992:23).

6. In the split between progressive and traditional Native Americans, even progressive Native Americans often retained some of their customary ways. William Wash, an early Native American twentieth-century stock raiser, played a dual role, by first enriching himself, and second defending tribal land against outsiders (Lewis 1991:139). Leadership also consisted of passing that role on to younger men who had proved themselves, in this case among the Shawnee in battle against their enemies, white settlers invading their lands (Eckert 1992:337).

A council had been held and speaker after speaker had risen to extol the courage of their son who had gone away a boy and returned home not just a man, but as a warrior among warriors. Old Chief Spotka—Hanokula—had been last to speak and the words he said had been most important.

"I have always been a warrior," the messenger had quoted the elderly chief as having said, "and in my youth I won great honors and excelled beyond those with whom I lived and for this I was finally made a chief. At that time I said that when a warrior rose among us who was as I was then, to him I would give over my chieftainship. Chaubenee is such a one—not only as I was then, but even more. From this day forward, he is your chief." (Ibid.)

For a discussion of the conflict between individual and societal needs, see Turnbull 1984 and Bellah et al. 1986.

7. Among modern industrialized nations, it is only in the United States that economic ideology embodies the belief that capitalism, unencumbered by "government interference," produces good jobs for all who want to work. In France, for example, for those unable to find a job, a law of December 1988 known as the R.M.I. (*revenue minimum d'insertion*), provides a monthly stipend of about $400 per month, or somewhat less than what would be earned at the minimum wage. This law takes its rationale from Article 25 of the Universal Declaration of Human Rights (which the United States has never ratified), adopted in 1948 by the United Nations General Assembly, stating:

(1) Everyone has the right to a standard of living adequate for the health and well-being of himself and of his family, including food, clothing, housing and medical care and necessary social services, and the right to security in the event of unemployment, sickness, disability, widowhood, old age, or other lack of livelihood in circumstances beyond his control. (Osmańczyk 1990:402)

Such provision for the whole population is not unknown in our society. In the 1930s depression era, the garment workers' union developed "entire chains of regional medical centers for their members [and] [m]aintained their own summer resorts, children's camps, and mother-and-child centers, their own life-insurance companies, their own cooperative workers housing projects in New York and Chicago" (Sachar 1992:462).

8. One of the greatest contradictions in today's society is the high youth unemployment in inner-city neighborhoods side by side with decaying housing, garbage-strewn lots and streets, abandoned cars, and burned-out buildings. In other words, there is plenty of work for idle hands but no way within our present economic scheme to employ them. The despair resulting from these conditions has been used to explain "why disadvantaged kids become addicts. The problem is not drugs. . . . The problem is all these people who don't have enough reasons not to do drugs . . . [o]r enough of an alternative not to sell drugs. . . . [L]ife is a complete dead-end routine, and [a kid] gets a crack high and it's the best thing he ever felt. . . . And the question is: Why shouldn't he?" (Balliett 1992: 176).

9. Fanelli (1990:106), in a description of life in a New York City lower-class neighborhood, observes that if youth are not provided a constructive way to use their energies they will find a destructive way.

When a metal doorframe in an empty apartment was bent and twisted in an effort to get at what remained, I could not help but imagine what the same expenditure of energy could have created. When a gang of 14 year olds tore the marble slabs from the hallway walls, that was a graphic demonstration of their need to have something against which to test their strength. If young men and women were not given the chance to be a constructive part of their community, then they would surely become its liability.

10. One of the most successful of these community institutions has been the South Shore Bank in Chicago, which in the mid-1970s replaced a defunct bank that made few loans to its own black low-income community. Since then the South Shore Bank has made a total of 300 million dollars in loans to rebuild community houses and businesses, and has made a substantial contribution to the rehabilitation of the community.

11. Among Native Americans "more important" than accumulation "was the distribution of wealth as a means of securing the obligations and respect of friends and kinsmen. Personal valor, wisdom and generosity were more highly regarded as virtues than the hoarding of natural wealth. Prior to the 1770s, that is, the influence of white cultural values, upon death, most of a man's person-ally-acquired property was buried with him so that it could be enjoyed in the next life (Champagne 1992:34). When, however, there is unequal distribution of wealth, such "community" qualities become problematic. Summarizing a num-

ber of studies on role model behavior in inner-city poverty-stricken areas, it was hypothesized (Duneir 1992:180 n.7):

(1) When neighbors set social standards for one another or create institutions that serve the entire neighborhood, affluent neighbors are an advantage. (2) When neighbors compete with one another for a scarce resource, such as social standing, good high school grades, or teenage jobs, affluent neighbors are a disadvantage.

12. Many of these community institutions are already in place. Since the late 1960s family care and community health centers have been present in cities throughout the United States. John M. Silva, executive director of such a center in South St. Louis, states: "Only through a community-directed, community-supported and community-involved model will grass-roots activities necessary to ensure access to qualified primary health care for all succeed" (Silva 1992:3c). Fifteen hundred such centers, serving six million low-income people, exist in the United States (Pear 1992:14). "In Chicago, every public school is now run by a council of six parents; two community members, elected by community residents; two teachers, elected by the school staff; and the principal. This council acts as a board of directors: it hires the principal . . . , prepares a school improvement plan, and prepares the school budget" (Osborne and Gaebler 1992:54). In San Francisco, a prison counselor has organized community gardens tended by recently released prisoners (Gross 1992:A8). It is estimated that there are 800 such gardens, in "green-neighborhoods" programs, in New York City (Hiss 1992:101); and in New York City, a new class of taxis, "community cabs," would be permitted to pick up riders at newly created hack stands (Finder 1992:B1). In communities such as the Bronx, Chicago, and Milwaukee, among others, community problems have been attacked

on several fronts at once [by] training a few people to monitor the health of their neighbors, hiring others to cajole their neighbors into participating in meetings about the future; and creating a day care center where mothers are asked for volunteer time in lieu of payment; and trying to enable people to buy homes and keep them. . . . [Y]ou rebuild the physical infrastructure, the social fabric, and you create a viable neighborhood out of one that is demolished. . . . To rebuild communities you've got to see them as a whole. What are the building blocks? Good schools. Job opportunities. An economic stake in the community. Home ownership. (Barringer 1992:1,30)

13. "Public Safety Coordinating Councils," which "would fund local coordinating councils," would "bring together representatives of all providers (the county sheriffs, state attorneys, U.S. district attorneys, public defenders, police chiefs and) some of the customers (the civic coalitions, neighborhood organizations, superintendent of schools)" (Osborne and Gaebler 1992:320).

14. In one such exercise, law enforcement personnel, in cooperation with a community organization, conducted studies of the political, economic, social and historical characteristics of the neighborhoods they patrolled (Robinson 1988).

REFERENCES

Adams, Robert. 1966. *The Evolution of Urban Society: Early Mesopotamia and Prehistoric Mexico*. Chicago: Aldine.

Alpert, Geoffrey, and Roger G. Dunham. 1988. *Policing Multi-ethnic neighborhoods, The Miami Study and Findings for Law Enforcement in the United States*. New York: Greenwood Press.

Anderson, Gary Clayton. 1986. *Little Crow, Spokesman for the Sioux*. St. Paul, Minn.: Minnesota Historical Society Press.

Andreski, Stanislav. 1968. *Military Organization and Society*. Berkeley: University of California Press.

Ash, William. 1964. *Marxism and Moral Concepts*. New York: Monthly Review Press.

Ashburn, F. G. 1967. "A Study of Differential Role Expectations of Police Patrolmen in the Manila Police Department, Republic of the Philippines." Ph.D. diss., Florida State University.

Badura, Bernhard. 1986. "Social Networks and the Quality of Life." In *The Quality of Urban Life, Social, Psychological, and Physical Conditions*, ed. Dieter Frick, 55–60. New York: Walter de Gruyter.

Balandier, Georges. 1970. *Political Anthropology*. Trans. from the French by A. M. Sheridan Smith. New York: Pantheon Books.

Balliett, Whitney. 1992. "Rewinding 'clockers.' " *The New Yorker*, Oct. 5, pp. 174–176.

Banton, M. 1964. *The Policeman in the Community*. New York: Basic Books.

Bard, M. 1969. "Family Intervention Police Teams as a Mental Health Resource." *Journal of Criminal Law, Criminology and Police Science* 60: 247–250.

Bard, M., and B. Berkowitz. 1967. "Training Police as Specialists in Family Crisis Intervention: A Community Psychological Action Program." *Community Mental Health Journal* 3:315–317.

Barringer, Felicity. 1992. "Shift for Urban Renewal: Nurture the Grass Roots." *New York Times*, November 29, pp. 1,30.

Bayley, David H. 1988. "Community Policing: A Report from the Devil's Advocate." In *Community Policing: Rhetoric or Reality*, ed. Jack R. Greene and Stephen D. Mastrofski, 225–238. New York: Praeger.

Becker, H. K., and G. T. Felkenes. 1968. *Law Enforcement: A Selected Bibliography*. Metuchen, N.J.: Scarecrow Press.

Bellah, Robert N., Richard Madsen, William M. Sullivan, Ann Swidler, and Shawn M. Tipton. 1991. *The Good Society*. New York: Knopf.

_____. 1986. *Habits of the Heart, Individualism and Commitment in American Life*. New York: Harper and Row.

Bennett, Trevor. 1990. *Evaluating Neighbourhood Watch*. Aldershot, England: Gower.

Bittner, Egon. 1967. "The Police on Skid Row: A Study of Peace Keeping." *American Sociological Review* 32:699–715.

_____. 1990. *Aspects of Police Work*. Boston: Northeastern University Press.

Black, Donald. 1976. *The Behavior of Law*. New York: Academic Press.

Bohannan, Paul. 1968. "Law and Legal Institutions." In *International Encyclopedia of the Social Sciences*, 73.

Boserup, Ester. 1970. *Women's Role in Economic Development*. London: Allen & Unwin.

Boulding, Kenneth E. 1981. *Evolutionary Economics*. New York: Sage.

Bouza, Anthony V. 1990. *The Police Mystique, An Insider's Look at Cops, Crime and the Criminal Justice System*. New York: Plenum Press.

Brodeur, John-Paul. 1991. "Police l'apparence." *Canadian Journal of Criminology* 33:285–332.

Bukowczyk, John J. 1984. "The Decline and Fall of a Detroit Neighborhood: Poletown vs. G. M. and the City of Detroit." *Washington & Lee Law Review* 41:49–76.

Campbell, Joseph. 1959. *The Marks of God: Primitive Mythology*. New York: Viking Press.

Carneiro, Robert L. 1970. "A Theory of the Origin of the State." *Science* 169: 733–738.

Center for Research on Criminal Justice. 1977. *The Iron Fist and Velvet Glove*. 2nd ed. Berkeley: Center for Research on Criminal Justice.

Chambliss, William J. 1975. *Criminal Law in Action*. Santa Barbara: Hamilton.

Champagne, Duane. 1992. *Social Order and Political Change, Constitutional Governments among the Cherokee, the Choctaw, the Chickasaw and the Creek*. Stanford, Calif.: Stanford University Press.

Chen, H. 1963. *A Comparative Study of Police Systems of China and the United States*. Taipei, China: Police Friends Journal.

Claessen, Henri J. M. 1978. "The Early State: A Structural Approach." In *The Early State*, ed. Henri J. M. Claessen and Peter Skalník, 533–596. The Hague: Mouton.

Claessen, Henri J. M., and Peter Skalník. 1978a. "The Early State: Models and Reality." In *The Early State*, ed. Henri J. M. Claessen and Peter Skalník, 637–650. The Hague: Mouton.

_____. 1978b. "The Early State: Theories and Hypotheses." In *The Early State*, ed. Henri J. M. Claessen and Peter Skalník, 3–29. The Hague: Mouton.

_____. 1978c. "Limits: Beginning and End of the Early State." In *The Early State*, ed. Henri J. M. Claessen and Peter Skalník, 619–635. The Hague: Mouton.

Clairmont, Don. 1991. "Community-Based Policing: Implementation and Impact." *Canadian Journal of Criminology* 33:469–484.

Clinton, William. 1992. "Excerpts from the Victory Speech by President-Elect Clinton." *New York Times*, November 4, p. B3.

Coats, G. Y. 1969. "The Philippine Constabulary: 1901–1917." Ph.D. diss., Ohio State University.

Cohen, Ronald. 1978a. "State Foundations: A Controlled Comparison." In *Origins of the State: The Anthropology of Political Evolution*, ed. Ronald Cohen and Elman R. Service, 141–160. Philadelphia: Institute for the Study of Human Issues.

_____. 1978b. "State Origins: A Reappraisal." In *The Early State*, ed. Henri J. M. Claessen and Peter Skalník, 31–76. The Hague: Mouton.

Cohen, Ronald, and Elman R. Service. 1978. *Origins of the State: The Anthropology of Political Evolution*. Philadelphia: Institute for the Study of Human Issues.

Cohen, Stanley. 1985. *Visions of Social Control, Crime, Punishment and Classification*. Cambridge, England: Polity Press.

Collins, Hugh. 1982. *Marxism and Law*. New York: Oxford University Press.

Colson, E. 1953. "Social Control and Vengeance in Plateau Tonga Society." *Africa* 23:199–212.

Copet-Rougier, Elizabeth. 1986. " 'Le Mal Court': Visible and Invisible Violence in an Acephalous Society—Mkako of Cameroon." In *The Anthropology of Violence*, ed. David Riches, 50–69. Oxford, England: Basil Blackwell.

Corrigan, Philip, and Derek Sayer. 1985. *The Great Arch, English State Formation as Cultural Revolution*. Oxford, England: Basil Blackwell.

Critchley, T. A. 1967. *A History of Police in England and Wales, 900 to 1966*. London: Constable and Co.

Cumming, Elaine, Ian Cumming, and Laura Edell. 1965. "Policeman as Philosopher, Guide and Friend." *Social Problems* 12:276–286.

Curran, Ron. 1992. "Native Sun." *Mother Jones*, Sept./Oct., 23–25.

Dalton, Michael 1975 [1618]. *The Countrey Justice*. Reprint. Norwood, N.J.: Walter L. Johnson.

Diakonoff, I. M. 1969. "The Rise of the Despotic State in Ancient Mesopotamia." In *Ancient Mesopotamia: Socio-Economic History. A Collection of Studies by Soviet Scholars*, ed. I. M. Diakonoff, 173–203. Moscow: "Nauka" Publishing House.

Diamond, Stanley. 1971. "The Rule of Law versus the Order of Customs." In *The Rule of Law*, ed. Robert Paul Wolff. New York: Simon and Schuster.

Dissertation Abstracts. International Retrospective Index. 9 vols. University Microfilms, Ann Arbor, Mich.

Duffee, David E. 1990. *Explaining Criminal Justice, Community Theory and Criminal Justice Reform.* Prospect Heights, Ill.: Waveland Press.

Duneier, Mitchell. 1992. *Slim's Table, Race, Respectability, and Masculinity.* Chicago, Ill.: University of Chicago Press.

Earle, T. K. 1977. "A Reappraisal of Redistribution: Complex Hawaiian Chiefdoms." In *Exchange Systems in Prehistory,* ed. T. Earle. New York: Academic Press.

Eckert, Alan W. 1992. *A Sorrow in Our Heart: The Life of Tecumseh.* New York: Bantam Books.

Edwards, G. 1968. *The Police on the Urban Frontier.* New York: Institute of Human Relations Press.

Ehle, John. 1988. *Trail of Tears: The Rise and Fall of the Cherokee Nation.* New York: Doubleday.

Eisenstadt, S. N. 1963. *The Political Systems of Empires.* New York: Free Press of Glencoe.

Ellickson, Robert C. 1991. *Order without Law, How Neighbors Settle Disputes.* Cambridge, Mass.: Harvard University Press.

Engels, Frederick. 1972. *The Origin of the Family, Private Property and the State.* New York: International Publishing.

Fallers, Lloyd A. 1964. "Social Stratification and Economic Processes." In *Economic Transition in Africa,* ed. Melville J. Herkovits and Mitchell Harwitz. Evanston: Northwestern University Press.

_____. 1969. *Law without Precedent.* Chicago: University of Chicago Press.

Family Crisis Intervention Unit. n.d. "Training Police as Specialists in Family Crisis Intervention." Report to the Office of Law Enforcement Administration, Grant #157.

Fanelli, Vincent. 1990. *The Human Face of Poverty, A Chronicle of Urban America.* New York: Bootstrap Press.

Finder, Alan. 1992. "Dinkins Narrows Plan for Improving Taxi Service." *New York Times*, October 13, p. B1.

Finley, M. I. 1973. *The Ancient Economy.* Berkeley: University of California Press.

Fischer, Claude S. 1982. *To Dwell Among Friends: Personal Networks in Town and City.* Chicago: University of Chicago Press.

Flannery, Kent V. 1972. "The Cultural Evolution of Civilizations." *Annual Review of Ecology and Systematics* 3:399–426.

Flannery, Kent V., and M. Coe. 1968. "Social and Economic Systems in Formative Mesoamerica." In *New Perspectives in Archeology,* ed. S. and L. Binford. Chicago: Aldine.

Foran, W. R. 1962. *The Kenya Police 1887–1969.* London: Robert Hale.

Fox, Richard G. 1971. *Kin, Clan, Raja and Rule: State-Hinterland Relations in Pre-Industrial India*. Berkeley: University of California Press.

_____. 1976. "Lineage Cells and Regional Definition in Complex Societies." In *Regional Analysis*, vol. 2 of *Social Systems*, ed. Carol A. Smith, 95–121. New York: Academic Press.

Fried, Morton H. 1967. *The Evolution of Political Society*. New York: Random House.

Gabel, Creighton. 1967. *Analysis of Prehistoric Economic Patterns*. New York: Holt, Rinehart and Winston.

Galliher, John F. 1971. "Explanation of Police Behavior: A Critical View and Analysis." *Sociological Quarterly* 12: 308–318.

Geschiere, Peter. 1982. *Village Communities and the State: Changing Relations Among the Maka of South-Eastern Cameroon since the Colonial Conquest*. Trans. James J. Ravell. London: Kegan Paul.

Gluckman, M. 1955. *The Judicial Process among the Barotse of Northern Rhodesia*. Manchester, U.K.: Manchester University Press.

Godelier, Maurice. 1972. *Rationality and Irrationality in Economics*. Translated from the French by Brian Pearce. London: NLB.

_____. 1977. *Perspectives in Marxist Anthropology*. Trans. Robert Brain. New York: Cambridge University Press.

_____. 1982a. *La Production des Grands Hommes: Pouvoir et domination masculine chez les Baruya de Nouvelle-Guinee*. Paris: Fayard.

_____. 1982b. "Social Hierarchies among the Baruya of New Guinea." In *Inequality in New Guinea Highland Society*, ed. Andrew Strathern. Cambridge: Cambridge University Press.

_____. 1986. *The Making of Great Men: Male Domination and Power among the New Guinea Baruya*. Translated from the French by Rupert Swyer. Cambridge: Cambridge University Press.

Godelier, Maurice, and Marilyn Strathern, eds. 1991. *Big Men and Great Men: Personifications of Power in Melanesia*. Cambridge: Cambridge University Press.

Goldman, Irving. 1955. "Status Rivalry and Cultural Evolution in Polynesia." *American Anthropologist* 57:680–697.

_____. 1970. *Ancient Polynesia Society*. Chicago: University of Chicago Press.

Goldstein, H. 1967. "Toward a Redefinition of the Police Function." Paper Presented to the Southern Regional Education Board Seminar on the Administration of Justice, Institute of Government, University of North Carolina.

Gonzalez, David. 1992. "Sliwa Admits Faking Crimes for Publicity." *New York Times*. November 25, Section B1, p. 1.

Greenberg, Douglas. 1976. *Crime and Law Enforcement in the Colony of New York 1691–1777*. Ithaca, N.Y.: Cornell University Press.

Greenberg, Martin Alan. 1984. *Auxiliary Police, the Citizen's Approach to Public Safety*. Westport, Conn.: Greenwood Press.

Greene, Jack R. 1981. "Changes in the Conception of Police Work: Crime Control vs. Collective Goods." In *Crime and Criminal Justice in a Declining Economy*, ed. Kevin N. Wright, pp. 233–256. Cambridge, Mass.: Oelgeschlager, Gunn and Hain.

Grinnel, George B. 1956. *The Fighting Cheyennes*. Norman: University of Oklahoma Press.

Gross, Jane. 1992. "A Jail Garden's Harvest: Hope and Redemption." *New York Times*, September 3, p. A8.

Gulliver, P. H. 1971. *Neighbors and Networks: The Idiom of Kinship in Social Action among the Ndendeuli of Tanzania*. Berkeley: University of California Press.

Haas, Jonathan. 1982. *The Evolution of the Prehistoric State*. New York: Columbia University Press.

Hagan, W. T. 1980 [1966]. *Indian Police and Judges: Experiments in Acculturation and Control*. Reprint. New Haven, Conn.: Yale University Press.

Handy, E.S.C., and E. G. Handy. 1972. *Native Planters in Old Hawaii: Their Life, Love and Environment*. Bernice P. Bishop Museum Bulletin 233. Honolulu, Hawaii.

Harding, Alan. 1966. *A Social History of English Law*. Baltimore: Penguin Books.

Harrington, Christine. 1985. *Shadow Justice: The Ideology and Institutionalization of Alternatives to Court*. Westport, Conn.: Greenwood Press.

Harris, Marvin. 1975. *Culture, People, Nature: An Introduction to General Anthropology*. New York: Thomas Y. Crowell.

Hendrix, Llewellyn, and Zakir Hossain. 1988. "Women's Status and Mode of Production: A Cross-Cultural Test," *Signs: Journal of Workers in Culture and Society* 13:437–453.

Henry, Howell N. 1968 [1914]. *The Police Control of the Slave in South Carolina*. Reprint. New York: Negro University Press.

Hewitt, W. H. 1965. *A Bibliography of Police Administration, Public Safety and Criminology*. Springfield, Ill.: Charles C Thomas.

Hindess, Barry, and Paul Q. Hirst. 1975. *Pre-Capitalist Modes of Production*. London: Routledge and Kegan Paul.

———. 1977. *Critique of Pre-Capitalist Modes of Production*. London: MacMillan Press.

Hiss, Tony. 1992. "An Ecologist at Large." *The New Yorker*, October 26, 1992, 101–102.

Hoebel, E. Adamson. 1978. *The Cheyennes: Indians of the Great Plains*. New York: Holt, Rinehart and Winston.

———. 1983 [1954]. *The Law of Primitive Man: A Study in Comparative Legal Dynamics*. Reprint. New York: Atheneum.

Hofrichter, Richard. 1987. *Neighborhood Justice in Capitalist Society*. Westport, Conn.: Greenwood Press.

Holden, Richard N. 1986. *Modern Police Management*. Englewood Cliffs, N.J.: Prentice Hall.

Holmberg, Allan R. 1969 [1950]. *Nomads of the Long Bow, the Sirono of Eastern Bolivia.* Reprint. Garden City, N.Y.: The Natural History Press.

Hostetler, John Andrew. 1980. *Amish Society.* 3d ed. Baltimore, Md.: Johns Hopkins University Press.

———. 1992. *Amish Children, Education in the Family, School, and Community.* Rev. ed. of: *Children in Amish Society.* Fort Worth, Tex.: Harcourt Brace Jovanovich.

International Police Association. 1968. *International Bibliography of Selected Police Literature.* 2nd ed. London: M & W Publications.

Irving, Barrie L., Cathy Bird, Malcolm Hibberd, and Jon Wilmore. 1989. *Neighbourhood Policing, the Natural History of a Policing Experiment.* London, England: Police Foundation.

Jeffery, C. Ray. 1957. "The Development of Crime in Early English Society." *Journal of Criminal Law, Criminology and Police Science.* 47:647–666.

Jeudwine, J. W. 1917. *Tort, Crime, and Police in Medieval Britain: A Review of Some Early Law and Custom.* London: Williams and Norgate.

Jones, Jacqueline. 1992. *The Dispossessed Americans Underclass from the Civil War to the Present.* New York: Basic Books.

Kelling, George L., and Mark H. Moore. 1988, January. "The Evolving Strategy of Policing." In *Perspectives on Policing.* Washington, D.C.: National Institute of Justice.

Kent, Joan R. 1986. *The English Village Constable 1580–1642, a Social and Administrative Study.* Oxford, England: Clarendon Press.

Khazanov, Anatoli M. 1978. "Some Theoretical Problems of the Study of the Early State." In *The Early State*, ed. Henri J. M. Claessen and Peter Skalník, 77–92. The Hague: Mouton.

Kirsch, Patrick V. 1989 [1984]. *The Evolution of the Polynesian Chiefdoms.* Reprint. New York: Cambridge University Press.

Klockars, Carl B. 1988. "The Rhetoric of Community Policing," In *Community Policing: Rhetoric or Reality*, ed. Jack R. Greene and Stephen D. Mastrofski, 239–258. New York: Praeger.

Koch, K.- F. 1974. *War and Peace in Jalémó: The Management of Conflict in Highland New Guinea.* Cambridge, Mass.: Harvard University Press.

Konig, Rene. 1968. *The Community.* Translated from German by Edward Fitzgerald. London: Routledge and Kegan Paul.

Krader, Lawrence. 1968. *Formation of the State.* Englewood Cliffs, N.J.: Prentice Hall.

———. 1976. *Dialectic of Civil Society.* Amsterdam: Van Gorcum, Assen.

———. 1978. "The Origin of the State among the Nomads of Asia." In *The Early State*, ed. Henri J. M. Claessen and Peter Skalník, 93–107. The Hague: Mouton.

Kurtz, Donald V. 1978. "The Legitimation of the Aztec State." In *The Early State*, ed. Henri J. M. Claessen and Peter Skalník, 169–189. The Hague: Mouton.

Lane, Roger. 1967. *Policing the City.* Cambridge, Mass.: Harvard University Press.

Latham, Ronald, trans. 1958. *The Travels of Marco Polo*. London: Penguin.

Law Enforcement Assistance Administration (LEAA). 1978. *Criminal Justice Research Solicitation: Citizen/Police Relations in Police Policy Setting*. Washington, D.C.: National Institute of Law Enforcement and Criminal Justice.

Leacock, Eleanor B. 1972. Introduction and Notes to Frederick Engels, *The Origin of the Family, Private Property and the State*. New York: International Publishers.

Lee, Richard. 1968. "What Hunters Do for a Living, or How to Make Out on Scarce Resources." In *Man the Hunter*, ed. R. Lee and I. DeVore, 30–48. Chicago: Aldine.

———. 1979. *The !Kungsan: Men, Women and Work in a Foraging Society*. Cambridge: Cambridge University Press.

Lee, W. L. Melville. 1971 [1901]. *A History of Police in England*. Reprint. Montclair, N.J.: Patterson Smith.

Leighton, Barry N. 1991. "Visions of Community Policing: Rhetoric and Reality in Canada." *Canadian Journal of Criminology* 33:485–522.

Lenski, Gerhard E. 1966. *Power and Privilege: A Theory of Social Stratification*. New York: McGraw-Hill.

Lewis, Dan A., Jane A. Grant, and Dennis P. Rosenbaum. 1988. *The Social Construction of Reform, Crime Prevention and Community Organizations*. New Brunswick, N.J.: Transaction Books.

Lewis, David Rich. 1991. "Reservation Leadership and the Progressive-Traditional Dichotomy: William Wash and the Northern Utes." *Ethnohistory* 38:124–148.

Lewis, Flora. 1983. "The Quantum Mechanics of Politics." *New York Times Magazine*, November 6, 1983, 98.

Lewis, I. M., ed. 1968. *History and Social Anthropology*. London: Tavistock Publications.

Light, Ivan H. 1972. *Ethnic Enterprise in America*. Berkeley: University of California Press.

Llewellyn, K. M., and E. Adamson Hoebel. 1941. *The Cheyenne Way: Conflict and Case Law in Primitive Jurisprudence*. Norman: University of Oklahoma Press.

Lloyd, P. C. 1968. "Conflict Theory and Yoruba Kingdoms." In *History and Social Anthropology*, ed. I. M. Lewis, 25–61. London: Tavistock Publications.

Lowie, Robert H. 1927. *The Origin of the State*. New York: Harcourt, Brace and World.

———. 1935. *The Crow Indians*. New York: Farrar and Rinehart.

Loyn, H. R. 1984. *The Governance of Anglo-Saxon England, 500–1087*. Stanford: Stanford University Press.

MacLeod, William C. 1924. "The Origin of the State, Reconsidered in the Light of the Date of Aboriginal North America." Ph.D. diss., University of Pennsylvania.

———. 1931. *The Origin and History of Politics*. New York: Wiley.

_____. 1937 "Police and Punishment among Native Americans of the Plains." *Journal of the American Institute of Criminal Law and Criminology* 28:181–201.

Mair, Lucy. 1964. *Primitive Government*. Baltimore: Penguin Books.

Malinowski, Bronislaw. 1921. "The Primitive Economics of the Trobriand Islanders." *Economic Journal* 31:116.

_____. 1922. *Argonauts of the Western Pacific*. New York: E. P. Dutton.

_____. 1926. *Crime and Custom in Savage Society*. London: Routledge and Kegan Paul.

Mallon, Florencia E. 1983. "Murders in the Andes: Patrons, Clients and the Impact of Foreign Capital." *Radical History Review* 27:79–98.

Malo, D. 1951. *Hawaiian Antiquities*. Honolulu: Bishop Museum Press.

Mandel, Ernest. 1968. *Marxist Economic Theory*. Vol. 1. Trans. Brian Pearce. New York: Monthly Review Press.

Manning, Peter K. 1979. *Police Work: The Social Organization of Policing*. Paperback. Cambridge, Mass.: MIT Press.

_____. 1988. "Community Policing as a Drama of Control." In *Community Policing: Rhetoric or Reality*, ed. Jack R. Greene and Stephen D. Mastrofski, 27–46. New York: Praeger.

Martin, Douglas. 1992. "One New York City Landlord's Lament: From Riches to Rags." *New York Times*. October 26, p. A13.

Marx, Karl. 1964. *Pre-Capitalist Economic Formations*. Translated by Jack Cohen; edited and with an introduction by E. J. Hobsbawm. New York: International.

Mastrofski, Stephen D. 1988. "Community Policing as Reform: A Cautionary Tale." In *Community Policing: Rhetoric or Reality*, ed. Jack R. Greene and Stephen D. Mastrofski, 47–68. New York: Praeger.

Matthiessen, Peter. 1984. *Indian Country*. New York: Viking Press.

McGehee, A. L. 1970. *Police Literature: An Annotated Bibliography*. Athens: University of Georgia, Institute of Government.

Meier, August, and Elliot Rudwick. 1970. *From Plantation to Ghetto*. Rev. ed. New York: Hill and Wang.

Meillassoux, Claude, ed. 1964. *L'Anthropologie économique des Gouro de Côte D'Ivoire*. Paris: Mouton.

Miller, Joseph C. 1977. "Imbangala Lineage Slavery (Angola)." In *Slavery in Africa: Historical and Anthropological Perspectives*, ed. Suzanne Miers and Igor Kopytoff, 205–233. Madison: University of Wisconsin Press.

Monkkonen, Eric H. 1981. *Police in Urban America, 1860–1920*. Cambridge: Cambridge University Press.

Moore, John H. 1987. *The Cheyenne Nation, a Social and Demographic History*. Lincoln: University of Nebraska Press.

Moore, Mark H., Robert C. Trojanowicz, and George L. Kelling. June 1988. "Crime and Policing." In *Perspectives on Policing*. Washington, D.C.: National Institute of Justice.

Morgan, L. H. 1964. *Ancient Society*. Cambridge, Mass.: Belknap Press of Harvard University Press.

Murdock, G. P. 1967. "Ethnographic Atlas." *Ethnology*. Pittsburgh, Penn. Vol. 6, no. 2.

Murdock, G. P., and D. R. White. 1969. "Standard Cross-Cultural Sample." *Ethnology* 8:329–369.

Murphy, Christopher. 1988a. "Community Problems, Problem Communities, and Community Policing in Toronto," *Journal of Research in Crime and Delinquency* 25:392–410.

_____. 1988b. "The Development, Impact, and Implications of Community Policing in Canada." In *Community Policing: Rhetoric or Reality*, ed. Jack R. Greene and Stephen D. Mastrofski, 177–190. New York: Praeger.

Mydans, Seth. 1992. "Los Angeles Riot Anger Spills into Competition for Jobs." *New York Times*, August 30, p. 10.

Nader, Laura, and H. S. Todd. 1978. *The Disputing Process: Law in Ten Societies*. New York: Columbia University Press.

National Institute of Justice. 1991. *Evaluation Plan: 1991*. Washington, D.C.: U.S. Department of Justice.

Neely, Richard. 1990. *Take Back Your Neighborhood: A Case for Modern-Day "Vigilantism."* New York: Donald I. Fine.

Newman, Katherine S. 1983. *Law and Economic Organization: A Comparative Study of Preindustrial Societies*. New York: Cambridge University Press.

Nie, Norman H. 1975. *SPSS: Statistical Package for the Social Sciences*. New York: McGraw-Hill.

Nielsen, Marianne. 1982. "Informal Social Control—Its Role in Crime Prevention in Traditional Native Culture." Discussion paper, 1982 American Society of Criminology, Toronto, Ontario.

Olivero, J. Michael. 1990. "A New Look at the Evolution of Police Structure." *Journal of Criminal Justice* 18:171–176.

Osborne, David, and Ted Gaebler. 1992. *Reinventing Government: How the Entrepreneurial Spirit Is Transforming the Public Sector*. Reading, Mass.: Addison-Wesley.

Osmańczyk, Edmund Jan. 1990. *The Encyclopedia of the United Nations and International Relations*. New York: Taylor and Francis.

Parkinson, C. Northcote. 1958. *The Evolution of Political Thought*. New York: Viking Press.

Patterson, Orlando. 1991. *Freedom Vol. I: Freedom in the Making of Western Culture*. New York: Basic Books.

Payne, Dennis M., and Robert C. Trojanowicz. 1985. "Performance Profiles of Foot Versus Motor Officers." Community Policing Series No. 6. East Lansing, Mich. National Neighborhood Foot Patrol Center, Michigan State University.

Pear, Robert. 1992. "Congress Passes Bill to Widen Health-Care Access." *New York Times*, October 18, p. 14.

Pearce, Frank. 1976. *Crimes of the Powerful: Marxism, Crime and Deviance.* London: Pluto Press.

Perry, David C. 1975. *Police in the Metropolis.* Columbus, Ohio: Charles E. Merrill.

Petty, E. A. 1961. "Directed Change and Culture Adhesion: A Study of Functional Integration in the Police Administration of Tapan." Ph.D. diss., University of Southern California.

Phillips, Kevin. 1993. *Boiling Point, Republicans, Democrats, and the Decline of the Middle Class.* New York: Random House.

Polanyi, Karl. 1957. *The Great Transformation: The Political and Economic Origins of Our Time.* Boston: Beacon Press.

———. 1968. "Anthropology and Economic Theory." In *Readings in Anthropology*, ed. Morton H. Fried, Vol. 1, 215–238. New York: Thomas Y. Crowell.

Police Foundation. 1981. *The Newark Foot Patrol Experiment.* Washington, D.C.

Pollock, Frederick, and Frederick William Maitland. 1968. *The History of English Law before the Time of Edward I.* Vol. 1. Cambridge: Cambridge University Press.

Pospisil, Leopold. 1971. *Anthropology of Law: A Comparative Study.* New York: Harper and Row.

President's Commission on Law Enforcement and Administration of Justice. 1967. *The Challenge of Crime in a Free Society.* Washington, D.C.: Government Printing Office.

Preyer, Kathryn. 1983. "Crime, the Criminal Law and Reform in Post-Revolutionary Virginia." *Law and History Review* 1:54–85.

Price, Barbara J. 1978. "Secondary State Formation: An Explanatory Model." In *Origins of the State: The Anthropology of Political Evolution*, ed. Ronald Cohen and Elman R. Service, 161–186. Philadelphia: Institute for the Study of Human Issues.

Priestley, H. E. 1967. *Britain under the Romans.* London: Frederick Warne.

Provinse, J. H. 1937. "The Underlying Structures of Plains Indian Culture." *Social Anthropology of North American Tribes*, ed. F. Eggan, 341–374. Chicago: University of Chicago Press.

Pryor, Frederick L. 1977. *The Origins of the Economy: A Comparative Study of Distribution in Primitive and Peasant Economies.* New York: Academic Press.

Radelet, Louis A. 1986. *The Police and the Community.* 4th ed. New York: Macmillan.

Radzinowicz, Leon. 1956. *A History of English Criminal Law and Its Administration from 1750.* Vol. 2, *The Clash Between Private Initiative and Public Interest in the Enforcement of the Law.* London: Stevens and Sons.

Rattray, R. S. 1929. *Ashanti Law and Constitution*. Oxford, England: Kumasi, Basel Mission Book Depot.

Reid, John Phillip. 1970. *A Law of Blood, the Primitive Law of the Cherokee Nation*. New York: New York University Press.

Reiner, Robert. 1978. "The Police in the Class Struggle." *British Journal of Law and Society* 5:166–184.

Reith, Charles. 1952 (1975, reprint). *The Blind Eye of History: A Study of the Origins of the Present Police Era*. London: Faber and Faber. Reprint. Montclair, N.J.: Patterson Smith.

_____. 1956. *A New Study of Police History*. London: Oliver and Boyd.

Richardson, James F. 1970. *The New York Police: Colonial Times to 1901*. New York: Oxford University Press.

_____. 1979. "Historical Perspectives on the Police." Paper presented at the Academy of Criminal Justice Sciences, Cincinnati, Ohio, March 1979.

Rivet, A.L.F. 1958. *Town and Country in Roman Britain*. London: Hutchinson and Co.

Robinson, Cyril D. 1975. "The Mayor and the Police—The Political Role of the Police in Society." In *Police Forces in History*, ed. George L. Mosse, 277–315. Beverly Hills: Sage.

_____. 1977. "Historical and Economic Underpinnings to Police-Community Relations." Monograph presented at the Annual Meeting of the Society for the Study of Social Problems, New York, New York.

_____. 1978. "The Deradicalization of the Policeman: A Historical Analysis." *Crime and Delinquency* 24:129–151.

_____. 1979. "Ideology as History: A Look at the Way Some English Police Historians Look at the Police." *Police Studies* 2:35–49.

_____. 1983. "Criminal Justice History Progress in the United States." *Criminal Justice History*. Vol. 3, 1982, 97–124.

_____. 1984. *Legal Rights, Duties and Liabilities of Criminal Justice Personnel: History and Analysis*. Springfield, Ill.: Charles C Thomas.

_____. 1985. "Criminal Justice Research: Two Competing Futures." *Crime and Social Justice* 23:101–128.

_____. 1988. "Police-Community Relations through Community History." *Social Justice* 15:179–196.

_____. 1993. "The Production of Black Violence in Chicago." In *Crime and Capitalism*, ed. David Greenberg. Philadelphia: Temple University Press.

Rocher, Guy. 1972. *Talcott Parsons and American Society*. Trans. Barbara Mennell and Stephen Mennell. London: Nelson and Sons.

Rock, Paul. 1983. "Law, Order and Power in Late Seventeenth- and Early Eighteenth-Century England." In *Social Control and the State: Historical and Comparative Essays*, ed. Stanley Cohen and Andrew Scull, 191–221. Oxford, England: Martin Robertson.

Romay, F. L. 1963–1966. *Historia de la Policia*. 5 vols. Federal Argentina, Biblioteca Polical.

Ropers, Richard H. 1991. *Persistent Poverty; the American Dream Turned Nightmare.* New York: Plenum Press.

Rosenbaum, Dennis. 1986. *Community Crime Prevention: Does It Work?* Beverly Hills, Calif.: Sage.

Ross, Marc Howard. 1983. "Political Decision Making and Conflict: Additional Cross-Cultural Codes and Scales." *Ethnology* 22:169–192.

Rounds, J. 1979. "Lineage, Class, and Power in the Aztec State." *American Ethnologist* 6:73–86.

Rueschemeyer, Dietrich, and Peter B. Evans. 1985. "The State and Economic Transformation: Toward an Analysis of the Conditions Underlying Effective Intervention." In *Bringing the State Back In*, ed. Peter B. Evans, Dietrich Rueschemeyer and Theda Skocpol, 44–77. Cambridge, U.K.: Cambridge University Press.

Ruyle, Eugene E. 1973. "Slavery, Surplus, and Stratification of the Northwest Coast: The Ethnoenergetics of an Incipient Stratification System." *Current Anthropology* 14:603–630.

———. 1976. "On the Origins of Class Rule." *Thoughtlines* 1:21–28.

Sachar, Howard M. 1992. *A History of the Jews in America.* New York: Knopf.

Sacks, Karen. 1979. *Sisters and Wives: The Past and Future of Sexual Equality.* Westport, Conn.: Greenwood Press.

Sahlins, Marshall. 1958. *Social Stratification in Polynesia.* Seattle: American Ethnological Society.

———. 1963. "Poor Man, Rich Man, Big-Man, Chief: Political Types in Melanesia and Polynesia." *Comparative Studies in Society and History* 5:285–303.

———. 1972. *Stone Age Economics.* Chicago: Aldine-Atherton.

Sanders, William T., and Barbara J. Price. 1968. *MesoAmerica: The Evolution of a Civilization.* New York: Random House.

Saxe, Arthur A. 1977. "On the Origin of Evolutionary Processes: State Formation in the Sandwich Islands, a Systematic Approach." In *Explanation of Prehistoric Change*, ed. James N. Hill, 105–151. Albuquerque: University of New Mexico Press.

Scaglion, R. 1973. "Report of the Police-Community Relations Project." (Pamphlet.) Pittsburgh.

Schaedel, Richard P. 1978. "Early State of the Incas." In *The Early State*, ed. Henri J. M. Claessen and Peter Skalník, 289–320. The Hague: Mouton.

Schapera, I. 1938. *A Handbook of Tswana Law and Custom.* London: Oxford University Press for the International African Institute.

Schlegel, Alice. 1992. "African Political Models in the American Southwest: Hopi as an Internal Frontier Society." *American Anthropologist* 94:376–397.

Schwartz, Richard D., and James C. Miller. 1964. "Legal Evolution and Societal Complexity." *American Journal of Sociology* 70:159–169.

Schwarz, John E. and Thomas J. Volgy. 1992. *The Forgotten Americans.* New York: W. W. Norton Co.

Sedov, Leonid A. 1978. "Angkor: Society and State. In *The Early State*, ed. Henri J. M. Claessen and Peter Skalník, 111–130. The Hague: Mouton.

Sellin, Thorsten J. 1976. *Slavery and the Penal System*. New York: Elsevier Scientific Publishing.

Seneviratne, H. 1978. *Rituals of the Kandon State*. New York: Cambridge University Press.

Service, Elman R. 1962 [1967]. *Primitive Social Organization: An Evolutionary Perspective*. New York: Random House.

_____. 1975. *Origins of the State and Civilization: The Process of Cultural Evolution*. New York: W. W. Norton.

Silva, John M. 1992. "A Community Model for Health Care." *St. Louis Post Dispatch*, September 11, p. 3c.

Skalník, Peter. 1978. "The Early State as a Process." In *The Early State*, ed. Henri J. M. Claessen and Peter Skalník, 597–618. The Hague: Mouton.

Skogan, Wesley G. 1990. *Disorder and Decline: Crime and the Spiral of Decay in American Neighborhoods*. New York: Free Press.

Skolnick, J. 1968. "The Police and the Urban Ghetto." *Research Contributions to the American Bar Foundation*, No. 3.

Skolnick, Jerome H., and David H. Bayley. 1986. *The New Blue Line: Police Innovation in Six American Cities*. New York: Free Press.

_____. 1988. *Community Policing: Issues and Practice Around the World*. Washington, D.C.: National Institute of Justice.

Smith, Carol A. 1976. "Exchange Systems and the Spatial Distribution of Elites: The Organization of Stratification in Agrarian Societies." In *Regional Analysis*, vol. 2, *Social Systems*, ed. Carol A. Smith, 309–374. New York: Academic Press.

Sparrow, Malcolm K., Mark H. Moore, and David M. Kennedy. 1990. *Beyond 911: A New Era for Policing*. New York: Basic Books.

Spitzer, Steven. 1983. "The Rationalization of Crime Control in Capitalist Society." In *Social Control and the State*, ed. Stanley Cohen and Andrew Scull, 312–333. Oxford, England: Martin Robertson.

St. Louis Metropolitan Police Department. n.d. "The St. Louis Detoxification and Diagnostic Evaluation Center." Report to the Law Enforcement Administration, Grant No. 284.

Stampp, Kennett M. 1956. *The Peculiar Institution: Slavery in the Antebellum South*. New York: Vintage Books.

Steele, Marilyn. 1987. "Mott Foundation Support Helps CP Grow." In *Footprints, the Community Policing Newsletter*. National Neighborhood Foot Patrol Center, Michigan State University, East Lansing, Mich.

Strathern, Andrew, ed. 1982. *Inequality in New Guinea Highland Societies*. Cambridge: Cambridge University Press.

Stubbs, William. 1874. *The Constitutional History of England*. Vol. 1. Oxford, England: Clarendon Press.

Swanton, J. R. 1911. "Indian Tribes of the Lower Mississippi Valley." *Bulletins of the Bureau of American Ethnology* 43:1–387.

Tacitus, Cornelius. 1942. *The Complete Works of Tacitus*. New York: The Modern Library.

Taylor, Ian. 1987. "Theorizing in Canada." In *State Control, Criminal Justice Politics in Canada*, ed. R. S. Ratner and John L. McMullan, 198–224. Vancouver, Canada: University of British Columbia Press.

Terray, Emmanuel. 1972. *Marxism and Primitive Societies: Two Studies*. New York: Monthly Review Press.

_____. 1974. "Long Distance Exchange and Formation of the State: The Case of Abron Kingdom of Gyaman." *Economy and Society* 3:313–345.

Thompson, E. P. 1966. *The Making of the English Working Class*. New York: Vintage Books.

Thurnwald, Richard. 1969 [1932]. *Economics in Primitive Communities*. Reprint. London: Oxford University Press.

Tigar, Michael E., and Madeleine Levy. 1974. "Long Distance Exchange and Formation of the State: The Case of Abron Kingdom of Gyaman." *Economy and Society* 3:313–345.

_____. 1977. *Law and the Rise of Capitalism*. New York: Monthly Review Press.

Tooker, Elisabeth. 1988. "The United States Constitution and the Iroquois League." *Ethnohistory* 35:305–336.

Trevelyan, G. M. 1953. *History of England*. Vol. 1. Garden City, N.Y.: Anchor Books.

Trojanowicz, Robert, and Bonnie Bucqueroux. 1990. *Community Policing: A Contemporary Perspective*. Cincinnati, Ohio: Anderson.

Trojanowicz, Robert, and David Carter. 1988. "The Philosophy and Role of Community Policing." Community Policing Series No. 13. National Neighborhood Foot Patrol Center, Michigan State University, East Lansing, Mich.

Trojanowicz, Robert, Richard Gleason, Bonnie Pollard, and David Sinclair. 1987. "Community Policing: Community Input into Police Policy-Making." Community Policing Series No. 12. National Neighborhood Foot Patrol Center, Michigan State University, East Lansing, Mich.

Trojanowicz, Robert C., and Mark H. Moore. 1988. "The Meaning of Community in Community Policing." Community Policing Series No. 15. National Neighborhood Foot Patrol Center, Michigan State University, East Lansing, Mich.

Tuden, Arthur, and Catherine Marshall. 1972. "Political Organization: Cross-Cultural Codes 4." *Ethnology* 11:436–464.

Turnbull, Colin. 1968 [1961, 1962]. *The Forest People*. Reprint. New York: Simon and Schuster.

_____. 1983. *The Mbuti Pygmies: Change and Adaptation*. New York: CBS College Publishing.

_____. 1984. "The Individual Community and Society: Rights and Responsibilities from an Anthropological Perspective." *Washington and Lee Law Review* 41:77–132.

Turner, V. W. 1957. *Schism and Continuity in an African Society: A Study of Ndembu Village Life*. Manchester: Manchester University Press.

Vanderwood, P. J. 1970. "The Rurales: Mexico's Rural Police Force, 1861–1914." Ph.D. diss., University of Texas at Austin.

Vera Institute of Justice. 1969. "First Annual Report of the Manhattan Bowery Project." New York.

Vinogradoff, Paul. 1920. *Outlines of Historical Jurisprudence*. Vol. 1. London: Oxford University Press.

Von Rosensteil, E. B. 1971. "The Proposal to Separate the Police Law Enforcement and Peace-Keeping Functions: A Consideration of Some of the Issues." Master's thesis, University of Pittsburgh.

Walker, Samuel. 1977. *A Critical History of Police Reform*. Lexington, Mass.: Lexington Books.

———. 1984. " 'Broken Windows' and Fractured History: The Use and Misuse of History in Recent Police Patrol Analysis." *Justice Quarterly* 1:75–90.

Walter, Eugene V. 1969. *Terror and Resistance: A Study of Political Violence*. London: Oxford Press.

Weber, Max. 1976. *The Agrarian Sociology of Ancient Civilization*. London: NLB.

White, Leslie. 1959. *The Evolution of Culture: The Development of Civilization to the Fall of Rome*. New York: McGraw-Hill.

Whitelock, Dorothy. 1968. *The Beginnings of English Society*. Vol. 2. 2nd ed. London: Penguin Books.

Williams, Hubert, and Patrick V. Murphy. 1990. "The Evolving Strategy of Police: A Minority View." In *Perspectives on Policing*. Washington, D.C.: National Institute of Justice.

Wilson, J. Q. 1968. *Varieties of Police Behavior*. Cambridge, Mass.: Harvard University Press.

Winks, Robin W., ed. 1972. *Slavery: A Comparative Perspective: Readings on Slavery from Ancient Times to the Present*. New York: New York University Press.

Wittfogel, Karl A. 1957. *Oriental Despotism: A Comparative Study of Total Power*. New Haven: Yale University Press.

Wolf, Eric. 1959. *Sons of the Shaking Earth*. Chicago: University of Chicago Press.

Wood, Gordon A. 1992. *The Radicalism of the American Revolution*. New York: Knopf.

Wright, Burton, and Vernon Fox. 1978. *Criminal Justice and the Social Sciences*. Philadelphia: W. B. Saunders.

Wright, Henry T. 1977. "Toward an Explanation of the Origin of the State." In *Explanation of Prehistoric Change*, ed. James N. Hill, 215–230. Albuquerque: University of New Mexico Press.

———. 1986. "The Evolution of Civilizations." In *American Archeology Past and Future*, ed. David J. Meltzer, Don D. Fowler, and Jeremy A. Sabloff, 323–365. Washington, D.C.: Smithsonian Institution Press.

INDEX

About the Authors

CYRIL D. ROBINSON, Professor Emeritus, Center for the Study of Crime, Delinquency, and Corrections at Southern Illinois University at Carbondale, has long specialized in criminal law and police-community relations. His most recent book is *Legal Rights, Duties and Liabilities of Criminal Justice Personnel: History and Analysis* (1992).

RICHARD SCAGLION is Associate Professor in Anthropology at the University of Pittsburgh. He specializes in tribal societies. He is the editor of "Customary Law and Legal Development in Papua, New Guinea" *(Journal of Anthropology*, volume 6, nos. 1 and 2, 1987) and author of numerous articles on travel societies, customary law, and police-community relations.

J. MICHAEL OLIVERO is Associate Professor and Chairman of the Department of Law and Justice at Central Washington University in Ellensburg. His most recent book is *Honor, Violence, and Upward Mobility: Chicago Gangs, 1970s - 1980s* (1992).